T0210903

IFIP Advances in Information and Communication Technology

407

IFIP – The International Federation for Information Processing

IFIP was founded in 1960 under the auspices of UNESCO, following the First World Computer Congress held in Paris the previous year. An umbrella organization for societies working in information processing, IFIP's aim is two-fold: to support information processing within its member countries and to encourage technology transfer to developing nations. As its mission statement clearly states,

> IFIP's mission is to be the leading, truly international, apolitical organization which encourages and assists in the development, exploitation and application of information technology for the benefit of all people.

IFIP is a non-profitmaking organization, run almost solely by 2500 volunteers. It operates through a number of technical committees, which organize events and publications. IFIP's events range from an international congress to local seminars, but the most important are:

- The IFIP World Computer Congress, held every second year;
- Open conferences;
- Working conferences.

The flagship event is the IFIP World Computer Congress, at which both invited and contributed papers are presented. Contributed papers are rigorously refereed and the rejection rate is high.

As with the Congress, participation in the open conferences is open to all and papers may be invited or submitted. Again, submitted papers are stringently refereed.

The working conferences are structured differently. They are usually run by a working group and attendance is small and by invitation only. Their purpose is to create an atmosphere conducive to innovation and development. Refereeing is also rigorous and papers are subjected to extensive group discussion.

Publications arising from IFIP events vary. The papers presented at the IFIP World Computer Congress and at open conferences are published as conference proceedings, while the results of the working conferences are often published as collections of selected and edited papers.

Any national society whose primary activity is about information processing may apply to become a full member of IFIP, although full membership is restricted to one society per country. Full members are entitled to vote at the annual General Assembly, National societies preferring a less committed involvement may apply for associate or corresponding membership. Associate members enjoy the same benefits as full members, but without voting rights. Corresponding members are not represented in IFIP bodies. Affiliated membership is open to non-national societies, and individual and honorary membership schemes are also offered.

Pedro Campos   Torkil Clemmensen
José Abdelnour Nocera   Dinesh Katre
Arminda Lopes   Rikke Ørngreen (Eds.)

Human Work Interaction Design

Work Analysis and HCI

Third IFIP WG 13.6 Working Conference, HWID 2012
Copenhagen, Denmark, December 5-6, 2012
Revised Selected Papers

 Springer

Volume Editors

Pedro Campos
Arminda Lopes
Madeira Interactive Technologies Institute, Funchal, Portugal
E-mail: pcampos@uma.pt; aguerralopes@gmail.com

Torkil Clemmensen
Copenhagen Business School, Frederiksberg, Denmark
E-mail: tc.itm@cbs.dk

José Abdelnour Nocera
University of West London, UK
E-mail: jose.abdelnour-nocera@uwl.ac.uk

Dinesh Katre
Centre for Development of Advanced Computing, Pune, India
E-mail: dinesh@cdac.in

Rikke Ørngreen
Aalborg University, Copenhagen, Denmark
E-mail: rior@learning.aau.dk

ISSN 1868-4238   e-ISSN 1868-422X
ISBN 978-3-662-52513-5   e-ISBN 978-3-642-41145-8
DOI 10.1007/978-3-642-41145-8
Springer Heidelberg New York Dordrecht London

CR Subject Classification (1998): H.5, J.4, K.4, K.8, J.3

Typesetting: Camera-ready by author, data conversion by Scientific Publishing Services, Chennai, India

Printed on acid-free paper

Springer is part of Springer Science+Business Media (www.springer.com)

Preface

The Human Work Interaction Design Working Group (HWID) was founded in September 2005 under the auspices of IFIP, the International Federation for Information Processing, and was registered as the WG 13.6. With the primary goal of encouraging empirical studies and conceptualizations of the interaction among humans, their variegated social contexts and the technology they use both within and across these contexts, HWID today is more significant than ever, since it remains a true challenge to design applications that support users of technology in complex and emergent organizational and work contexts. This complexity has been constant, and although today we have many tools, techniques, and approaches to aid the interaction design tasks, the technology itself has also changed rapidly, as well as the nature of human work itself.

Seven years after its establishment as a working conference, it is with great pleasure that we find ourselves as a healthier, skillful group than we were some years ago. Attesting that fact is the current edition of the 3rd HWID conference that is held at the place of its birth, Copenhagen, Denmark. The range of contributions published in this 3rd conference reflect many different areas and address many complex and diverse work domains, ranging from medical user interfaces, work and speech interactions at elderly care facilities, greenhouse climate control, navigating through large oil industry engineering models, crisis management, library usability, mobile probing, and others.

Just like science itself, HWID is also condemned to the joyful curse of being eternally young. Therefore, we hope that this conference will become again another opportunity to reflect about the past and most importantly to craft novel research initiatives, address more challenges and continually improve the state of the art regarding the way the design and use of technology mediates the interaction between humans and specific work contexts.

August 2013

Pedro Campos
Torkil Clemmensen
José Abdelnour-Nocera
Dinesh Katre
Arminda Lopes
Rikke Ørngreen

Organization

Organizing Committee

Torkil Clemmensen	Copenhagen Business School, Denmark
José Abdelnour-Nocera	University of West London, UK
Pedro Filipe Pereira Campos	Madeira Interactive Technologies Institute, Portugal
Dinesh Katre	C-DAC, India
Arminda Lopes	Madeira Interactive Technologies Institute, Portugal
Annelise Mark Pejtersen	Center of Cognitive Systems Engineering, Denmark
Rikke Ørngreen	Aalborg University at Copenhagen, Denmark

Program Committee

Ebba Þóra Hvannberg	University of Iceland, Iceland
Virpi Roto	Aalto University, Finland
Pernille Bjorn	IT University at Copenhagen, Denmark
William Wong	Middlesex University, UK
Pradeep Yammiyavar	Indian Institute of Technology, India
Thomas Visby Snitker	UX alliance, Denmark
Shailey Minocha	The Open University, UK
Anirudha Joshi	Indian Institute of Technology, India
Morten Hertzum	Roskilde University, Denmark
Anant Bhaskar Garg	University of Petroleum & Energy Studies, India, and Jt.Hony.Sec., The Institu, India
Sergio España	Universitat Politècnica de València, Spain
Paola Amaldi	UK

Sponsors

IFIP International Federation for Information Processing
Copenhagen Business School
SnitkerGroup

Sources of Support

Copenhagen Business School

Table of Contents

Cognitive Work Analysis: New Dimensions

Catherine Burns

Department of Systems Design Engineering, University of Waterloo, Waterloo Canada
catherine.burns@uwaterloo.ca

Abstract. Cognitive work analysis (CWA) originated in the late 1970's and 1980's through the work of Jens Rasmussen, being collected and built into an effective methodology through the 1990's work of Kim Vicente, and culminating in his book Cognitive Work Analysis [1]. Since that time, CWA, and in particular its derivative design approach Ecological Interface Design (EID), has been widely applied in a vast range of complex, control-oriented systems. Since the 1990's however, there has been an explosion of a new type of system – networked and distributed systems. These systems are characterized by their highly social dimension, resulting in new challenges in team problem solving, community building, and trust allocation across distributed teams. Our recent work in CWA has focused on adapting CWA to face these new challenges and provide a solution that fits a truly social technical system.

Keywords: cognitive work analysis, interface design, task analysis, human-computer interaction.

1   Introduction

In 1999, Vicente published his seminal book, Cognitive Work Analysis (CWA) [1]. This book brought together several analytical views of cognitive work that had been developed earlier by Jens Rasmussen and his associates at the Riso National Laboratory in Denmark [2-4]. The application of CWA as a method was demonstrated through the use of the method on a sample experimental process control system, DURESS [5]. DURESS was later used through multiple studies to confirm and to test the principles of CWA and Ecological Interface Design. While DURESS served as a solid test bed for validating the new approach, DURESS had limitations due to its simplicity compared to real world systems. In particular, DURESS could be operated with a single operator, and with relatively low competency levels, which meant that while this system could demonstrate the first three phases of CWA, Work Domain Analysis (WDA), Control Task Analysis (ConTA) and Strategies Analysis (StA), it remained a weak example for the last two phases, Social Organizational Analysis (SOA) and Worker Competency Analysis (WCA) [1].

For many years, as CWA was becoming more established, this pattern continued. Multiple researchers demonstrated WDA, ConTA and in some cases StA, gradually refining these methods, making them simpler and building a set of examples [6,7]. These first three phases were also demonstrated in design, showing that they could

P. Campos et al. (Eds.): HWID 2012, IFIP AICT 407, pp. 1–11, 2013.

effectively define useful design requirements and develop designs that were often more effective than existing designs. Essentially, through time, the value proposition for using CWA as a method became more convincing as more examples and designs emerged. In the background, however, the two final phases of CWA languished with little attention and poor development. In many cases, researchers made cursory statements that "of course" systems operated in a social-organizational context and "of course" the business would ensure workers had adequate competencies to operate the design. It was assumed, in fact, that in most cases, social-organizational factors, and worker competencies were out of the scope of the designer and were essentially elements of context that could not be changed.

Behind the scene, however, the world was changing. In 2002 LinkedIn was created and in 2004 Facebook was started. While it would be several years before these sites had become established, the reality was that the technology of social connectivity had arrived. Social connectivity meant that quick and fast access to people, as well as the development of new flexible social structures in the form of social networks. Social networks began among groups of friends but before long the business world had also adopted chats and social groups. Social networking allowed for faster and more flexible teamwork, mentoring and the rich access to expertise. Even a plant operator worked in a team, had email and chat to others in his or her organization, and talked to other operators and colleagues in his or her profession. Social organizational factors were becoming more important.

Early attempts to apply CWA to team situations produced a variety of results. Hadjukiewicz et al. [8] mapped work domain zones in the operating room. We adopted this for a multiple objective domain in a military context [9]. Naikar developed the contextual activity template as an approach for teams [10, 11] and Jenkins and Stanton showed various team roles across different phases of CWA [12]. Through this work it became apparent that as CWA tackled social questions, a variety of approaches would be needed. We decided to focus on the development of a range of CWA inspired social methods to help tackle these new questions. We identified different needs for teams and for communities. In this paper we are defining teams as relatively small, goal focused work teams. In contrast communities are larger, more open, and less tightly focused. Team CWA is discussed first and in the following section, community based CWA is discussed. While Team CWA is fairly well developed, we are just beginning to explore CWA for community-based design.

2 Team CWA

Several Team CWA as an approach recognizes that in many cases, people do not work in isolation but function with others to achieve goals. In designing systems for teams, many questions arise such as "what view should team leaders have of team member work?" "What do people need to know of each other's work" and "how do we facilitate effective communication between team members?". Traditional CWA as a base provides a useful structure for gathering requirements, but does not particularly lead analysts towards developing the models or exploring the requirements that would answer these questions.

In developing Team CWA, we quickly realized that team concerns influenced all levels of the analysis and could not be easily reduced to a single analysis phase [13]. In fact, isolating team requirements from the primary CWA could be ineffective and lead to a loss of information. We argue that, when design for a team is required, that team requirements can be handled through the traditional CWA phases with some modifications. We suggest a full four phases looking at team WDA, team ConTA, team StrA, and team Competency Analysis (Figure 1). In the next sections these phases are described, in the context of a healthcare example taken from [13].

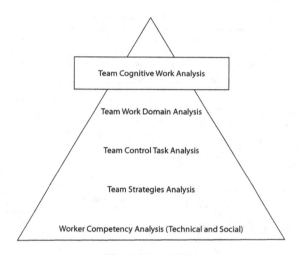

Fig. 1. Team CWA

The basics of the team CWA analyses are discussed below.

2.1   Team Work Domain Analysis

The objective of Team WDA is to understand how work domain constraints influence a team. There are several distinct possibilities:

1. Team members may have shared objects or processes.
2. Team members may have objects or processes that are not shared.
3. Team members may have shared purposes.
4. Team members may have different or conflicting purposes.

When team members have their own individual scope of control that is distinct from others, team work is relatively simple. However, when team members share objects or processes, team relevant design requirements become important. Must team members share object x? or pass it between them? Do they use it for different purposes? Do they have different information needs from object x? Similarly, which team members have shared purposes? And which team members may have conflicting purposes? Team members with shared purposes may find it useful to see how they are each contributing to the shared goal, while team members with conflicting purposes may need to accommodate each other to achieve overall success. Team members with individual and unshared purposes may need to focus on their own part of the work domain, with less distraction from the team. Using a basic WDA, team WDA can use maps of team member zones on the work domain, contextual activity templates, or collaboration tables to keep track of various team interactions in the work domain. Below (Figure 2) we show an example of mapped zones in a healthcare domain.

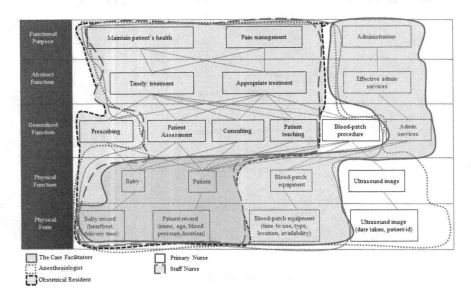

Fig. 2. Team member mappings on a work domain model

2.2   Team Control Task Analysis

Team ConTA should identify how control tasks are shared across team members. It is also an opportunity to identify when various team collaborate on tasks synchronously, or across time, asynchronously. The contextual activity template can be used for this, multiple decision ladders, and we have recently explored the development of a decision wheel (Figure 3). The decision wheel has some advantages in showing individual team members as slices and separate teams as wheels. As well, the wheel tends to concentrate the evaluation processes into the bulls-eye, helping to identify key team members involved in more complex decision-making. We have also used this structure to show synchronous and asynchronous activity. Sample wheels are shown in Figure 3.

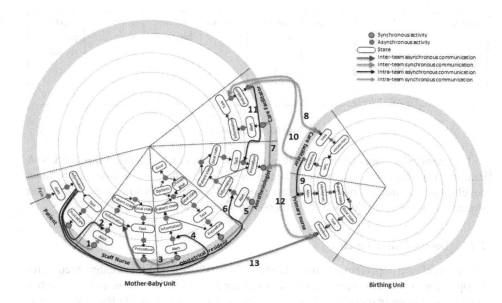

Fig. 3. The decision wheel (from Ashoori and Burns, Journal of Cognitive Engineering and Decision Making in press), copyright ©2012 Human Factors and Ergonomics Society. Reprinted by Permission of SAGE Publications.

2.3   Team Strategies

Strategies, in CWA are alternative ways of achieving control tasks. While we see individual strategies shift with factors like expertise and workload, we also see teams show strategies. To respond to different work constraints, teams may adopt different configurations, roles, and expertise levels. The example below in Figure 4 shows different team structures under normal and emergency situations in the mother-baby unit example. Note that in emergency situations, the team shifts to highly experienced personnel, different types of expertise, and has access to different resources.

Situation	Team Structure	Resource Access	Expertise Level	Task Priority	Location	Duration	Systems used
Emergency	Paediatrician Staff nurse Obstetrical resident Anaesthesiologist Primary nurse	Full access	Expert	High	Mother-baby unit with transfer as needed	Quick response	Electronic patient record and others

Fig. 4. Team strategies

Normal	Staff Nurse Obstetrical resident Anaesthesi-ologist Primary nurse	Limited access	Novice and expert	Medium	Mother-baby unit	5-10 min-utes	Electronic patient record

Fig. 4. (*Continued*)

In general, there are different kinds of strategies that can be modeled through CWA strategy analysis, from structural strategies provided by the work domain itself, team development strategies, operational strategies, and coordination strategies. The team strategies in this example are a case of coordination strategies.

2.4   Social Competencies

Where worker competencies would define the skills, rules and knowledge needed for an operator to perform their job, social competencies define the skills and capabilities needed in various team roles. Some team members need to provide leadership, some mentorship, some negotiation, and others need to take direction and understand objectives. In the next two tables, we include the worker competencies (Table 1) and the social competencies (Table 2) from the mother-baby unit observations. It is clear from this example, that different social capabilities are required for different roles and an incorrect assignment of people to roles could significantly affect the coordination and performance of the team.

Table 1. Worker competencies

Actions	Skill-based behavior	Rule-based behavior	Knowledge-based behavior
Collecting information	An experienced obstetrical resident should be aware of the symptoms and know what signs and symbols to observe.	The obstetrical resident should be able to look up the fact sheets or best practices to find a list of signs and symbols to observe.	The obstetrical resident should be able to analyze the symptoms and plan for further assessments, if required.
Identifying the reason for the pain	An experienced obstetrical resident should know that a lumbar puncture can cause a headache.	The obstetrical resident should be able to look up the fact sheets, best practices, or instructions to find the cause for a post-dural puncture headache.	Severe headache on the day of surgery can have many reasons. The obstetrical resident should be able to analyze supplementary information and make a decision about the cause of the headache.

Table 1. (*Continued*)

Consulting with the rest of the team to verify that reason and discuss possible prescriptions	An experienced obstetrical resident should know the best person to get opinion from. He should know what sort of information should be provided for effective discussion.	The obstetrical resident should be aware of the fact sheets and the best practices and be able to discuss them with the peers.	The obstetrical resident should be able to effectively describe the observation, discuss the options with the peer, analyze the situation, and make a decision about the reason for the pain.

Table 2. Social competencies

Function Role	Team role	Social skills required (Belbin,1981)
Care facilitator at MBU	Coordinators	Mature, confident, a good chairperson, should be able to clarify goals, promote decision making, and delegate well
Care facilitator at BU		
Primary nurse	Team-workers	Cooperative, perceptive and diplomatic. Should be able to listen, build, and avert friction
Staff nurse		
Anesthesiologist	Specialists	Single-minded, self-starting, dedicated to providing knowledge and skills in rare supply
Obstetrical resident		

3   CWA in Communities

While improving CWA for teams is effective for smaller, more goal directed situations, there are cases where one can be asked to develop new designs for larger communities. Designing for communities can be a challenge as there are very few human factors methods that suit these kinds of problems. To work with CWA in communities, we explored community of practice concepts (CoP) [14]. The CoP ideas originate from the work of Wenger [15] and seek to understand why communities exist and how they grow. A difficulty with using the CoP concepts is that they were never developed for design. In the example below we show the use of CoP concepts in WDA. In this case, we were designing a social networking environment for a development organization. The key to CWA in community contexts is realizing that while a community has goals (in this case meeting certain development goals, the left hand column of the WDA in Table 3), a community also has a need to build and sustain itself as an entity (the right hand column of the WDA in Table 3). The CoP concepts were very helpful in understanding community-building requirements. In this sense, and in the terminology of WDA, a community has purposes, values and principles, processes, and people working together. Note that it can be helpful in this context to adjust the labels of the WDA to fit with more community relevant terms.

Table 3. Work domain analysis including community domain elements (Euerby, Burns Journal of Cognitive Engineering and Decision Making 6 (2), 194-213. © 2012 by Human Factors and Ergonomics Society. Reprinted by Permission of SAGE publications.

	Domain	Community	
Functional Purpose	Achieve the UN Millennium Development Goals (MDGs)	Agreed upon role in the larger context; Strength in relationships to actively discuss differences with respect to the domain and practice; Established what knowledge should be shared and how to share it.	**Desired State of the Learning Community**
Value and Priority Measures	Span of the external network vs. strength of the connections; Social action vs. research results; Power of the researcher vs. power of the communities. Mobilize knowledge and mobilize communities; Bring awareness about MDGs and impel collective social action toward their achievement; Educate, engage and empower communities.	Participation vs. reification; Designed vs. emergent; Identification vs. negotiability; Local vs. global. Increase alignment, engagement and imagination.	**Tradeoffs and Priorities of the Negotiation of Meaning**
Processes	Building formal partnerships, hosting networking and public outreach events, collaborating with partners.	Building connections between the core participants, identifying opportunities to provide value in the larger context, finding the ideas and insights that are worth sharing with other members, identifying gaps in the knowledge, refining the CoP's role in the larger context	**Practices**
People, Relationships, Projects, Events	Network Facilitator, Executive Team Members, Regional Coordinators, peripheral members, Knowledge Partners, Organizational Partners, Memorandums of Agreement with Organizational Partners, Executive Meetings, Stand-Up Against Poverty Events, Bridging the World virtual events.		**People, Relationships, Projects, Events**

In this particular case, this analysis was used to redesign a site for the community. Over a six-month longitudinal study, significant improvements in community structure and presence were obtained [16, 17]. This provides early encouragement that this approach to design for communities may be effective.

4   Discussion: When to Use What?

The intention of this work is not to turn CWA into a massive analysis of individual, team and community, multiplied by 4 phases of analysis. But given systems with different needs, CWA needs to provide a responsive methodology to help designers to face these new systems. CWA is a toolbox and while doing every analysis at every level of detail is ideal, it is also unrealistic in many cases.

Designers need to understand the scope of their design problem, its scale, and the key objectives of the redesign. There are many examples of successful designs developed solely from WDA. We have also had strong success using ConTA and StA to inform design in environments like healthcare where work domain information can be difficult to obtain. Just as the traditional phases of WDA can be applied in part to solve a design problem, so too can a more team or community oriented view be adopted if that suits the problem at hand. Figure 5 below provides some guidance on how to choose approaches.

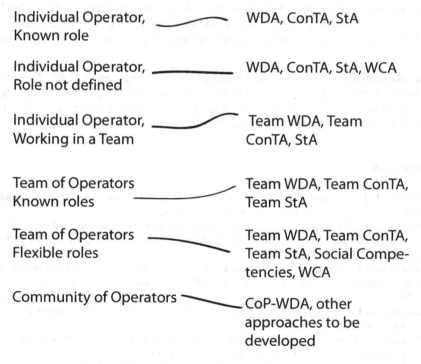

Individual Operator,   WDA, ConTA, StA
Known role

Individual Operator,   WDA, ConTA, StA, WCA
Role not defined

Individual Operator,   Team WDA, Team
Working in a Team   ConTA, StA

Team of Operators   Team WDA, Team ConTA,
Known roles   Team StA

Team of Operators   Team WDA, Team ConTA,
Flexible roles   Team StA, Social Compe-
                                            tencies, WCA

Community of Operators   CoP-WDA, other
                                            approaches to be
                                            developed

Fig. 5. Choosing CWA approaches

5   Conclusion: Next Steps

Evolving CWA, and indeed Human Factors Engineering to tackle modern sociotechnical systems is just beginning. There are, at this point, still relatively few methods adapted for social or team systems and few examples. The work presented here is also preliminary, but expected to be a core research direction for the Advanced Interface Design Lab over the next few years. Several key research directions are apparent.

First, further method development is possible. We have not yet integrated the ideas of macro cognition and emergent team processes into CWA and there is evidence that these processes play an important role. Further, the community building approach could be deepened through an understanding of community processes, strategies, and competencies. Completing these directions would provide a rich analytical approach to understanding cognitive work in a variety of environments.

Understanding the design support for these environments is critical. Drawing from a base the ecological psychology foundation of ecological interface design, we anticipate a new class of affordances, social affordances that need to be understood. These affordances already exist, and we use them every day (friend counts, like buttons, mail and chat are just a few), but a systematic understanding of the influence of these affordances and how to best use them in design does not exist. Furthermore, there are social processes such as trust and engagement that are very influential in encouraging, or discouraging human behaviour that are amenable to influence by design but remain poorly understood. We intend over the next few years to explore the design of social affordances as well as how trust and engagement are influenced through design.

Acknowledgments. This work was made possible through an NSERC Discovery Accelerator Supplement Award to Catherine Burns. The Accelerator Supplement Award identifies Canadian researchers who are most likely to become world class researchers and make a lasting impact in their field.

References

1. Vicente, K.J.: Cognitive Work Analysis, Toward Safe, Productive, and Healthy Computer-based Work. Lawrence Erlbaum Associates, NJ (1999)
2. Rasmussen, J.: Skills, rules, and knowledge; signals, signs, and symbols, and other distinctions in human performance models. IEEE Transactions on Systems, Man, and Cybernetics 13, 257–266 (1983)
3. Rasmussen, J.: The role of hierarchical knowledge representation in decision making and system management. IEEE Transactions on Systems, Man and Cybernetics 15, 234–243 (1985)
4. Rasmussen, J., Jensen, A.: Mental procedures in real-life tasks: A case study of electronic trouble shooting. Ergonomics 17, 293–307 (1974)
5. Vicente, K., Rasmussen, J.: Ecological interface design: Theoretical foundations. IEEE Transactions on Systems, Man and Cybernetics 22, 1–18 (1992)
6. Burns, C.M., Hajdukiewicz, J.R.: Ecological Interface Design. CRC Press, Boca Raton (2004)
7. Bisantz, A.M., Burns, C.M.: Applications of Cognitive Work Analysis. CRC Press, Boca Raton (2008)

8. Hajdukiewicz, J.R., Vicente, K.J., Doyle, D.J., Milgram, P., Burns, C.M.: Modeling a medical environment: An ontology for integrated medical informatics design. International Journal of Medical Informatics 62, 79–99 (2001)
9. Burns, C.M., Torenvliet, G., Chalmers, B., Scott, S.: Work domain analysis for establishing collaborative work. In: Proceedings of the 53rd Annual Meeting of the Human Factors and Ergonomics Society, pp. 314–318 (2009)
10. Naikar, N., Pearce, B., Drumm, D., Sanderson, M.P.: Designing teams for first-of-a-kind, complex systems using the initial phases of Cognitive Work Analysis: Case study, human factors. Human Factors 45, 202–217 (2003)
11. Naikar, N., Moylan, A., Pearce, B.: Analyzing activity in complex systems with cognitive work analysis: Concepts, guidelines, and case study for control task analysis. Theoretical Issues in Ergonomics Science 7, 371–394 (2006)
12. Jenkins, D.P., Stanton, N.A., Salmon, P.M., Walker, G.H., Young, M.S.: Using Cognitive Work Analysis to explore activity allocation within military domains. Ergonomics 51, 798–815 (2008)
13. Ashoori, M., Burns, C.M.: Team Cognitive Work Analysis: Structure and tasks. Journal of Cognitive Engineering and Decision Making (in press)
14. Euerby, A., Burns, C.M.: Designing for social engagement in online social networks using communities of practice theory and cognitive work analysis: A case study. Journal of Cognitive Engineering and Decision Making 6, 194–213 (2012)
15. Wenger, E.: Communities of practice: Learning, meaning, and identity. Cambridge University Press, Cambridge (1998)
16. Euerby, A., Burns, C.M.: Improving social connection through a communities of practice inspired Cognitive Work Analysis approach. Human Factors (submitted)
17. Euerby, A., Burns, C.M.: Increasing social activity through a Community of Practice inspired design. Advances in Human-Computer Interaction (submitted)

On the Usage of Different Work Analysis Methods for Collaborative Review of Large Scale 3D CAD Models

Pedro Campos and Hildegardo Noronha

Madeira Interactive Technologies Institute, University of Madeira
Campus Universitário da Penteada, 9000-390 Funchal, Portugal
pcampos@uma.pt, hildnoronha@gmail.com

Abstract. Human work interaction design is an emerging discipline that aims to encourage empirical studies and conceptualizations of the interaction among humans, their variegated social contexts and the technology they use both within and across these contexts. In this paper we describe and elaborate around the usage of different work analysis methods in a complex, real world work domain: collaborative review of large-scale 3D engineering models. The analysis is based on (i) input from experts in the oil platform engineering field, (ii) previous and related work and (iii) application of different methods considering the recent advances in technology. We conclude that hierarchical task analysis was not effective in obtaining a clear, common vision about the work domain. Storyboarding was the most useful technique as it allowed discovering novelty factors that differentiate the solution and improve the usability of the product, thereby supporting the human work at offshore engineering design and review sessions.

1   Introduction

Human work interaction design [1] is an emerging research field within HCI that is focused on the user's experience of tasks (procedures) and the artifact environment (constraints in the work domain). That analysis and interpretation of human work is eventually manifested in the design of novel, technology-based products, systems and applications [1]. In this paper, we report on a seven-month research study around the requirements elicitation, scenario design and storyboarding processes for creating a new Virtual Reality (VR) distributed application to support a complex work domain: the collaborative review of large scale 3D engineering models, in the context of the oil and gas industry at a very large organization [2].

The current way of designing industrial plants relies on the communication among experts in several areas of the field, and on tools that allow the specification and simulation of the site. VR resources are used to visualize and interact with complex 3D environments in real time. Several engineering simulations employ VR to foresee the results of complex industrial operations.

In this paper, we analyze the user tasks at stake during collaborative sessions of 3D CAD models design and review in the specific context of the oil and gas industry. By studying the users' work and needs, the related existing work and the possibilities that

P. Campos et al. (Eds.): HWID 2012, IFIP AICT 407, pp. 12–21, 2013.

recent advances in multimodal technologies, we expect to shed new light into how an integrated environment should be conceived and designed in order to positively influence the collaboration levels between dispersed teams of engineers that need to review oil platform problems and to design solutions for those problems.

Our main contribution to the Human Work Interaction Design (HWID) field is the comparison of the effectiveness of different work analysis and design methods towards establishing a common vision regarding a new product for the oil and gas industry engineering models' review, in a collaborative manner. This is especially important for gaining new insight about the relative advantages between the different methods in a highly complex, real world work domain.

2   Background and Related Work

Human Work Interaction Design (HWID) is an emerging approach that promotes a better understanding of the relationship between work-domain based empirical studies and the iterative design of prototypes and new technologies [1]. HWID's goal is to encourage empirical studies and conceptualizations of the interaction among humans, their variegated social contexts and the technology they use both within and across these contexts.

To achieve this, HWID promotes the use of knowledge, concepts, methods and techniques that enable user studies to procure a better apprehension of the complex interplay between individual, social and organizational contexts and thereby a better understanding of how and why people work in the ways they do. Therefore, one of the main characteristics of HWID as an interaction design approach is to focus the analysis on the how's and why's of people's work. HWID also tries to promote a better understanding of the relationship between work-domain based empirical studies and iterative design of prototypes and new technologies [12]. HWID's roots lie in Cognitive Work Analysis (CWA) [1, 6]. Cognitive Work Analysis (CWA) is a multidisciplinary framework for the analysis, design, and evaluation of human work developed by Rasmussen, and colleagues [7]. Its purpose is to guide the design of technology for use in the work place. CWA helps an analyst identify the activities and agents that are needed for a system to effectively fulfill its functional purpose. CWA can also be regarded as a formative process that focuses on an ever-increasing number of dynamic constraints that systems present nowadays, rather than prescriptive methods of working.

Storyboarding [4] is a common technique in HCI and design for demonstrating system interfaces and contexts of use. Despite its recognized benefits, novice designers still encounter challenges in the creation of storyboards. Many researchers have studied the benefits and disadvantages of storyboards, including Truong and colleagues [4], who presented two formative studies designed to uncover the important elements of storyboards.

Activity-based analysis [5], in particular activity theory methods, incorporates the notions of intentionality, history, mediation, motivation, understanding, culture and community into design. In particular, it provides a framework in which the critical issue of context can be taken into account.

In hierarchical analysis [3], another work analysis method, the instructional designer breaks down a task from top to bottom, thereby, showing a hierarchical relationship amongst the tasks, and then the instruction is sequenced bottom up. Task analysis often results in a hierarchical representation of what steps it takes to perform a task for which there is a goal and for which there is some lowest-level "action" that is performed [3].

3   Usage of Different Work Analysis Methods

In the offshore engineering field, the project of deep-water production systems, including oil platforms, ships and all the subsea equipment that plays a part in the production process, is currently designed by means of complex computer modeling systems. The design of a new production unit is a lengthy and expensive process, which can last many years and consume hundreds of millions of dollars, depending on the complexity of the unit and the maturity of the technology required to make the project technically and economically feasible.

Offshore engineering projects involve not only geographically distributed teams but also teams of specialists in different areas using different software tools, both commercial and internally developed. While the interoperability of those tools is still an issue, it is a mandatory requirement for any collaborative solution.

One of the objectives we had was to establish a sound requirements document stating clearly the desired project's objectives, requirements and specifications, as well as outlining scenarios for the solutions proposed and their evaluation procedures.

We used the resources available at Tecgraf-PUC Rio (the research arm of Brazil's largest oil industry company, Petrobrás) [2] to conduct user observations and informal interviews with the engineers involved in collaborative engineering design and review activities. The final result we obtain is very important, since it allows us to understand: (i) the application domain, (ii) the problem of designing and reviewing CAD models, and (iii) the needs and constraints of the system's stakeholders. Additionally, and perhaps most importantly, we elaborate on the relative advantages and disadvantages we faced when applying different work analysis methods: activity-based analysis [5], hierarchical analysis [3] and storyboarding as a way to understand the value of possible solutions [4].

3.1   Activity-Based Analysis

Activity 1: Designing and Reviewing Engineering Models. Design review is the process of checking the correctness and consistency of an engineering project while making the necessary adjustments [2]. In the session, users can manipulate objects, highlight and create annotations, do measurements, check the proper ergonomic design. The ability to move, rotate and scale objects is important for various purposes, such as joining models, viewing hidden areas, planning the placement of new devices, and simulating a maintenance or intervention operation in a process plant. Moreover, integration with an engineering database from the CAD system is useful to create annotations emphasizing critical parts (Figure 1). Comments attached to objects can also be used as recommendations for project management. Figure 1 shows a measurement taken for planning the movement of a large tank in a production unit. Users create annotations to guide the maintenance procedure and animate the entire operation. Finally it is possible also to confirm if the space distribution of the engineering devices conforms to the ergonomic needs for operation and maintenance.

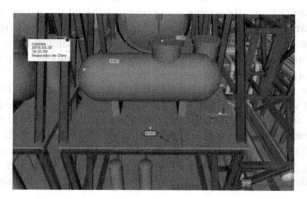

Fig. 1. Annotating and measuring activities involved during design and review

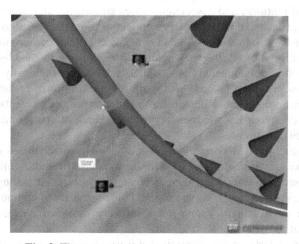

Fig. 2. The second activity identified: riser analysis

Activity 2: Riser Analysis Workflow. An important step in deep-water oil exploitation is the elevation of the oil from depths over one thousand meters to the surface. Oil platforms use ascending pipes, called risers, which are tubular structures that convey oil and/or gas from the wellhead on the sea floor to the platform's separator system tanks [2]. To certificate the operation of the risers for their entire lifecycle

(30 years or so), simulations of the stress applied to the riser system are conducted based on meteo-oceanographic data about wind, tide and water currents. Simulations are made under extreme environment conditions to test stress resistance. It is important to perform fatigue analysis studies to evaluate the most critical regions of the risers affected by cyclical stress in order to guarantee their integrity during their lifetime.

Conclusions after the Activity Analysis. The problem of providing engineering teams with effective tools for collaborative work is becoming increasingly important, not only because teams are increasingly working distributed throughout the world, but also because current tools still lack support for collaborative engineering design and review, either in co-located or distributed settings. The oil industry is especially well positioned as a potential demonstrator for research developments in this field, since it's one of the largest user bases of high-end hardware and software.

Collaborative Virtual Environments (CVEs) place the emphasis on providing a common virtual space of interaction to distributed teams, a space where they can meet as if they were face to face, while sharing and manipulating the relevant work artifacts, in real time. In the case of this application domain, the oil industry, there is a relevant issue that motivates this project: the working force is aging, and the industry is not attracting younger generations of workers. Therefore, the trend of conceiving "digital oil fields" capable of being controlled remotely is becoming strategic for oil companies.

The essential scenario for solving this problem is a 3D interactive environment that represents the oil platform and associated subsea equipment, in a multi-touch virtual control room approach. The oil industry application domain, as referred in the previous section, fits well into the design and evaluation of novel environments, because of several factors. First of all, the very nature of the work performed by the engineers themselves, which is often carried out in collaborative, geographically apart settings. Secondly, because they can provide real world data in the form of large-scale CAD models, thus acting as reliable demonstrators of the project's results. And finally, because there are - to our knowledge - very few research efforts specifically targeted at this application domain.

The final product the team performing this work analysis identified is essentially a large-scale virtual environment based on multi-touch and remote collaboration features for increased awareness and increased sense of presence among teams of oil industry engineers. The final prototype should consist of a set of computer clusters for multi-projection environments running the software designed, developed and evaluated throughout the project.

The main idea underlying this vision is that if we provide engineers with multitouch collaborative tables and walls, we can achieve a state-of-the-art environment with an interesting application to the oil industry: a system that finally allows these users to find, navigate and visualize their complex CAD models' data in a much more satisfying and effective way. This goal can be measured in two dimensions: the usability dimension, making use of well-know Human-Computer Interaction (HCI) evaluation methods and the collaborative dimension, using traditional measures for determining the levels of remote collaboration between geographically dispersed teams.

3.2   Hierarchical Task Analysis

In this work analysis, the hierarchical task breakdown was actually the first step the team took. The analysis was based on input from experts in the oil platform engineering field, several brainstorming sessions, semi-structured interviews and other meetings. The result (after many iterations) is shown in Figure 3. One of the positive aspects was the fact that the team was able to identify the most important tasks and the most intense tasks from a cognitive perspective. The downside was that the team remained without a clear picture about what should be designed and implemented, what was more important and what was less relevant. Other methods, as we will see in the next section, proved far more efficient in gaining a common vision.

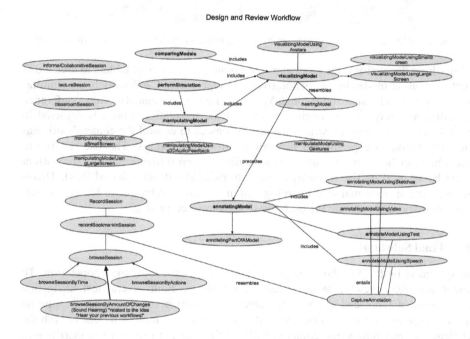

Fig. 3. Task case map for our work domain analysis

3.3   Storyboard-Based Analysis

Since the team had difficulties in synthesizing the work of offshore engineering design and review teams, we decided to employ storyboards [4] to facilitate the ideation process as well as to better explore the possible design concepts. Figure 4 illustrates a particular one (textual descriptions omitted for brevity).

Storyboarding was particularly beneficial to this project's HCI design. It allowed matching the possibilities offered by recent advances in mobile, multitouch technologies with the cognitive tasks at stake.

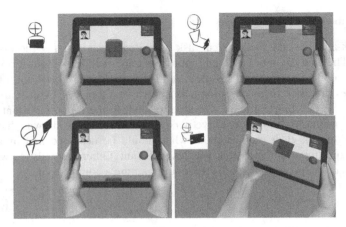

Fig. 4. A particular part of the storyboards created, illustrating one of the navigation modes

After long discussions, the team chose to employ the power of tablets to create different navigation modes in a collaborative prototype where CAD models are simultaneously shared and visualized through Wi-Fi, while the user can also videoconference with other remotely located engineers. One of the navigation modes is depicted in Figure 4. The storyboard illustrates the use of sensors to control the camera's orientation. Translations are performed through multi-touch gestures. The user is free to work whenever he wishes to, which is a significant step further regarding the current system being used by the company (based on traditional desktop-based PCs). Therefore, we can conclude that storyboarding was an effective technique to identify novelty factors that could enhance the usability of the proposed product.

3.4   Final Solution

The system is built upon the concepts of intuitive visualization and cooperation. To achieve our objectives while using those concepts we built several test navigation modes. Two of them ended up being selected for further improvement. Despite an apparent similarity on interaction styles, the two modes are quite different in both the technical and user interaction components: The first version uses built-in inertial sensors to position the virtual camera in a first person view manner, just as if the user was holding a real video camera and filming around. To allow the user to move around, it uses an in-screen touch-based joystick. The second version uses the tablet's camera to track its position and orientation, relative to a tracker. It works as if the user was filming the object on top of a table allowing all the natural movements he would do.

The second version can't use the built-in inertial sensors exclusively as none of them gives translation (the position can be doubly integrated from acceleration but the errors and drift are too significant to be useful). GPS, another possible alternative, can only work outdoors and doesn't have enough accuracy for this problem. The solution is to use the camera to track an object and from that deduce the tablet's position and orientation. The camera tracking is a suitable solution as it provides a surprisingly accurate translation, rotation and, indirectly, zooming without the need of another artificial input (like the virtual joystick on the first-person view navigation mode). The first-person version can be shared between multiple tablets allowing one user to guide or show some feature on the model to the other users. Figure 5 illustrates this. The microphones and the front cameras are shared between multiple tablets, creating a videoconference that improves the cooperativeness of the system. A minor feature (freezing the camera) was also implemented. It allows users to freeze the current view and move around the tablet without fearing that the movements performed will change the camera's position and without stressing body positions. This feature can be used when showing certain features on the models or even when working on the models themselves on future work.

Fig. 5. Two engineers engaged in a co-located collaborative design and review session

4   Comparison between the Different Methods

Hierarchical task analysis was the first method employed in this product's HCI design. Perhaps because of that it was the method that required more effort in order to produce a reasonable set of artifacts describing the engineers' work.

Task analysis taken from a hierarchical perspective had its advantages. First, it allowed the entire team to understand the priorities in the design that should be taken into account. It also had the advantage of promoting discussion around a single diagram, which made it easier to reason about human work without losing the "big picture". However, this method was the least efficient of all. The team remained without a completely clear picture about what should be designed and implemented, what was more important and what was less relevant.

Secondly, the method for trying out a more efficient work analysis was activity-based analysis. We tried to write a complete, detailed description of the collaborative engineering activities that are performed by offshore engineering teams, working both in the oil platform as well as in the central company's offices.

The activity-based analysis effort was overall positive. By forcing a detailed description of the activities at stake, the team spent a lot of time and effort, but at least was able to reach a better work analysis. It allowed identifying a final, concrete product, essentially a large-scale virtual environment based on multi-touch and remote collaboration features for increased awareness and increased sense of presence among teams of oil industry engineers. The disadvantage we encountered was the fact that activity-based analysis did not allow the identification of novel ideas, and the brainstorming processes that usually lead to better UI designs was not well undertaken.

As mentioned before, storyboarding was the most useful technique as it allowed discovering novelty factors that differentiate the solution and improve the usability of the product, thereby supporting the human work at offshore engineering design and review sessions.

5   Conclusions

Supporting the needs of offshore engineering teams is an important industrial problem that should be addressed taking into account the rapid evolution in user interaction styles available. The potential for innovative solutions that is brought by tablet-based computing is enormous. In this paper, we described the industrial creation and evaluation experience of a new mobile system for collaboratively navigating and reviewing 3D engineering models, applied to the oil industry. We highlight that storyboards and scenarios were an effective way to elicit requirements together with oil industry experts, as opposed to high-level task analysis.

Our main contribution to the Human Work Interaction Design (HWID) field is the comparison of the effectiveness of different work analysis and design methods towards establishing a common vision regarding a new product for the oil and gas industry engineering models' review, in a collaborative manner. This is especially important for gaining new insight about the relative advantages between the different methods in a highly complex, real world work domain.

Acknowledgments. This work was supported by Portuguese national funds through Fundação para a Ciência e Tecnologia (FCT), under project PTDC/EIA-EIA/116070/2009.

References

1. Katre, D., Orngreen, R., Yammiyavar, P., Clemmensen, T. (eds.): HWID 2009. IFIP AICT, vol. 316. Springer, Heidelberg (2010)
2. Santos, I., Soares, L., Carvalho, F., Raposo, A.: A collaborative VR visualization environment for offshore engineering projects. In: Proceedings of the 10th International Conference on Virtual Reality Continuum and Its Applications in Industry (VRCAI 2011), pp. 179–186. ACM, New York (2011)

3. Annett, J., Duncan, K.D.: Task analysis and training design. Journal of Occupational Psychology 41, 211–221 (1967)
4. Truong, K.N., Hayes, G.R., Abowd, G.D.: Storyboarding: an empirical determination of best practices and effective guidelines. In: Proceedings of the 6th Conference on Designing Interactive systems (DIS 2006), pp. 12–21. ACM, New York (2006)
5. Uden, L., Helo, P.: Designing mobile interfaces using activity theory. International Journal of Mobile Communications 6(5), 616–632 (2008)
6. Vicente, K.: Cognitive Work Analysis: Towards Safe, Productive, and Healthy Computer-Based Work. L. Erlbaum Assoc. Inc., Hillsdale (1999)
7. Rasmussen, J., Pejtersen, A., Goodstein, L.: Cognitive systems engineering. Wiley, New York (1994)

'Adaptation' in Children – A GUI Interaction Based Task-Performance Study

Yogesh Deshpande[1], Pradeep Yammiyavar[1], and Samit Bhattacharya[2]

[1] Department of Design, Indian Institute of Technology Guwahati, India
{d.deshpande,pradeep}@iitg.ernet.in
[2] Department of Computer Science & Engineering,
Indian Institute of Technology Guwahati, India
samit@iitg.ernet.in

Abstract. This paper describes an exploration of how children adapt their interactions with different graphical user interfaces (GUIs) in varied task situations. The effect of computer exposure, computer knowledge, attitude and motivation (computer-friendliness) on childrens' (age 13-15 years) adaptations and performance was studied. No significant effect of computer-friendliness was found influencing their adaptations and task-performance. The participants were exposed to two different known graphical user interfaces (GUIs). The empirical data shows that participants performed equally well on both the GUIs by adapting their interactions. Also it was observed that a GUI which is rich in features facilitates user adaptations in coping with differences in task complexities. Thus between-task adaptations and adaptivity can emerge as a new usability measure for comparing alternate GUI designs, for users of all age group.

Keywords: Human-Computer-Interaction, User Adaptations, Graphical User Interfaces, Task Performance, Children.

1   Introduction

Coping with different kinds of computing devices has become an essential skill for users of all ages including children. It has now become necessary for a child as young as 6 years of age to interact with various computing devices and interfaces especially in a learning environment.

As new computing and communication devices and software applications replace older ones a greater ability to adapt or discard them would be demanded of human skills. This study focuses on knowing what, when and how do children adapt to graphical user interfaces (GUIs). We have explored adaptations in interaction behaviour and task performances of children in changing situations.(Adaptation means modification in behaviour for improving performance due to change in environment.)

Empirical research work on user adaptations in interaction behaviour has been reported widely as seen in published literature some of which is reviewed below.

P. Campos et al. (Eds.): HWID 2012, IFIP AICT 407, pp. 22–34, 2013.

1.1   Related Work

Attempts have been made by researchers to capture factors affecting learner's task performance and to find relationships among these factors. Personal goals, computer self efficacy,[1][2] motivation,[3] computer usage, anxiety,[4] age, [5] internet efficacy and attitude[6] have been reported to influence user interactions and satisfaction which may affect the success and failure of a task. A user with high computer self-efficacy or skills may also exhibit poor performance [2]. Inability to adapt to situations causes such perception-performance difference. A review of research on types, causes, effects and adapting ability of users is presented in following paragraphs.

Some researchers have tried to characterize or model these user-adaptations. Gray et al. [7] incorporated a new fuzzy based credit assignment scheme to model user's adaptations in strategy selection. Freed et al. [8] proposed a new way of cognitive modelling i.e. modelling adaptations in one's cognitive architectures in response to changing task characteristics or situations.

In coping with different task demands users adapt their strategies and levels in using software features. Heshan Sun [9] investigated the causes of "feature-use adaptations". The observed causes were a new task, other person's influence, change in working environment, discrepancy in system response and self deliberate initiative. Hayama et al.[10] found a new way to measure user's adaptivity to software feature-use. They applied simple compression algorithm (LZW) to the user's operation log to compute compression rate i.e. user's adaptivity. Thus a new metric of measuring user's interaction adaptivity was contributed. Schmitz et al. [11] used task-technology-fit theory to explain these adaptations. They segregated task adaptations(operational adaptations) from technology adaptations(software adaptations) and additionally found their strong relationship with perceived performance.

Smith et al. [12] found a novel mechanism of detecting drop in a search engine's performance by monitoring change in user's adaptations in querying instructions. They proposed that monitoring the querying behaviour of user can be used unobtrusively to indicate failure in system and adaptively upgrade the system.

In e-learning domain Merri et al. [13] investigated adaptations in selecting a learning-task using a shared-control (user+system) mechanism. In the experimental system a personalized learning-task list is first presented by the system and later user selects his learning-task from this list. The results showed benefit of this mechanism of user-adaptation and control in enhancing task involvement and motivation. Pieschl et al.[14] processed an e-learner's interaction log and found that they adapt their learning process(time and interactions) to complexity of learning task. Between task adaptations were computed and summed to get a single score called "adaptation score" for each interaction variable. They concluded that adaptations in judged task complexity(JTC), number of accessed nodes (NAN) and use of hierarchical commands(HC) were significantly related in improving learner's performance. We have used this adaptation score (AS_X – refer section 2.1) as a measure to find magnitude of adaptations in search, modify and delete operations of users.

Grayson et al. [15] recorded eye-movement data to find whether unconventional interface design layout triggers an adaptation of visual search behaviour during repeated trials. Results of their experiment show influence of design characteristics like size, colour , boldness and location on adaptation of visual search behaviour.

The reviewed work shows no specific research related to adaptations in children using computers. Most of the findings were related to adaptations to task characteristics. Not much research has been reported about adaptations to system or interface characteristics or user's personality. The authors of this paper have therefore chosen to research on adaptation phenomena in children.

2   Research Questions

This study therefore focuses on investigating adaptations in children to different graphical user interfaces through tasks. The aim was to establish relationship between adaptations and task performance. Children prefer drawing and gaming activities on computers the most. The authors have investigated childrens' drawing skills on computers with different levels of task complexity and using different drawing tools(GUIs).

Terms relevant in this document are defined as follows by the authors.

i. **Computer-friendliness**= (Computer   exposure)+(Computer knowledge)+
(Motivation to use computer)+(Attitude towards computer)

ii. **Adaptation Score** (AS_X) of   an operation X   is

$$AS_X = (\,|\,X_{T1}\text{-}X_{T2}\,|\,) + (\,|\,X_{T2}\text{-}X_{T3}\,|\,) + \dots\dots \; + (\,|\,X_{Ti\text{-}1}\text{-}X_{Ti}\,|\,) \qquad \dots\dots\dots\dots [14]$$

Where X_{Ti} = number of X operations during task T_i assuming tasks T_1, T_2, T_3 ... T_i are executed in sequence.

iii. **Adaptivity** is the ability of adapting as well as achieving an ideal performance level within minimum trials in response to change in surrounding environment.

We have investigated following research questions.

RQ1=Does children's computer-friendliness significantly affect their drawing performance?

RQ2 = Does task or interface complexity (tool used) significantly affect children's' drawing performance?

RQ3=Does task or interface complexity (tool used) significantly affect children's' interaction behaviour or adaptations?

3   Method

3.1   Participants

Participants of this study were 40 students of two different English medium schools situated in Indian cities of Pune and Guwahati. The participants were familiar with Paint and PowerPoint software interfaces. The schools had computer education inbuilt in their curriculum. Details of participants are shown in Table 1.

Table 1. The participants

School	Number / Sex	Age	Class	Computer Experience
Jnana Prabodhini , Pune	10 Boys+10 Girls	Mean=13.98	8 + 9	5 yrs
Kendriya Vidyalaya IITG	10 Boys+10 Girls			

3.2   Material

Drawing Tools (Graphical User Interfaces - GUI). The drawing tools used were Paint(PNT) and PowerPoint(PPT). Paint was included because of its simplicity and familiarity. PowerPoint was included because of its popularity and ease-of-use. During informal group discussions with participants they were asked to give feedback on their perceptions about the two interfaces. These were counter checked with the task evaluator's opinions. They are summarized qualitatively in Table 2.

Table 2. Comparision of the drawing tools

Parameter	Paint	PowerPoint
Major use	Drawing	Slides
Features	Low	High
Complexity	Low	High
Ease-of-use	High	Low

Computer-Friendliness Preset Questionaries. Two questionnaires were designed for scaling computer-friendliness.

Questionnaire (Q1). – Consisted of 14 objective and 3 subjective items grouped into two scales capturing computer-exposure and computer-knowledge. Computer exposure was measured as usage in hours/week at home and at school. Computer knowledge was measured as knowledge of computer hardware, internet and applications.

Questionnaire (Q2). – Consisted of 15 objective and 1 subjective items grouped into two scales capturing computer-motivation and computer attitude. Motivation was measured in terms of motivation for e-learning, computer affinity and possessiveness. Computer attitude was measured in form of beliefs and initiatives.

Target Tasks. Total four drawing tasks T1,T2,T3,T4 were administered to the child subjects as shown in Table 3.

Table 3. The drawing tasks

Task	Diagram	Drawing Tool	Time Allotted
T1	D1(Simple)	PowerPoint (PPT)	5 minutes
T2	D2(Complex)	Paint (PNT)	5 minutes
T3	D2(Complex)	PowerPoint (PPT)	5 minutes
T4	D1(Simple)	Paint (PNT)	5 minutes

Task-Performance Evaluation. To remove variability or bias in task evaluation, three evaluators evaluated the tasks of each participant. Average age of evaluators was 28 with experience of two years in design. Drawings were evaluated on the basis of how close the final outcome matches with the master-drawings D1 and D2 in all aspects. Each drawing task was evaluated using a 10 point scale. Average of evaluator's scores was treated as task-performance score for that task.

3.3   Procedure

Twenty boys (20 numbers) and girls (20 numbers) from class 8 and 9 of two schools (Table 1) were chosen for the experiments. Participants were chosen randomly by the class-teacher. They were briefed about the study and asked to complete two questionnaires Q1 and Q2. After the questionnaire survey participants were given drawing tasks on computers. They were asked to complete four tasks as mentioned in Table 3 using appropriate drawing tools (refer Fig. 1.). Total time consumed for the entire experiment was around 1 hour. To judge drawing performance, drawing outputs were evaluated by expert evaluators having design expertise. (Refer *Task-Performance Evaluation* paragraph in previous section).

Fig. 1. Participants performing tasks

Semi-structured group interviews in two groups, were conducted to understand childrens' mental model, beliefs and perceptions about GUI features.

All drawing tasks were recorded using CamStudio Version 2.00 (Copyright 2001-2003 by RenderSoft). The full-screen region was recorded with Microsoft Video-1 compression format, square yellow highlighted cursor without audio recording.

4   Results and Discussions

Encoded questionnaire data was entered into statistical software (SPSS version-17) for analysis. Task performance scores were also computed and entered into SPSS.

The participants' computer exposure, knowledge, motivation and attitude data was normalized to 10. The statistics of this data for the entire sample population is summarized in Fig. 2. and Table 4.

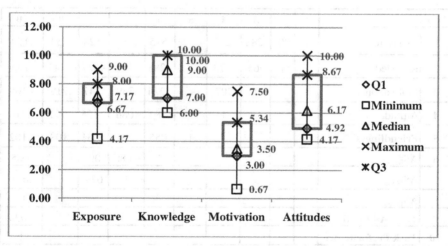

Fig. 2. Comparison of computer-friendliness constructs of sample population

Table 4. Computer friendliness constructs of sample population

Statistic	Exposure	Knowledge	Motivation	Attitude
Mean (SD)	**7.15** (1.10)	**8.50** (1.34)	**3.65** (1.63)	**6.57** (1.99)
Range	4.83	4.00	6.83	5.83

Results show that students have good knowledge of computers, high exposure to computers and possess positive attitudes towards computers. What lacks is motivation to learn. It is posited here that learning programs on computers need to be engaging and motivating for continuous learning.

4.1   Research Questions

Does Childrens' Computer-friendliness Significantly Affect their Drawing-Performance (RQ1)?. To answer this question correlation was done between computer-friendliness constructs and drawing performance scores of each task and average performance as well. Average task-performance (max=10) was computed as average of task-scores of T1, T2, T3 and T4. Computer friendliness (max=40) was computed as sum of scores of computer exposure, knowledge, motivation and attitude.

The results in Table 5 indicates that none of the factors contributing to computer-friendliness viz. computer exposure, knowledge, motivation and attitude influence the task-performance significantly. To a certain extent when seen in depth computer-friendliness partially influences complex task performance.

Table 5. Correlation Coefficients   (Computer-Friendliness, Performance ,Adaptations)

NO		1	2	3	4	5	6	7	8	9	10
1	Exposure	1	.207	.288	.217		.515	.138	.128	.353	.179
2	Knowledge		1	.665*	.473		-.288	.086	-.327	-.243	.166
3	Motivation			1	.707*		-.224	.389	.247	.218	-.105
4	Attitudes				1		.184	.086	-.126	.060	-.316
5	Friendliness					1	.055	.205	-.031	.108	-.102
6	AS$_{Search}$						1	-.080	.097		.065
7	AS$_{Modify}$							1	.679*		.033
8	AS$_{Delete}$								1		-.140
9	Total Adaptations									1	-.024
10	Task Performance										1

Figures from Table 5 indicates partial relationship between computer knowledge and motivation as well as between motivation and attitudes. Computer-friendliness has no direct influence on adaptations to GUIs. Therefore user's adaptations to GUI may be connected with factors like interface design, task complexity, time constrain and interest in topic or motivation. This is investigated further in next section of this paper.

RQ1 : Computer-friendliness does not significantly affect the task-performance.

**Does Task or Interface Complexity (Tool Used) Significantly affect Childrens'
Drawing Performance (RQ2)?.** Dependant t-test (paired-samples t-test in SPSS) was
conducted to see the effect of task-complexity on the drawing performance. For
Paint with two independent tasks (simple, complex) the t statistics was $t_{paint}(36)$ =
5.561, P < 0.0005 and for PowerPoint it was $t_{powerpoint}(37)$ = 3.553, P < 0.001.This
shows that user's drawing performance is dependent on how complex is the drawing task. Which is evident in Fig. 3. Also the influence of task complexity on performance is more in Paint than in PowerPoint. This may be accounted to PowerPoint
having more features to accommodate ease-of-change during complex tasks. An interesting hypothesis arises here: Do more features in a GUI lead to faster adaptation?

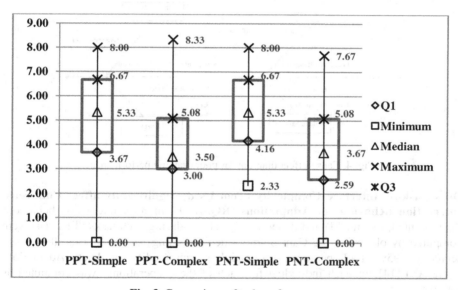

Fig. 3. Comparison of task performances

   The mean task-performance in case of simple task for PPT=4.9297 and PNT=5.3338.
Similarly mean task-performance in complex task situation for PPT=3.8676 and
PNT=3.8429. This shows that task-performance is not influenced much by the GUI. A
similar t-test was conducted to see the effect of interfaces on the drawing performances.
For simple-task with two independent interfaces (Paint, PowerPoint) the t statistics was
$t_{simple}(36)$ = 1.321, P < 0.195 and for complex task it was $t_{complex}(37)$ = - 0.113, P <
0.911. This reassures that interface is not influencing the drawing performance to that
extend. This is because in difficult task situations, users adapt their GUI interactions,
and thereby achieve their goal successfully and efficiently. These user-adaptations can
be at two levels (a)cognitive level and (b) interaction level. The second one is explored
further in this paper.

RQ2 : The results of this experiment show that children once familiar with a particular GUI show differences in their performances only because of complexity of task executed and not the GUI. They adjust very well to the complexity of known GUIs in keeping performances same. Therefore when exposed to a new interface a child will adapt and perform well (do less errors and take less time) after some trials or learning period. In this case what matters is how quickly he can adapt (adaptivity) to an interface. Are these adaptations or adaptivity dependant on interface characteristics or does it depend on individual abilities needs investigation.

Semi structured interviews of participants were conducted to investigate their perceptions and belief in this regards. These are depicted in the cause-effect diagram (Fig. 4).

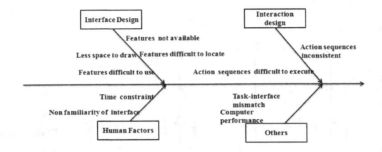

Fig. 4. Cause-effect diagram for poor drawing performance

Does Task or Interface Complexity (Tool Used) Significantly affect Childrens' Interaction Behaviour or Adaptations (RQ3)?. To monitor interaction behaviour the search(S), modify(M) and delete(D) operations during each tasks (T1 .. T4) were computed by observing the Cam Studio video recordings of these tasks. It was observed that 95% of all operations were mainly search, modify and delete. Adaptation-Score(AS) [14] for each individual for each of these operations was computed as follows

$$AS_{search} = (| S_{T1}-S_{T2} |) + (| S_{T2}-S_{T3} |) + (| S_{T3}-S_{T4} |)$$
$$AS_{modify} = (| M_{T1}-M_{T2} |) + (| M_{T2}-M_{T3} |) + (| M_{T3}-M_{T4} |)$$
$$AS_{delete} = (| D_{T1}-D_{T2} |) + (| D_{T2}-D_{T3} |) + (| D_{T3}-D_{T4} |)$$

The statistics obtained for the entire group is shown in Table 6 and Fig. 5.

Table 6. Adaptation Scores Statictics

Statistic	AS_{Search}	AS_{Modify}	AS_{Delete}
MEAN (SD)	**11.55** (6.409)	**17.36** (7.270)	**15.00** (7.253)
RANGE	17	22	22

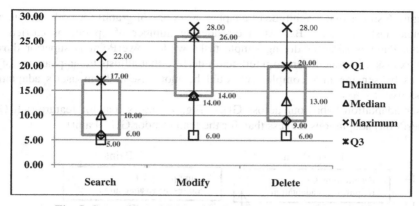

Fig. 5. Comparison of Adaptation Scores of interaction variables

Figure 5. shows high adaptation score for 'modify' operations compared to 'delete' and 'searches'. It means that a child shows more adaptation in 'modify' behaviour while drawing. Therefore if a drawing tool gives a good support and flexibility of modifying drawing elements, it will prove to be a better interface when adapting to different situations. Similarly operations showing more between-task adaptations can be identified for e-learning interfaces as inputs to UI designers.

Figures of mean search, modify and delete operations in all tasks (T1..T4) were used to draw graphs (Fig. 6.) and analyse the trend in user adaptations across tasks and GUIs. The slope of graph reflects magnitude of between-task adaptations. Steep slope means large adaptations in behaviour to cope with new exposed task or interface.

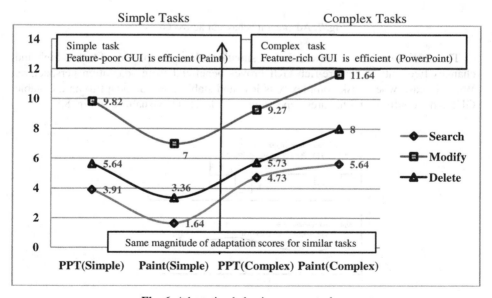

Fig. 6. Adaptation behaviour across tasks

Figure 6 shows that magnitude of adaptations (slope of graph) for both (simple and complex) tasks is same. But when considering number of operations carried out (clicks), Paint is superior during simple tasks while PowerPoint is superior during complex tasks. In conclusion an intelligent interface that adjusts the appearance of its features by sensing task complexity would be more useful from user's adaptation perspective.

User adaptation behaviour across GUIs (Fig. 7) shows that for feature-rich GUI (PowerPoint) adaptations are less than for the feature-poor GUI (Paint).

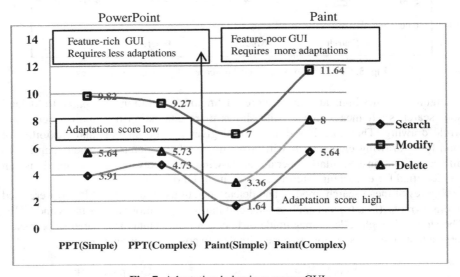

Fig. 7. Adaptation behaviour across GUIs

The conclusion we can draw is that, in situation where complexity of task is high and changes frequently a feature-rich GUI proves beneficial from adaptation perspective. While in case where task complexity is low and stable user can adapt to an adaptable GUI and reconfigure UI features depending on task. This is visualized in Fig. 8.

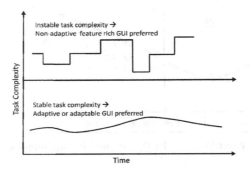

Fig. 8. Task characteristics favourable for adaptations

E-learning interfaces should fall in this second category where learning tasks vary slowly in their complexity levels influenced by the learner's strategies and style.

RQ3: The answer to this question emerges that the adaptations shown in handling simple or complex tasks are same between interfaces. (Fig. 6). However between-task adaptations (from simple to complex) show significant difference among two GUIs i.e. Paint and PowerPoint. (Fig.7). Practical implication of this is that between-task adaptation can be used as a usability measure in evaluating usefulness of alternative interface designs.

5   Conclusions and Future Scope

This study shows that childrens' drawing performance is neither influenced by their computer-friendliness nor by the GUI they use. Task characteristics affect the performance to a large extent.

Results also point to the fact that children show adaptations in their interactions to cope up with difficult task situations. Amount of features available in a GUI may influence these adaptations and adaptivity to changing task situations. A further study can be undertaken on this.

Lastly it was seen that a specific functionality or feature of an interface influences ease-of-adaptations like modify feature of a drawing tool. Interface designers therefore can make use of user's adaptation patterns and limits, in building "adaptation-friendly interfaces". A task-sensitive adaptive interface may be more useful in personalization and can support adaptivity in a better way.

This paper contributes to an idea of using between-task-adaptation score as a usability measure in evaluating usefulness of alternate interface designs. Can we also make use of user's adaptation pattern as a tool for cognitive modelling is an interesting question that arises.

An investigation into interface characteristics influencing user-adaptivity is required. We need to study whether features available in interface or information architecture of interface or interaction design influences adaptivity. Cognitive adaptivity and interaction adaptivity can be two promising directions for future research.

Acknowledgements. The authors would like to acknowledge the help extended by the Principals of Jnana Prabodhini , Pune and Kendriya Vidyalaya IIT Guwahati. We are thankful to the additional support we got from computer teaching staff Ms. Rohini Dhavale, Mr. Rajeev Patel and Mr. Lukman Khan of these schools. We would like to thank all the participating   students in this study.

References

1. Yi, M.Y.: Predicting computer task performance: Personal goal and self-efficacy. J. Organizational and End User Computing 16(2), 20–37 (2004)
2. Smith, S.: An examination of computer self efficacy and computer-related task performance relationship. J. Continuing Higher Education 47306(765) (2005)

3. Artis, S.: In Thesis: The Effects of Age, Computer Self-Efficacy, and the Design of Web-Based Training on Computer Task Performance (2005)
4. Veena, D., Joseph, S.: The effects of motivation and computer usage policies and procedures on task performance. In: ECIS 2006 Proceedings, Sweden, paper 36 (2006)
5. Pak, R., Czaja, S.J., Sharit, J., Rogers, W.A., Fisk, A.D.: The role of spatial abilities and age in performance in an auditory computer navigation task. J. Computers in Human Behavior 24(6), 3045–3051 (2008)
6. Sun, P.-C., Tsai, R.J., Finger, G., Chen, Y.-Y., Yeh, D.: What drives a successful e-Learning? An empirical investigation of the critical factors influencing learner satisfaction. J. Computers & Education 50(4), 1183–1202 (2008)
7. Gray, W.D., Schoelles, M.J., Sims, C.R.: Adapting to the task environment: Explorations in expected value. J. Cognitive Systems Research 6(1), 27–40 (2005)
8. Freed, M., Matessa, M., Rehling, J., Remington, R., Vera, A.: Human-Task Adaptations: The Next Step for Cognitive Modelling. In: IICM 2001 Proceedings, pp. 423–425. Virginia, USA (2001)
9. Sun, H.: Adaptive system use; An investigation at the system feature level. In: ICIS 2008 Proceedings, Paris, paper 170 (2008)
10. Hayama, H., Ueda, K.: Evaluation of Users' Adaptation by Applying LZW Compression Algorithm to Operation Logs. In: Negoita, M.G., Howlett, R.J., Jain, L.C. (eds.) KES 2004. LNCS (LNAI), vol. 3215, pp. 625–631. Springer, Heidelberg (2004)
11. Schmitz, K.: Exploring Technology and Task Adaptation Among Individual Users of Mobile Technology. In: ICIS 2010 Proceedings, St. Louis, paper 57 (2010)
12. Smith, C.L., Kantor, P.B.: User adaptation: good results from poor systems. In: SIGIR 2008 Proceedings, Singapore, pp. 147–154 (2008)
13. Corbalan, G.: Selecting learning tasks: Effects of adaptation and shared control on learning efficiency and task involvement. J. Contemporary Educational Psychology 33(4), 733–756 (2008)
14. Pieschl, S., Stahl, E.: Is adaptation to task complexity really beneficial for performance? J. Learning and Instruction 22(4), 281–289 (2011)
15. Tzanidou, E., Petre, M., Minocha, S., Grayson, A.: Combining Eye Tracking and Conventional Techniques for Indications of User-Adaptability. In: Costabile, M.F., Paternó, F. (eds.) INTERACT 2005. LNCS, vol. 3585, pp. 753–766. Springer, Heidelberg (2005)

Work and Speech Interactions among Staff at an Elderly Care Facility

Tetsuro Chino[1], Kentaro Torii[1], Naoshi Uchihira[1], and Yuji Hirabayashi[2]

[1] Corporate R&D Center, Toshiba Corporation, Kawasaki, Japan
[2] Institute of Technology, Shimizu Corporation, Tokyo, Japan
`tetsuro.chino@toshiba.co.jp`

Abstract. We observed bathing assistance, night shift operations, and handover tasks at a private elderly care home for 8 days. We collected approximately 400 h of recorded speech, 42,000 transcribed utterances, data from an indoor location tracking system, and handwritten notes by human observers. We also analyzed speech interaction in the bathing assistance task. We found that (1) staff members are almost always speaking during tasks, (2) remote communication is rare, (3) about 75% of utterances are spoken to the residents, (4) the intended recipient of utterances is frequently switched, and (5) about 17% of utterances contain personal names. We also attempted clustering utterances into passages, and about 33% of passages contained only one person's name. These results should be applicable in semi-automatic long-term care record taking.

Keywords: cooperative work, speech interaction, care.

1 Introduction

Japan's increasingly aging population is an important issue, one urgent aspect of which is caring for elderly persons with disabilities. Nowadays, care services are often provided by the devoted efforts of care staff at long-term care facilities. Care services are characterized by what we call "action-oriented intellectual services." Care staff makes many decisions regarding medical care which require specialized knowledge. They also assist elderly persons with disabilities in many activities of daily living. Care service staff members have many types of professions and specialties. Also, care services must operate at all hours, throughout the year, and successfully doing so requires a high degree of information sharing among staff, for example, keeping records of care performed. [1] pointed out that medical staff spend much time on indirect care, including record keeping and information sharing. Conventional IT systems are fundamentally designed for desk work, however, and do not support the needs for hands-free and eyes-free operations suited to action-oriented intellectual services.

[2] and [3] proposed a "voice tweet system" to overcome these problems. In that system, "voice tweets" spoken by a staff member are tagged with the staff member's

P. Campos et al. (Eds.): HWID 2012, IFIP AICT 407, pp. 35–45, 2013.

location and motion, spoken keywords, and associations with background knowledge, and based on these tags, the tweets are automatically delivered to an appropriate staffer. This system provides semi-hands-free and eyes-free communication among medical and care staff. Such a system requires knowing what kind of speech communication supports cooperative work in medical and care domains. We therefore performed field studies at an elderly care home in Japan to analyze cooperative work and speech interaction among care staff.

We report on a series of field studies and the insights extracted from analysis of the collected data. The remainder of this paper is organized as follows. Section 2 describes previous works. Section 3 describes the field and the tasks examined. Section 4 describes the study methodology, and Section 5 presents an analysis of the collected data. Finally, Section 6 gives our conclusions and proposed areas for future study.

2   Related Works

[4] analyzed dynamically formed teams in a hospital emergency room, and identified three key factors in the design of team communication technology: (1) maintaining awareness within the team, (2) making informative interruptions, and (3) supporting role-based calling. However, this study was limited to a few directly connected rooms on a single floor. Further investigation of more distributed locations, such as in larger hospitals or care facilities with multiple stories, may therefore be necessary.

[5], [6], and [7] reported on the use of a commercial voice communication system named "Vocera" in actual hospitals. They pointed out (1) that selecting communication artifacts is necessary, (2) that person-locating features can reduce human movement, and (3) that remote voice communication has positive effects on the prioritization and scheduling of tasks. They also described risks and problems associated with voice communication devices.

[8] reported on an analysis of nurse-patient conversations in a Japanese hospital. They found that most utterances effective for risk sharing are spoken by nurses who are highly skilled at risk recognition and communication. In the "voice tweet system" described above, sharing this kind of informative utterances as "voice tweets" can have positive educational effects for the whole team.

3   Study Location

3.1   Care Facility

We performed field studies at a Japanese elderly care home over 8 days between September 2011 and February 2012. Figure 1 shows an overview of the study location. The building has four stories, with 40 private resident rooms, common living and dining rooms, 1 care station, 1 bath area, and other rooms and spaces. Corridors, elevators, and stairways connect the rooms.

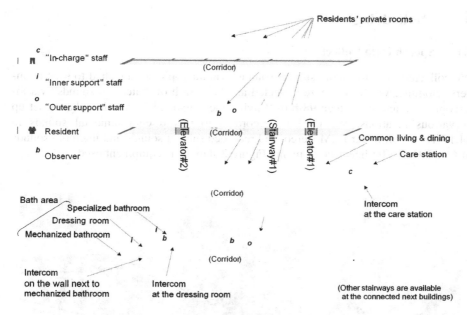

Fig. 1. Overview of the elderly care facility

3.2   Residents with Disabilities

About 30 residents were living in this building during our field study. For convenience, we classify residents into the following groups:

— **Residents with slight disability** are independently mobile with the aid of a device such as a cane or walker.
— **Residents with moderate disability** require a wheelchair and staff assistance to move around.
— **Residents with severe disability** are bedridden, and can only be moved by multiple staff using specially designed devices such as a stretcher.

3.3   Target Tasks

We observed and collected data on 3 tasks.

— The **bathing assistance task** involves bathing residents on the first floor of the building, and is performed by a special day shift team.
— The nighttime staff performs **night shift tasks**, which involve monitoring resident sleep, performing evening and morning care, checking vital signs on a schedule, responding to nurse and sensor calls, and attending to other needs as they arise.
— At scheduled shift changes, leaders of the incoming and outgoing shift personnel perform the **handover task**.

4   Methodology

4.1   Speech Data Collection

We collected over 142 h of "subject sounds" via microphones attached to staff members' clothing. We furthermore collected another 142 h of "intercom sounds" via intercom lines, and more than 98 h of "environmental sounds" via microphones set up at various locations. We used IC recorders to record environmental sounds in 44.1 KHz 16-bit linear PCM stereo, and recorded subject sounds and intercom sounds in 44.1 KHz 16-bit linear PCM mono. Figure 2 shows the equipment used.

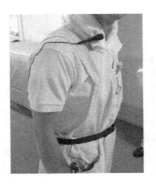

(a) Subject sounds   (b) Intercom sounds   (c) Environmental sounds

Fig. 2. Sound data collection equipment

4.2   Extraction and Transcription of Utterances

About half of the audio data was selected and automatically split into sound fragments. We set the threshold parameter for length of silence between fragments to 500 ms, and human transcribers flagged fragments that were human utterances. Finally, the human utterances were transcribed with time stamps and speaker identifiers. This resulted in more than 42,000 transcribed utterances.

4.3   Other Collected Data

We collected more than 64,000 staff location samples using a Bluetooth-based indoor location tracking system that we developed. Human observers traced staff movements onto paper, and investigated their actions. The observers recorded the time, place, participants, media, and a brief memo on the content of observed conversations involving staffers. Observers also videotaped subjects to get precise movement data with timestamps.

5   Work and Speech Interaction Analysis

5.1   Work Analysis of the Bathing Assistance Task

We chose the **bathing assistance task** for analyzing work and speech interactions, because this was the most complicated collaborative activity among our target tasks. The following is an overview of the bathing assistance task.

1. An **"inner support" staff** in the dressing room determines the next resident to be bathed according to a schedule. Staff performs the bathing task according to the disability level of the resident as follows:

- For **residents with slight disability**, the inner-support staff calls the resident's room via intercom and asks the resident to come to the bath area.

- For **residents with moderate disability**, one or two "outer support" staff members go to the resident's room, check vital signs, and then ask the resident to come to the bath area by wheelchair with their assistance. If the resident agrees, then the staff members assist the resident from the bed to the wheel chair, and bring the resident to the bath area on the first floor.

- For **residents with severe disability**, two or three outer support staff members go to the resident's room with a stretcher designed for bathing bedridden residents, and check vital signs. If the resident agrees and conditions are met, then the staff members assist the resident from the bed to the stretcher, and bring the resident to the bath area on the first floor.

2. After arriving at the bath area, the resident undresses with inner or outer staff assistance, according to need and availability.

3. Assisting staff also check the resident's body and apply ointments or medicines if necessary.

4. The inner support staff helps the resident bathe in a specially designed barrier-free bathroom or a mechanized bathroom, as needed.

5. After bathing, mainly inner support staff helps the resident get dressed.

6. Outer support staff assists the resident from the first-floor dressing room to the second-floor common living and dining rooms.

7. In the living and dining room, other staff members provide support by drying the resident's hair, bringing food, or helping the resident rest in the living room.

8. Finally, staff helps the resident return to his or her room.

Since multiple residents bathe at the same time, some procedures are performed simultaneously. Many factors can force changes in procedure. For example, residents may not be in their rooms, or their mental or physical condition may preclude bathing.

It is worth noting that the tasks of getting dressed and undressed provide residents with valuable opportunities to train and maintain their physical and intellectual abilities, so the staffers provide minimal support and focus on safety. The time needed for getting dressed and undressed differs from resident to resident and can reach 30 min in the longest case, but *efficiency is not the primary consideration in providing high-quality services at elderly care facilities.* Flexible collaboration is therefore necessary to ensure these tasks are performed smoothly.

5.2   Utterances Spoken during Bathing Assistance

We choose one bathing assistance task involving all female residents for our speech interaction analysis. The task was performed over one morning, and represents about 10% of the speech data described in section 4.1.

According to records provided by the elderly care home, 6 staff members had bathing assistance duties that morning. Among them, we focused on two outer support staff members, who we refer to as A and B. We selected them because they moved throughout the study location and interacted with many residents in many different situations at multiple times and places. Table 1 shows a summary of utterances by A and B and other staff and residents.

Table 1. Summary of the extracted utterances

Table 1. Number and length of extracted utterances of staffers A and B of the outer support staff and otehers (other persons, including other staff and residents).						
Speaker	Number	Percentage	Min.	Ave.	Max.	Stdev.
	Extracted utterances		Length of utterances (s)			
A	2,293	22.7%	0.074	**1.683**	5.697	1.214
B	1,692	16.8%	0.121	**1.724**	5.059	1.125
Others	6,110	60.5%	0.055	**1.635**	18.053	1.441
Total	**10,095**	100.0%	-	-	-	-

From the data, 10,095 utterances were extracted. The outer support staff spoke relatively more than others, perhaps because of numerous stock phrases used with residents. The lengths of each utterance were similar for all speakers, perhaps due in part to the influence of our automatic splitting process.

Table 2 shows the spatial conditions of each conversation participant. Almost all utterances (99.4%) were face-to-face communications. The proportion of remote communication was only 1.0% for staffer A, and 0% for staffer B. Inner support staff calls slightly disabled residents in this task, so there is little opportunity for remote communication by outer-support staff. Introducing the voice tweet system at this location would have a significant effect, because currently outer support staff does not have access to remote communication media, which may force unnecessary movement.

Table 2. Summary of special conditions of each conversation participant

Table 2. Spatial conditions of conversational participants in utterances of staffers A and B (outer support staff).							
Speaker	Number	Percentage	Number	Percentage	Number	Percentage
	Face-to-face		Remote		Total	
A	2,269	99.0%	24	1.0%	2,293	100.0%
B	1,692	100.0%	0	0.0%	1,692	100.0%
Total	3,961	99.4%	24	0.6%	3,985	100.0%

5.3   Frequency and Intended Recipients of Utterances

We analyzed utterance frequency and the intended recipients of each utterance to know how often and to whom the care staff talks during this task. Figure 3 shows a time plot of utterances spoken by outer support staffer A (the upper half of the graph) and staffer B (the lower half of the graph) during the 2.5 h of the bathing assistance task. Dots at the upper, middle, and lower positions denote utterances spoken to residents, other staff, and oneself (monologues), respectively. Both A and B are almost always speaking during the task, and the intended recipients quickly changes. In one instance, the collected data show an outer support staff's simultaneous conversation with a resident and other staff in the dressing room.

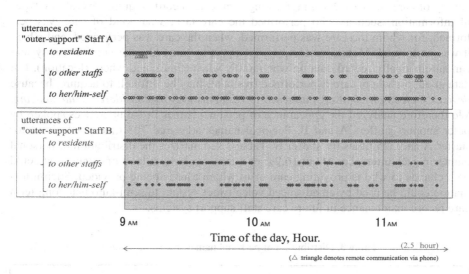

Fig. 3. Time plot and intended recipients of utterances

Figure 4 shows the distribution of intended recipients for utterances by staffers A and B. For both, about 75% of utterances are spoken to residents, about 17% to other staff, and the remaining utterances are monologues. The frequency of utterances to residents may be evidence of the importance of direct face-to-face verbal communication between staff and long-term residents.

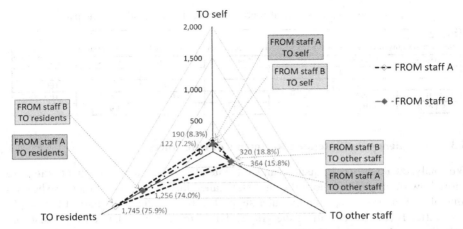

Fig. 4. Distribution of intended recipients of utterances of staffers A and B (outer support staff)

5.4   Names in Utterances

Accurate long-term care records are important for maintaining and improving the quality of care services. Meaningful long-term care records require several key types of information, such as who performed the care task, what kind of care was performed, for whom the care was performed, when the care was performed, and where it was performed. Mobile device–based support systems like the voice tweet system can automatically record data on who (staff), when (time), and where (location). But data about for whom care is performed (resident) may be difficult to acquire, because *devices such as physical tags attached to residents may be considered dehumanizing.* We therefore analyzed the appearance of personal names in the utterances spoken by outer support staffers A and B. Personal names appeared 703 times, 378 times for staffer A and 325 times for staffer B. Table 3 summarizes the distribution of personal names in each utterance. About 16.9% of utterances have at least one name that could be a clue as to who is providing care or to whom care is being provided. Such information could be used by an advanced voice tweet system to semi-automate long-term care record maintenance in future care staff support systems.

Table 3. Distribution of personal names in each utterance

Table 3. Distribution of number of presonal names in utterances of A (outer support staff A) and B (outer support staff B).								
Speaker	Number	Percentage	Number	Percentage	Number	Percentage	Number	Percentage
	No (0)		Only 1		2 or more		Total	
A	1,938	84.5%	335	14.6%	20	0.9%	2,293	100.0%
B	1,377	81.4%	305	18.0%	10	0.6%	1,692	100.0%
Total	3,315	83.2%	640	16.1%	30	0.8%	3,985	100.0%

5.5   Clustering Sequences of Utterances into Passages

To get more information about who provides care and for whom, from utterances for a semi-automatic long-term care record system, we attempted to cluster sequences of utterances into what we call "passages." A threshold parameter of the time gap between sequential utterances allows merging series of utterances spoken by each staffer into passages. Figure 5 shows distributions of passages with specified numbers of names, for 13 different settings (from 0.1 to 60 s) of the threshold for the time gap between passages.

Given an appropriate parameter value (3 s in this case, at the vertical dotted arrow in Figure 5.), the percentage of passages with only one person-name (shown as the solid line in the Figure 5.) can be dramatically improved from 16.1% (the unmerged utterances case in Table 3) to 32.6%, and the average time length of the passage will be 16.7 s. This rate is sufficiently high and this length is sufficiently short to be utilized for precise semi-automatic long-term care records in future care staff support systems.

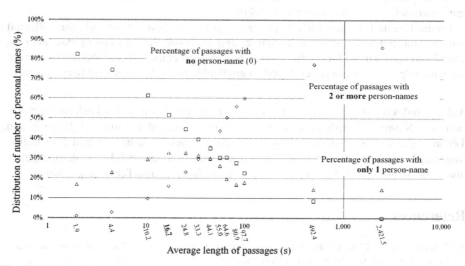

Fig. 5. Relation between the average length of passages (horizontal axis), and the distribution of passages with a specified number of personal names (vertical axis), for multiple thresholds

5.6   Possible Extensions and Applications

Background knowledge on each person who works or lives in the facility (e.g. name, role, gender, shift/work schedule, profession, behavioral preference or tendency, etc.) can be utilized to disambiguate the referent of each referring expression (e.g., personal names or pronouns) appearing in each utterance or passage. Based on this information, together with automatically acquirable information (e.g., who, where, and when) from a mobile device-based platform, the future stuff support system can generate and suggest estimated candidates or outlines of long-term care records to the responsible staff member, and ask for confirmation. This mechanism may contribute to lower costs and reduced load of care staff for the indirect care, as well as to improved quality of long-term care records.

6   Conclusions and Future Work

We reported on a series of field studies at an elderly care facility. For eight days we observed three tasks: bathing assistance, night shift operations, and shift handover. We collected approximately 400 h of recorded speech, 42,000 transcriptions, data from a location tracking system, and handwritten notes by human observers. We also analyzed speech interaction in a bathing assistance task. We found that (1) staff members are almost always speaking during the task, (2) remote communication is rare, (3) about 75% of staff utterances are spoken to residents, (4) utterance targets are frequently switched, and (5) about 17% of utterances contain at least one personal name. We also attempted clustering utterances into passages. The rate of passages with only one personal name can be raised to 33%. These results could be utilized in semi-automatic long-term care record taking.

Future targets for study include (1) an integrated analysis of not only the collected speech data, but also the location, action, and observed descriptions of staff actions, and (2) comparison with data from other hospitals to clarify differences and common aspects, helping to create general models applicable to the broader healthcare domain.

Acknowledgements. This project was joint research between the Toshiba Corporation, the Shimizu Corporation, and the Japan Advanced Institute of Science and Technology, and was supported by the Service Science, Solutions and Foundation Integrated Research Project Program of the Japan Science and Technology Agency under the Ministry of Education, Culture, Sports, Science and Technology, Japan.

References

1. Lemonidou, C., Plati, C., Brokalaki, H., Mantas, J., Lanara, V.: Allocation of nursing time. Scand. J. Caring Sci. 10(3), 131–136 (1996)
2. Naoshi, U., et al.: Innovation for Service Space Communication by Voice Tweets in Nursing and Caring: Concept and Approach in Japanese National Project. In: 20th Annual Frontiers in Service Conference (2011)
3. Torii, K., Uchihira, N., et al.: Service Space Communication by Voice Tweets in Nursing. In: Proc. of AHFE 2012 (July 2012)
4. Lee, S., Tang, C., et al.: Loosely Formed Patient Care Teams: Communication Challenges and Technology Design. In: Proc. of CSCW 2012, pp. 867–876 (February 2012)
5. Richardson, J.E.: The Effects of Hand Free Communication Devices on Clinical Communication: Balancing Communication Access Needs with User Control. In: Proc. of AIMA 2008, pp. 621–625 (2008)

6. Tang, C., Carpendale, S.: A Mobile Voice Communication System in Medical Setting: Love it or Hate It? In: Proc. of CHI 2009, pp. 2041–2050 (April 2009)
7. Tang, C., Carpendale, S., et al.: InfoFlow Framework for Evaluating Information Flow and New Health Care Technologies. Intl. Journal of Human-Computer Interaction 26(4), 477–505 (2010)
8. Nambu, M., Harada, E.T., et al.: Risk Sharing Communication in Medical Settings: Analysis of Nurses' Conversation. Cognitive Studies 13(1), 62–79 (2006) (in Japanese)
9. Alsos, O.A.: Awareness and Usability Issues in Clinical CSCW Systems. In: Proc. of CSCW 2010, pp. 501–502 (2010)

Usability Model for Medical User Interface of Ventilator System in Intensive Care Unit

Ganesh Bhutkar[1], Dinesh Katre[2], G. G. Ray[3], and Shahaji Deshmukh[4]

[1] IIT, Bombay and VIT, Pune, India
ganesh.bhutkar@vit.edu
[2] HCDC Group, C-DAC, Pune, India
[3] Industrial Design Centre, IIT Bombay, Mumbai, India
[4] Department of Surgery, BVUMC, Pune, India

Abstract. A usability model is a hierarchical structure encompassing the key elements such as users, user interface and interaction between them. It is a generic template which is independent of usability evaluation methods and provides flexibility for adaptation in different contexts and domains. In this paper, a usability model for medical user interfaces, especially for ventilator systems in Intensive Care Unit (ICU), is proposed based on Norman's action-oriented seven-step model to capture a related medical context. A ventilator system is a therapeutic device, which provides a respiratory support to critically-ill patients. Currently, a usability of user interfaces of ventilator systems is evaluated by typical usability evaluation methods from software industry. These evaluation methods miss out important elements in medical context. Therefore, a need for a specialized usability model for medical user interfaces is fulfilled with a proposed usability model encompassing vital elements such as medical user, user interface, ICU environment and time required. This usability model is validated first, through a human work analysis using videos of selected tasks with medical user interfaces and then, with an overview of critical factors affecting medical user interfaces in ICU. In future, a proposed usability model can be integrated with a suitable usability evaluation method for evaluating medical user interfaces to identify related medical usability problems more effectively.

Keywords: Usability Model, Medical User Interface, Human Work Analysis, Ventilator System, Intensive Care Unit, Usability Evaluation, Video Analysis.

1 Introduction

In Intensive Care Unit (ICU), there are several medical devices such as patient monitoring system, ventilator system, electrocardiogram (ECG) machine, syringe pump, arterial blood gas machine and defibrillator. Most of these medical devices have user interfaces along with related controls and buttons for interaction with medical users. Fig. 1 depicts a ventilator system with on-screen user interface. A ventilator system provides a respiratory support to critically-ill patients. Its user

P. Campos et al. (Eds.): HWID 2012, IFIP AICT 407, pp. 46–64, 2013.

interface helps medical users to input and control multiple and diversified system parameters during patient care [18]. The user interface also displays vital information related with critically-ill patients. This information includes numeric values, icons, options, menus, messages, graphs, tables or alerts [29] and is really important for communication with medical users.

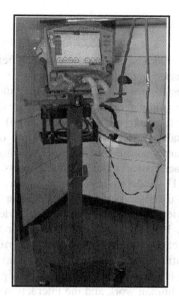

Fig. 1. Ventilator system with its user interface

There are various commonly observed usability problems with medical user interfaces in ICU such as poor legibility or contrast, right-handed design, lack of templates and intelligence, poorly distinguished alarms and alerts, no support in local language and poor feedback about device state and behavior [6, 27, 43]. Such problems may contribute to medical errors. Too many patients have been injured or died because someone pressed a wrong button, misread a number, misplaced a component, skipped a step or overlooked a warning [42] when using medical devices. In fact, medical error is a leading cause of death along with motor vehicle accidents, breast cancer and AIDS [45]. Many physicians, hospitals and even, manufacturers of medical devices may have to face medico-legal cases and liability claims.

Thus, usability of medical devices such as ventilator systems and their user interfaces, is evaluated using several usability evaluation methods such as heuristic evaluation, cognitive walk-through, rapid prototyping, field surveys, usability inspection, Goals, Operators, Methods and Selection rules (GOMS) analysis, computer-based video analysis, usability testing or think-aloud method [2, 19, 22]. Most of these usability methods are typical evaluation methods adapted by software industry and miss out important elements in medical context. Therefore, there is a need for a specialized usability model to bring such missed out medical context into usability evaluation of medical user interfaces in ICU.

In this paper, we have specifically considered touch-screen based ventilator systems. We have proposed a usability model for ventilator system, which encompasses the related medical context along with important elements affecting usability of medical user interfaces in ICU. This model can be used along with a suitable usability method for usability evaluation of medical user interfaces in ICU.

2   Related Work

There are several usability models proposed by researchers. These models are of different types and are discussed in this section.

Winter et al. have suggested two-dimensional quality meta-model of usability. It describes the user interface (input / output data and states) along with information about the situation of use (context and user knowledge) [44]. Abran et al. have provided a consolidated usability model with a baseline of ISO 9241-11 standard integrated with other relevant usability characteristics from ISO 9126 standard and other sources. These characteristics include effectiveness, efficiency, satisfaction, learnability and security [1]. Federici et al. have described integrated model of evaluation to measure the distance between the designer's and the user's mental models [12]. Ford has provided a detailed conceptual model of usability along with several classified variables. It has focused on three major types of contexts – user, task and environment, and each context is described in terms of classified variables. For example, user is identified with characteristics, knowledge and so on [14]. Clemmensen has proposed Human Work Interaction Design (HWID) model, which shows the characteristics of human work and the interaction during tasks and decision activities, individually or in collaboration. It also highlights impact of theory and environmental context on such interaction [10]. Rasmussen et al. have defined decision ladder model for representing the generic categories of activity that are necessary in a system and suitable for design and execution of actions [32]. A comprehensive study of usability models as briefly summarized above, has led to identification of common characteristics of models.

The usability model provides -

- broad elemental breakup of the activity.
- hierarchical structure between the key elements.
- a generic template which is independent of usability evaluation methods.
- flexibility for adaptation in different contexts and domains.

Table 1 depicts a comparison table for usability models differentiating among seven main models studied based on major aspects shown in first column of the table. Other columns represent usability models identified by names of authors proposing respective models. There are few observations realized during a comparison of usability models. The type of usability model is one from the related group - quality model, user-centered model, action-oriented model or work analysis model. Most of the models are non-iterative models expect Norman's model. Most of them do not consider work environment or time requirement during the analysis. Most of these models consider a restricted context in terms of task, situation or culture. None of the models consider medical context in usability analysis and evaluation.

Table 1. Comparison among usability models

Aspect of Comparison	Usability Models considered						
	Winter et al.	Ford	Federici et al.	Abran et al.	Clemmensen	Norman	Rasmussen et al.
Type of Model	Quality	User-centered	User-centered	Quality	Work Analysis	Action-oriented	Action-oriented
Levels of Details	Detailed	Abstract	Detailed	Abstract	Detailed	Abstract	Detailed
Iterative Approach	No	No	Partially	No	No	Yes	No
Work Environment	No	Considered	No	No	Considered	No	No
Time required	No	No	No	Indirectly	No	No	No
Context	Considered	Considered	No	No	Considered	No	Considered

Thus, though usability models are quite useful for usability analysis and evaluation, most of them are general-purpose and definitely miss out medical context. These models fail to identify usability problems and medical errors in ICU environment. Such failure may lead to patient injury or death [42]. Therefore, it puts forward an important research question:

How to Adapt the Usability Model in Medical Context?

A user interaction with medical devices through user interface is studied during usability evaluation. Such user interaction involves several tasks such as setting up a device, changing a device mode or parameters, updating patient record, monitoring patient's condition through alarms and alerts or generating reports [42, 45]. A task-oriented work analysis involving medical users can provide a better insight about usability problems as well as medical errors related with therapeutic devices such as ventilator systems. This aspect has directed a selection of Norman's action-based model during research work. This model is iterative and therefore, it can help in detecting usability problems in prototype design and subsequently, improving the prototype during several iterations. Also, it is possible to accommodate medical context in Norman's model in terms of necessary elements (discussed in next section) in ICU environment.

Norman has proposed a seven-stage action model, which is published in Psychological Review [30] and is represented in fig. 2, which was used initially to capture major action slips [31]. Norman's model starts with goal formation. The aspect of execution contains stages for the formulation of intentions to act, the planning of a sequence of actions, and the execution of actions, while the aspect of evaluation consists of observation of the result, interpreting it and evaluating it to create new goals, if required. **Till-date, many researchers have utilized and adapted Norman's action model with diversified perspectives in various domains such as Organizational Behavior, Telecommunication, Web Design, Public Interfaces, Computer Games, Aeronautics and Medicine** [3, 4, 13, 17, 25, 28, 34, 36, 39, 45].

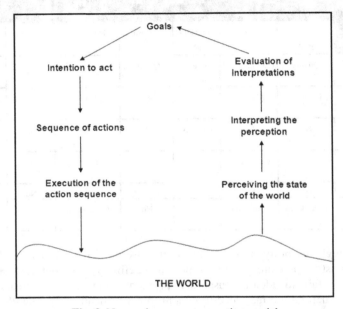

Fig. 2. Norman's seven-stage action model

Goldkuhl et al. have presented a general model of social action and have used it to characterize information systems as artifacts employed for organizational action [17]. This general model of social action is influenced by Norman's model. As part of the project AVANTI (AdaptiVe and Adaptable iNteractions for multimedia Telecommunication applIcation), the Norman Cognitive Walkthrough (NCW) method addresses the particular problem - the presence of design teams in different cities, even in different countries [34]. Babu et al. have used Norman's action model to conduct online assessments that guide in understanding the complete interaction between a blind user and the Web in performing an online task [3]. Finke et al. have reported on a series of experiments carried out to determine quantitative and qualitative effects on user performance when interaction is split across large public and smaller private screens. The experimentation is designed based on Norman's action model [13]. Kim et al. have introduced Eye Mouse and user's Thinking (EMT) System that tracks eye and mouse, and records user's thinking. For applying EMT system, EMT tool is developed to help a researcher to do usability test by recording the user's experience and reproducing it visually. For defining perception, recognition, and behavior of users' experience, Norman's action model is used along with other two models [25]. Salovaara has presented appropriation understood as interpretation process in which user perceives in a tool a new opportunity for action, thus acquiring a new mental usage schema that complements the existing uses [36]. This model is close to Norman's action model, but extended for learning during use. Barr has discussed implications of analyzing computer game actions using Norman's action model [4]. Sherry et al. have discussed about how pilots form 'mental models', the way system behaves and use these models to guide their interaction with the system based on Norman's action model [39].

Norman's action model has been also applied in medical domain. Zhang et al. have developed a preliminary action-based cognitive taxonomy of errors; both for slips and mistakes in the domain of medicine, based on Norman's action model [45]. Malhotra et al. have proposed a cognitive workflow model in critical care environment. The representation of medical users draws inspiration from data processing systems and Norman's action model, defining mental and system activities required for task completion [28].

Thus, Norman's action model has been widely accepted model in several studies as well as domains. This model is selected as it is iterative approach, which helps in identifying usability problems and subsequently improving the prototype design. Also, it is possible to accommodate medical context in the model in terms of necessary elements in ICU environment. The proposed usability model for medical user interface of ventilator system is discussed in the next section.

3   Proposed Usability Model for User Interface of Ventilator System

A usability model for medical user interface of ventilator system is proposed based on Norman's seven-stage action model as shown in fig. 3. In this usability model, all seven stages of actions highlighted in Norman's model are considered along with certain alterations and additions as discussed ahead:

- A 'medical user' is added and a 'physical system' is replaced by 'user interface'. These changes are required as the focus of proposed model is on usability, in which interaction among medical users and user interfaces of ventilator systems is dealt with. Thus, 'medical user' and 'user interface' are important elements in proposed usability model.
- Usability model starts and ends with 'goal' to complete the loop. The interaction with user interface of ventilator system is initiated by medical user, responded by user interface and evaluated again by the user for further action. The model also facilitates further iterations, if required.
- A 'response' is added next to 'user interface' as a response is always generated in the form of display of or change in numerical values, messages, graphs, alerts and alarms with medical user interfaces [29]. Such response is a basis for activities ahead such as perception, interpretation and evaluation

in usability model. The 'user interface' and 'response' are device-related items and therefore, grouped together as shown in fig. 3.

- Three important features observed with 'user interface' of ventilator systems are shown in the model – 'Combination of physical and onscreen interface', 'High risk' and 'Long-distance visibility' [5, 9, 23]. These features are shown connected with 'user interface' in the model.
- Along with elements - 'medical user' and 'user interface', other two vital elements - 'ICU environment' and 'time required' are also shown in the center of the model. These elements should be considered in each iteration of usability analysis to capture a related medical context.

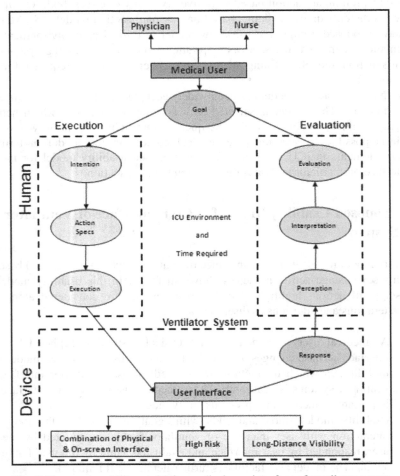

Fig. 3. Proposed usability model for medical user interface of ventilator system

The vital elements considered in usability model are discussed in this section in details.

3.1   Medical User

There are two major users of ventilator systems - physicians and nurses. They are primary users as they actually operate the devices during patient care in ICU [6]. Physicians and nurses differ from each other in mainly six aspects such as gender, language proficiency, education/training, eyesight, average work experience and numbers in ICU as shown in initial six rows of table 2. These comparative aspects are identified based on field study and profiles collected of 12 medical users including 6 physicians and 6 nurses working in intensive care units. The numbers indicated in brackets in table 2 represent positive entries of the related aspect. Remaining two aspects in table 2 depict roles and responsibilities of medical users identified in related literature survey [33, 37].

Table 2. Comparison between medical users – physicians and nurses

Aspect of Comparison	Physicians	Nurses
Gender	Mostly Male (5/6)	Mostly Female (5/6)
Proficiency of Language	English (6/6)	Mostly Hindi /Local Lang. (5/6)
Education / Training	4-8 Years (6/6)	2-4 Years (6/6)
Eyesight	Mostly Myopic (4/6)	Mostly Normal (5/6)
Average Work Experience	About 10 Years	About 5 Years
Number in ICU	Lesser (1 per 4 Patients)	More (1 per 2 Patients)
Role in Diagnosis	Decision-making	Assistive
Role in Therapy & Monitoring	Planning & Supervision	Execution

It can be observed that physicians and nurses differ significantly in their background and approach to patient care, which directly affects the manner in which they interact with medical devices in ICU. There is a noteworthy difference in a way in which they perform the task. For example, selection of ventilation mode may be executed by nurse, but it is generally on the advice of physician. This task is executed only by physicians in some intensive care units.

3.2   User Interface

The user interface considered in proposed model is for touch-screen based ventilator system. **Though ventilator system is mainly a therapeutic device, it also helps in**

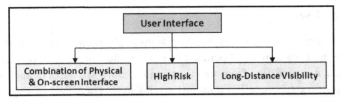

Fig. 4. Features of user interface with ventilator system

monitoring of critically-ill patients [11, 38]. It has a combination of onscreen and physical interface [18]. Physical interface includes a control panel with knobs, buttons, LEDs and/or indicator light. Being a therapeutic device in ICU, it is high-risk device. A long-distance visibility is involved in patient monitoring [9] with alarms and alerts of ventilator systems. These features are shown in fig. 4 and they should be considered in evaluation of user interfaces of ventilator systems.

3.3   ICU Environment

In ICU, several environmental factors affect user interaction with medical devices. These environmental factors include lighting condition, ICU layout, noise as well as interruptions and disruptions [9, 41]. There are three levels of lighting conditions in ICU. Low and average lighting conditions are observed at 0-100 lux and 101-500 lux respectively whereas extreme lighting condition is observed at higher range. These lighting conditions are derived based on light readings obtained from three intensive care units selected at various times of the day. The consultation with physicians and the observations of ICU layouts has led to three commonly observed viewing distances, which can be applied in long-distance visibility testing. The first level is 6 feet (1.83 m), which is the length of the bed. The next level is 13 feet (3.96 m), which is quite common monitoring distance in smaller intensive care units [9]. The highest monitoring distance suggested is 20 feet (6.10m) which can be observed in some bigger intensive care units. The next environmental factor is interruptions and disruptions, which include asking questions or for assistance, phone calls, exchange of information with others, presence of other patients [40] and movements of medical staff as well as devices. These environmental factors definitely affect user interaction with medical devices such as ventilator systems; especially during patient monitoring and can lead to medical errors harming patient life. Therefore, such factors are included in proposed usability model for medical user interface.

3.4   Time Required

In ICU, the time is a significant element during performance of tasks. The survival rates of patients are higher in hospitals and intensive care units where the emergency systems are efficient and quicker. In emergencies, physicians and nurses are required to provide a treatment to critically-ill patients in quick time. So, they interact with devices through user interfaces hurriedly during patient care. Such rapid and hasty execution of tasks during interaction increases the chances of medical errors as well as stoppages or delays creating a threat to patients' life. For example, to set couple of ventilation parameters, it takes about 10 seconds with user interface of ventilator system; but this task may be delayed if nurse fails to understand that screen is locked or there is a delay related with physician's advice. Therefore, a time required for a task is an important element in performance of task and is required to be considered in usability evaluation of user interface in medical devices such as ventilator systems.

4   Validation of Proposed Usability Model

The proposed usability model for medical user interface of ventilator system needs to be validated. This validation is performed using two methods - video analysis and overview of critical factors in ICU, which are described in this section ahead.

4.1   Human Work Analysis through Video Analysis

As proposed usability model is action-based model, one needs to capture and analyze action sequences of selected tasks. Therefore, video analysis method is selected for validation of model through human work analysis. A video provides a remarkably rich and vivid reproduction of an event. It also provides a permanent record of an event and supports reviewing and analysis of data at later times. Kaufman et al. have presented an approach to usability evaluation of computer-based healthcare systems designed for patient use in their homes. This approach includes a video analysis consisting of verbal and non-verbal analysis along with micro-level coding [24]. Rogers et al. have analyzed a blood glucose meter for its usability using video analysis, in which transcription and coding is used [35]. During this research work, selected task performances are video-recorded in real-time ICU environment. Such recordings have captured interaction of users with ventilator systems as well as related display screens in ICU environment. **The names of manufacturers, device models and user identities are not disclosed to maintain confidentiality.** Usability professionals also need to have basic domain knowledge about medical users and devices such as ventilator systems for applying the proposed usability model. This section includes necessary steps involved in video analysis.

4.1.1   Selection of Representative Users

There are two major types of users of ventilator systems - physicians and nurses in ICU. They are primary users and actually operate the ventilator systems during patient care. These users differ on range of aspects such as gender, language proficiency, education/training, eyesight, average work experience and numbers in ICU [33, 37] as seen in table 2. It is not possible to employ a fully representative sample and therefore, a convenient sampling method is used [26]. Two ventilator systems are studied and related videos are captured. Nurse is involved with videos of first ventilator system and physician is involved with videos of other ventilator system.

4.1.2   Selection of Representative Tasks

In patient care, several tasks are performed by physicians and nurses with ventilator systems in ICU. The list of tasks includes setting a system, pretesting of a system, setting a mode, changing parameter values, setting up alarms and alerts, patient monitoring, updating patient record and generating a diagnostic report [11, 38, 42, 45]. It is observed that two tasks - setting up a ventilator system and changing parameter values are most frequently employed tasks by medical users with ventilator systems. During these tasks, medical users extensively interact with ventilator systems though user interface. Such interactions often involve device displays, touch screen interaction or use of controls/knobs and may have effect of surrounding ICU environment. Therefore, these two tasks are selected for video-recording and related two videos are recorded for each ventilator system.

4.1.3   Conducting a Video-Recording

Setting ventilator systems and make them operational typically takes about 5-10 minutes if no other interruptions or distractions happen in ICU environment. Such setup is tested before video-recording the user interaction. It is very hectic and tricky challenge to get an access to busy intensive care units [8] and to obtain permission for video recording there. A problematic spatial layouts and noise in the surrounding also create hurdles for video-recording process. The primary focus of video-recording has been on tasks performed by medical users through user interaction with ventilator systems. Important activities such as hand movements of users, data presented, selection of options, responses displayed and delayed device responses are captured in video-recording. **The camera model used for video-recording is Pentax Optio M20 with resolution of 7 Megapixels. The file format of the recorded video file is .mov and the software used for video-logging is VLC Media Player 1.1.5.** The video-recording is conducted in late afternoon with an average lighting condition.

4.1.4   Preparation of Observation Table

For each video recorded, an observation table is prepared. A part of observation table related with a video of physician setting up a ventilator system is depicted in fig. 5. There is an attempt to realistically record the observations about interaction between medical users and ventilator system while performing the tasks. Few of the field observations and activities in surrounding environment during recording session are noted. The observation table shows a chronological sequence of activities involved in a particular task. The details of each activity are mapped onto various stages and vital elements of proposed usability model. During the mapping, the stages and elements are divided into five groups. This grouping can be noted in columns represented in the observation table of fig. 5. The grouping is mostly sequential as per the stages of the usability model.

Sr. No.	Start Time (Sec.)	Frame	Mapping with Usability Model for Medical User Interface				
			Medical User Type, Goal & Intention	Action Specifications (A) & Execution (E)	User Interface & Response (R)	ICU Environment & Time	Perception, Interpretation & Evaluation
1	0		Physician is *right-handed*. Physician is *setting up a ventilator system*.		R - Two green LEDs are ON. The screen is blank.	The LEDs can be observed from a *distance* (max. 6 feet) during patient monitoring.	Two green LEDs indicate 'Power ON' and 'AC' as a power source.
2	21			A - Physician presses a start button on side of the monitor using *index finger of right hand*.		A beep is heard.	A beep indicates a start of ventilator system.
3	23			A - Physician waits for system response.	R - Screen is still blank.	A physician is *waiting* for response on the screen. The LEDs can be observed from a *distance* (max. 6 feet) during patient monitoring.	
4	28				R – The icon 'lock' can be observed at top right corner with a start ventilation option on the screen. The option 'ACV' is also displayed.	The discussions among nurses and physicians can be heard generating some noise.	The 'Lock' icon does not look like a lock, more like a bag. Full form expression for describing the parameter is not available.
5	35			A - Physician unlocks the screen by touching the 'Lock' icon using index *finger of right hand*.			The screen is locked. *Information displayed* before setting ventilator system is *not helpful* to physicians.
6	37				R - Screen turns white.	A physician is *waiting* for response on the screen.	
7	40				R - The icon 'lock' can be observed at left-center position of the screen with handle open. Screen shows two options – 'ACV' and 'New Patient'.		The screen is unlocked and Icon – 'Lock' is shown at changed location in the center.
8	92		Physician requires to *select patient type*.	A - Physician selects an option – 'New patient' through touch with index *finger of right hand*.			
9	94				R - Screen shows four options – 'invasive', 'non-invasive', 'Paediatric' and 'Adult' for selection of patient configuration in capital letters.		It is not clear about how many options to be selected for patient configuration. The options are difficult to read.

Fig. 5. Part of observation table related with a video involving physician setting up a ventilator system

In the first column of mapping, medical user, goal and intention are grouped together as such details are necessary in a preparation before execution of task. The related entry in fig. 5 is - 'Physician is right-handed. Physician is setting a ventilator system'. The next column has two stages - Action specification (A) and Execution (E) as these are closely associated with execution of task. One such action is unlocking the screen. The next column has a group of entities related with user interface and related response. For example, on-screen user interface shows six options for selection of ventilation mode and selected mode is highlighted on the screen as a response.

The factors related with ICU environment and time required, are highlighted in fourth column. The LEDs for power source can be observed from a shorter distance (6-10 feet) during patient monitoring and therefore, are not suitable for long-distance visibility of alerts. Time required for an activity during user interaction is facilitated by a response provided through a user interface. At times, a physician needs to wait for few seconds to get the required response. The last column has a group containing stages - perception, interpretation and evaluation as these stages are related with evaluation of response provided by user interface. At times, an inquiry or a confirmation of details in this column is required and it is achieved through interviews of medical users. Physician has confirmed the confusion about how many options to be selected for patient configuration. The options displayed in capital letters for patient configuration are difficult to read. Also, icons are not used for providing these options though well-accepted icons for 'Paediatric' and 'Adult' [7] are easily available.

Thus, observation tables have several important observations about user interactions with ventilator system. These observations are analyzed to capture related medical context as discussed in next section.

4.1.5   Data Analysis

The details of activities segregated into five groups in observation table are studied and analyzed. Many observations in the table highlight some important usability problems associated with vital elements. The findings in data analysis are discussed in this section.

Medical User: In data analysis, many aspects of medical users are revealed. Nurse uses a middle finger; instead of index finger to operate touch screen as shown in fig. 6. But, other fingers are more error-prone than index finger during touch screen interaction [16]. The use of middle fingers by Indian nurses with touch screen interface may be associated with **'Kumkum/Bindi effect'** [20, 21] observed among Indian women. Traditionally, women apply kumkum on forehead of oneself or other women using a middle finger in India. Such effect may be carried over to interaction of nurses with interfaces of medical devices such as ventilator systems. Though nurse is right-handed, she has to operate the user interface using left hand due to space constraint. Nurse has also fumbled during selection of ventilation parameters as she failed to understand that screen is locked.

User Interface: In data analysis, many usability problems are identified in user interface of ventilator system. The arrangement of multiple options in menu can be improved. The three options in the dialogue box for 'Patient Select' are quite distant from each other and six options arranged in dialogue box - 'Screen select' are asymmetric as depicted in fig. 6.

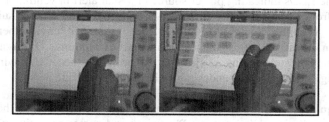

Fig. 6. Inappropriate grouping and symmetry of options in menu

Ventilator system is therapeutic device with important high-risk therapeutic tasks such as a selection of ventilator mode and setting up ventilation parameters. A confirmation of such tasks or actions is desirable, which is not provided in user interface of one of the ventilator systems studied.

ICU Environment: There are several factors related with ICU environment, which are highlighted in observation tables. The light reflections are noticed on and around the device screen and they obstruct the visibility of data on the screen. This is highlighted in the observation – 'Glossy screen reflects face of the nurse'.

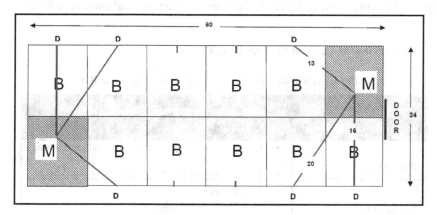

Fig. 7. Layout of ICU depicting dimensions and positions

Another factor highlighted in observations is ICU layout, which affects the viewing distance in ICU [9]. One of such ICU layouts, where this study is conducted, is provided in fig. 7. This layout is developed to understand the room dimensions and positions of doors, monitoring stations, beds as well as medical devices. In ICU layout, B stands for Bed position; D stands for Device position; M stands for

Monitoring station. The lines between monitoring stations (M) and devices (D) show the viewing distances in feet. The horizontal and vertical arrows depict the spatial dimensions of ICU in feet. A monitoring station is a place in ICU from where nurses or physicians monitor conditions of critically-ill patients. It is at minimum of 13 feet (3.96m) from devices as seen in fig. 7. From the observation table shown in fig. 5, it is clear that the LEDs indicating power source or visual alert in ventilator system can be observed from a short distance of 6 feet (1.83m) only and are not suitable for a long-distance visibility (upto 20 feet/ 6.10m). Another environmental factor highlighted in observations is interruptions and disruptions. Discussion among medical staff in a surrounding contributes to noise in the ICU environment as indicated in fig. 5. Multiple and undesirable alarms also generate noise.

Time Required: In time-critical environment like ICU, most of the tasks are performed hurriedly in minimum time. Physicians and nurses are quite often busy in patient care and dealing with emergency. A nurse or physician needs to wait as ventilator system takes time to start-up or boot-up. It makes the user little impatient.

4.1.6   Result

A data analysis of videos recorded shows that the proposed usability model is able to capture more aspects of medical context in ICU environment. Such aspects or observations include light reflections, noise, arrangements of options, use of different fingers with touch screens, therapeutic actions, long-distance visibility and delays in device responses. Thus, a proposed usability model is validated through human work analysis using videos and it definitely captures required medical context in ICU.

4.2   Overview of Critical Factors in ICU

Table 3. Critical factors related with distinct elements in ICU

Vital Element of Proposed Usability Model	Related Critical Factors in ICU
Medical User	• Physicians with varying levels of critical care training • Skills of nurses • Familiarity of equipment, procedure or environment
User Interface	• Therapy applied/ usage • Complex work and information flow • Design of alerts and alarms • Correctness of default thresholds
ICU Environment	• Interruptions and distractions • Lighting condition and noise • Room layout
Time required	• Emergency • Urgent high-risk decision making

A comprehensive overview of critical factors is taken with a literature survey of relevant research publications about ICU. The critical factors, which affect user interface design of medical devices such as ventilator systems, are identified. These critical factors are categorized with a due consideration to vital elements of proposed usability model such as medical user, user interface, ICU environment and time required. This categorization of critical factors is depicted in table 3.

The categorization of critical factors is discussed in this section. Few critical factors are related with medical users and may affect user interaction with medical devices. There are various types of physicians such as specialists, ICU physicians, resident physicians and interns with varying levels of critical care training. The 'skills of nurses' is a critical factor, which affects a patient care in ICU. These skills include safe medication, patient monitoring, respiratory or orthopedic care, record keeping, assistance to physicians and patient or family counseling [33]. Familiarity of equipment, procedure or environment of the medical user can affect one's task performance. Such user skills or features as highlighted by critical factors should be considered in design, analysis as well as evaluation of medical user interfaces.

Several critical factors affect the user interfaces of medical devices. Ventilator systems provide a respiratory support to critically-ill patients. A mode of usage or therapy applied is required to be considered in interface design of ventilator systems. A complex work and information flow provides a challenge for interface designers to incorporate it into effective user interface. Alert and alarm design demands a special attention as they are needed in patient monitoring in ICU. A correctness of default thresholds in parameter values is required for efficient patient care in ICU.

Environmental factors in ICU are also important. A major factor is interruptions and disruptions, which include questions asked for assistance, phone calls, exchange of information among medical staff [40], presence of other patients, noise from medical devices and surrounding people. Other environmental factors include lighting condition and ICU layout [41], which also affect the long-distance visibility of user interfaces in ICU.

Emergency with critically-ill patients puts a constraint on the time provided for performing a task by medical users. The tasks such as setting up a ventilator system providing respiratory support to patient need to be executed immediately. An 'urgent high-risk decision-making' is a factor affected by processes like cognitive tunneling, which is a tendency of physician to focus on only one hypothesis or solution at a time and ignoring other possibilities [15]. Such decisions affect the time required for a therapy provided by medical devices such as ventilator systems.

These critical factors in ICU affecting user interface can be categorized as per vital elements related with proposed usability model for medical user interface of ventilator system as observed in table 3. The consideration of vital elements in a proposed usability model can direct usability professionals to many of these critical factors affecting user interfaces of ventilator systems and can help in capturing a required medical context in ICU.

5   Conclusion and Future Work

Usability model for user interface of ventilator system is proposed based on Norman's seven-stage action model. This comprehensive model brings related medical context into human work analysis in terms of vital medical elements such as medical user, user interface, ICU environment and time required. It captures usability aspects like light reflections, noise, arrangements of options, use of different fingers with touch screens, therapeutic actions, long-distance visibility and delays in device responses. This model can be used as a template with medical user interfaces effectively by usability professionals for improved results. In future, a proposed usability model for ventilator system can be integrated with a suitable usability evaluation method to identify related usability problems with medical user interfaces more effectively.

Acknowledgements. We thank Prof. Torkil Clemmensen and IFIP officials for providing Ganesh Bhutkar, IFIP Developing Countries Support Committee (DCSC) grant to attend an International Conference - HWID 2012 at Copenhagen Business School, Denmark in Dec. 2012. We are grateful to Prof. Uday Athavankar for his critical comments and suggestions during Annual Progress Seminar (APS) presentations. We are also thankful to other Research Progress Committee (RPC) members - Prof. Ravi Poovaiah and Prof. Azizuddin Khan for their valuable support and guidance. We appreciate a cooperation extended by physicians – Dr. Shekhar Karmarkar, Dr. Ajit Adangale, Dr. Harshwardhan Anturkar and Dr. Rajiv Doshi along with the nursing staff during the field work and video-recording in intensive care units. We thank Ahmed Hamja - a photography enthusiast, for his support to research work through photography during the research. At last, we thank Uday Sagale and Dhiraj Jadhav for their assistive support in documentation and related editing during the paper writing.

References

1. Abran, A., Khelifi, A., Suryn, W., Seffah, A.: Consolidating ISO Usability Models. In: 11th International Software Quality Management Conference (2003)
2. Atyeo, M.: Usability Evaluation - Comparing Techniques. Presentation by Neo Insight (January 2006)
3. Babu, R., Singh, R., Ganesh, J.: Understanding Blind Users' Web Accessibility and Usability Problems. AIS Transaction on Human-Computer Interaction 2(3), 73–94 (2010)
4. Barr, P.: Usability and Value: Playing Computer Games (2003)
5. Bhutkar, G., Deshmukh, S.: Medical Devices in Intensive Care Unit. Medical Equipment and Automation (January-February 2012)
6. Bhutkar, G., Katre, D., Rajhans, N., Deshmukh, S.: Scope of Ergonomic and Usability Issues with Intensive Care Unit (ICU): An Indian Perspective. HFESA Journal - Ergonomics Australia 22(1), 26–32 (2008)
7. Bhutkar, G., Poovaiah, R., Katre, D., Karmarkar, S.: Semiotic Analysis combined with Usability and Ergonomic Testing for Evaluation of Icons in Medical User Interface. In: IndiaHCI 2011- Third International Conference on Human Computer Interaction, pp. 57–67. ACM, USA (2011)

8. Bhutkar, G., Rajhans, N., Katre, D., Dhabe, P., Dhore, M., Barbadekar, B.: Analysis and Design of ICU Knowledge Management System (IKMS) for Indian Environment with Usability Perspective. In: IEEE International Conference on Computer and Automation Engineering (ICCAE), Singapore, February 2, pp. 329–333 (2010)
9. Bhutkar, G., Ray, G., Katre, D., Deshmukh, S.: Long-Distance Visibility Testing of Visual Alerts in Medical User Interfaces in ICU. In: International Conference on Ergonomics and Human Factors - HWWE 2011, IIT Chennai (December 2011)
10. Clemmensen, T.: A Human Work Interaction Design (HWID) Case Study in e-Government and Public Information Systems. IJPIS 3, 105–113 (2011)
11. Draft Guidance-HUD Designations Guidance. FDA (2011)
12. Federici, S., Borsci, S.: Usability Evaluation: Models, Methods and Applications. International Encyclopedia of Rehabilitation (2010)
13. Finke, M., Kaviani, N., Wang, I., Tsao, V., Fels, S., Lea, R.: Investigating Distributed User Interfaces across Interactive Large Displays and Mobile Devices (2010)
14. Ford: Conceptual Model of Usability. Researching on the Effects of Culture on Usability, ch. 6, pp. 152–174 (2009)
15. Gokin, P.: Human Factor Issues in Designing Alarms and Monitors for Critical Care Environments. Course HF 755B (2005)
16. Forlines, C., Wigdor, D., Shen, C., Balakrishnan, R.: Direct Touch vs. Mouse Input for Tabletop Displays. In: Conference on Human Factors in Computer Systems (CHI) (April 2007)
17. Goldkuhl, G., Agerfalk, P.: Actability: A Way to Understand Information Systems Pragmatics. Coordination and Communication Using Signs: Studies in Organisational Semiotics (2000)
18. Gould, T., de Beer, J.: Principles of Artificial Ventilation. Anesthesia and Intensive Care Medicine 8(3), 91–101 (2007)
19. Hartson, H., Andre, T., Wellige, R.: Criteria for Evaluating Usability Evaluation Methods. International Journal of Human Computer Interaction 15(1), 145–181 (2003)
20. Hindu Janajagruti Samiti: What is the Benefit of Applying Kumkum than a Bindi?, http://www.hindujagruti.org/hinduism/knowledge/article/what-is-the-benefit-of-applying-kumkum-than-a-bindi.html (retrieved on December 24, 2012)
21. India Profile: Bindis - Traditional and Trendy, http://www.indiaprofile.com/fashion/bindis.htm (retrieved on December 24, 2012)
22. Jaspers, M.: A Comparison of Usability Methods for Testing Interactive Health Technologies: Methodological Aspects and Empirical Evidence. International Journal of Medical Informatics 78, 340–353 (2009)
23. Katre, D., Bhutkar, G., Karmarkar, S.: Usability Heuristics and Qualitative Indicators for the Usability Evaluation of Touch Screen Ventilator Systems. In: Katre, D., Orngreen, R., Yammiyavar, P., Clemmensen, T. (eds.) HWID 2009. IFIP AICT, vol. 316, pp. 83–97. Springer, Heidelberg (2010)
24. Kaufman, D., Patel, V., Hilliman, C., Morin, P., Pevzner, J., Weinstock, R., Goland, R., Shea, S., Starren, J.: Usability in the Real-World: Assessing Medical Information Technologies in Patients' Homes. Journal of Biomedical Informatics 36, 45–60 (2003)
25. Kim, B., Dong, Y., Kim, S., Lee, K.-P.: Development of Integrated Analysis System and Tool of Perception, Recognition, and Behavior for Web Usability Test: With Emphasis on Eye-Tracking, Mouse-Tracking, and Retrospective Think Aloud. In: Aykin, N. (ed.) HCII 2007. LNCS, vol. 4559, pp. 113–121. Springer, Heidelberg (2007)

26. Kothari C.: Research Methodology - Methods and Techniques, 2nd revised edn., p. 96. New Age International Publishers (2010)
27. Liu, Y., Osvalder, A., Dahlman, S.: Exploring User Background Settings in Cognitive Walkthrough Evaluation of Medical Prototype Interfaces: A Case Study. International Journal of Industrial Ergonomics 35, 379–390 (2005)
28. Malhotra, S., Jordan, D., Patel, V.: Workflow Modeling in Critical Care: Piecing your Own Puzzle. In: AMIA 2005, pp. 480–484 (2005)
29. Martin, J., Murphy, E., Crowe, J., Norris, B.: Capturing User Requirements in Medical Device Development: The Role of Ergonomics. Physiological Measurement 27(8), 49–62 (2006)
30. Norman, D.: Categories of Action Slips. Psychological Review 88(1), 1–15 (1981)
31. Norman, D.: The Design of Everyday Things, pp. 45–53. Basic Books (2002)
32. Rasmussen, J., Pejtersen, A., Goodstein, L.: Cognitive Systems Engineering. Wiley, New York (1994)
33. Reader, T., Flin, R., Mearns, K., Cuthbertson, B.: Interdisciplinary Communication in the Intensive Care Unit. British Journal of Anaesthesia 98(3), 347–352 (2007)
34. Rizzo, A., Marchigiani, E., Andreadis, A.: The AVANTI Project: Prototyping and Evaluation with a Cognitive Walkthrough based on the Norman's Model of Action. In: ACM Conference on Designing Interactive Systems, Amsterdam, Netherlands (August 1997)
35. Rogers, W., Mykityshyn, A., Campbell, R., Fisk, A.: Analysis of a Simple Medical Device. Ergonomics in Design, 6–14 (Winter 2001)
36. Salovaara, A.: Inventing New Uses for Tools: A Cognitive Foundation for Studies on Appropriation. Human Technology 4(2), 209–228 (2008)
37. Sayed, K., Sleem, W.: Nurse-Physician Collaboration: A Comparative Study of the Attitudes of Nurses and Physicians at Mansoura University Hospital. Life Science Journal 8(2), 141–146 (2011)
38. Serdijn, W.: Moving Therapeutic, Monitoring and Diagnostic Wireless Medical Devices into the Homes and into the Body. Handouts for ISMICT (April 2011)
39. Sherry, L., Feary, M., Polson, P., Mumaw, R., Palmer, E.: A Cognitive Engineering Analysis of the Vertical Navigation (VNAV) Function. Project Report NASA/TM (April 2001)
40. Smith, M., Higgs, J., Ellis, E.: Factors Influencing Clinical Decision Making, ch. 8, pp. 89–100 (2008)
41. Staggers, N., Troseth, M.: Group: Designing Usable Clinical Information Systems. The Tiger Initiative Usability Report, 1-25 (2009)
42. Wiklund, M., Kendler, J., Strochlic, A.: Usability Testing of Medical Devices. CRC Press, Taylor & Francis (2011)
43. Wiklund, M., Wilcox, S.: Designing Usability into Medical Devices. CRC Press, Taylor & Francis (2005)
44. Winter, S., Wagner, S., Deissenboeck, F.: A Comprehensive Model of Usability. In: Gulliksen, J., Harning, M.B., van der Veer, G.C., Wesson, J. (eds.) EIS 2007. LNCS, vol. 4940, Springer, Heidelberg (2008)
45. Zhang, J., Johnson, T., Patel, V., Paige, D., Kubose, T.: Using Usability Heuristics to evaluate Patient Safety of Medical Devices. Journal of Biomed. Informatics 36, 23–30 (2003)

A Game-Like Interactive Questionnaire for PV Application Research by Participatory Design

Zheng Dai[1] and Kasper Paasch[2]

[1] Realtime Targeting,
Antonigade 2, 1106 Copenhagen K, Danmark
twindai@gmail.com
[2] Mads Clausen Institute, University of Southern Denmark,
Alsion 2, 6400 Sønderborg, Danmark
paasch@mci.sdu.dk

Abstract. Questionnaire is a necessary method for investigation and research, but it often scares participants because of the impression of being long and boring. We developed a game-like questionnaire as an effective method to collect information and ideas from participants. In this paper, we describe the use of this tool to facilitate a photovoltaic (PV) application research, which is led by the University of Southern Denmark. The research is collaboration between local companies to popularize PV technology in both residential and the industrial markets. For such an innovative research, the interactive questionnaire developed by means of participatory design has helped us get a balanced perspective between user needs, market viability, and technical feasibility. Moreover, this tool guided our research focus on the artistic and usability aspects, and also raised design concepts and the concern of practice issues.

Keywords: Participatory design, Solar energy, Game-like questionnaire.

1 Introduction

The growing trend of solar energy attracts more companies and institutions to work together to catch the opportunities in the area of future energy supply. As to a general impression, solar energy has low efficiency, unstable current flow, and high price. But today, the fact is changing faster and faster. A well-designed system and a well-selected place will generate considerable power at a competitive price. A Photovoltaic (PV) system consists of several high technological components. They should be compatible with each other, adaptive to the installation environment, and accordant to the user's need. Participatory design balances the perspectives between different fields and involves more people to think together to contribute design concepts [1]. We believe that it was necessary to build an interactive tool that can facilitate usability research and idea generation effectively. The development of this tool and subsequent usability research is part of the Sunrise-PV project.

This Paper mainly introduces our development process of the interactive research tool, and the result of the tool. It also includes part of the research result from this

P. Campos et al. (Eds.): HWID 2012, IFIP AICT 407, pp. 65–72, 2013.

tool. This development process is dynamic, that means the tool is used in from the beginning of the research and was revised in each step.

The Sunrise-PV project is an industry-oriented project led by the Mads Clausen Institute (MCI) at the University of Southern Denmark and with the participation of Danfoss Solar Inverters A/S (DSI), Sydenergi (SE), Linak A/S, Esbensen Rådg. Ing. A/S and ProjectZero A/S. The project is partly funded of the Danish "Region Syddanmarks Vækstforum" and the European Regional Development Fund. Two large solar plants are party financed by the project, a 28 kW PV-plant on EUCSyd and a coming 80 kW plant at Produktionshøjskolen, both in Sønderborg, Denmark

The goal of the project is to develop new concepts, technologies and products in the field of PV systems with the main purpose of generating new jobs and companies in Southern Denmark. The activities in the project include both technical (inverter technology, tracking and control systems) as well as user oriented and design oriented activities with the focus on Building integrated Photo-Voltaic (BIPV).

To make full use of the particular advantage of solar energy, usability research is one of the essential sections in the Sunrise-PV project. We utilized the participatory design to promote the stakeholder and companies' cooperation, and to carry out a reasonable design solution, which fits the condition in Southern Denmark.

We defined one of our research questions as "How to improve the value and competences of solar energy for residential areas compared to other mainstream renewable power sources".

2   The Research

2.1   Research Issues

Basically, we can see that PV is having advantages regarding environmental acceptance, as they do not like wind energy produce shadow effects from wings or acoustic noise. They also have only little visual impact on the landscape. The demand of the place that fulfills the requirement of setting up a solar system is low. However these advantages are not common sense of the public. The focus of utilizing energy could be very practical like price, payback time, and how difficult to get. To take PV energy into mass markets, we need to facilitate from two directions. One is to hear the perspectives from end users, technicians, government, and scientists. The other is to popularize the knowledge and current state of PV to the public.

The initial focus was put on residential buildings. To get practical experience from private house owner and professional knowledge from stakeholders, questionnaire is necessary for the investigation. However the questionnaire has the impression of being long and boring, which scares participants and lowers the quality of the investigation. Therefore, we decided to develop a web-based program that is a game-like questionnaire to make participants enjoy the process of participating. The main questions for developing this program are how to choose the content and how to design the game-like interactions. The participatory design process provided rich materials to solve these two issues.

2.2   Approach for Participatory Design

The content of the interactive questionnaire is selected from the range of previous solar energy research that was focused on five basic fields. Much discussion has been on the balance between some of the following aspects: Economy, Ecology, Art, Technology, and Usability [1][4]. As the issues we mentioned above, solar energy has no significant predominance over wind power or waterpower in terms of economy, ecology, and technology. Governments or large companies always plan the construction of wind or waterpower. However, to mass market, the owner of a private house is more concerned about art and usability. Thus, we put the focus of the questionnaire on Art and Usability.

We followed serveral participatory design principal to design our research. As participatory design is a method through the whole process of an interaction design project, and the design is conducted in the working environment, users are part of design team [7]. Developing an interactive tool is also a user centered information design. Thus, besides user, we also involved other stakeholders including marketing specialist, usability manager, and technician in to the research [8]. The process of a participatory design can be inducted into 3 iterative steps: get public information, facilitate design workshop, and collect feedback [9]. To be specific in our research, we design following steps: investigation of the current situation and existing applications in Southern Denmark, the communication with local companies and private homeowners in four important towns from Southern Denmark, and the implementation of the web based questionnaire (game-like) for involving more participants. The outcome of each step contributed to the next step as design material. Finally, we presented one of the possible design concepts, as an example to inspire designers for later development. Through the process, we not only collected the knowledge and ideas for solar system, but also got the suggestions and ideas for designing the game-like questionnaire.

Besides the focused fields and the process, the groups of participants are also defined in our research. Essentially, there are four participants groups: end users, demonstration sites owners, technical support, and research specialists. Each group plays different roles in each step of the process. E.g. the end user group played a complimentary role during the investigation step, since the first step is put focus on studying and collecting fundamental knowledge about existing state of affairs of PV solar energy. But in the second step, the user is the core group to which we introduce the knowledge and send questionnaires to. User feedback is the significant part of the research output. The users list the priority between each research field, and speak out their own experience and story about solar and green energy.

In addition, the cooperation of the companies, in this study synthesized architectural design, user research, marketing investigation, and solar system testing. We have paid particular attention to technology development, sun tracking, green energy innovation, and building installation experience in our project. These professional participants contribute to knowledge in the five fields respectively. They provide and exchange rich information between each other and to the end users through the seminars. The information is also transferred to other participants by our web-based questionnaire.

3   Investigation, Communication, Implementation

Study and investigation is a usual start for an innovative project [6][9]. After the investigation of synthesizing data from Internet search, public research reports, and library resource, we build communication with experienced owners of solar plants. Danish town Skive have been placed several solar energy facilities on public buildings. All schools and many institutions currently receive energy from solar panels in Skive. According to the calculations, one of the projects, which were set up in 2009, is expected to have a payback time of approximately 12 year [2]. The experiences from Skive showed us an exemplification of utilizing solar system in the Danish geographical condition that it has relatively less sunshine in the world, and that daylight is much longer in summer. The top three remarkable aspects of Skive government are capacity, cost, and size, for which we particularly created one section in the interactive questionnaire to see other participants' perspective.

Our investigation also involved several conferences and seminars in Denmark to gain information about energy technology, economy, and policy. The Danish government has no special feed-in tariff for solar energy, but they allow a household photovoltaic installation, which is smaller than or equal to 6 kilowatts (kW), to use net metering. Net metering means that the contribution of a PV system will get the house energy meter to "turn backward" using the power grid as storage place for energy and can result in a zero-consumption of electricity on an annual basis [10]. The configuration of a 6.4 kWp PV system needs 41 square meters, and costs in the order of 126,000 DKK in 2012[3].

Building Integration Photovoltaic (BIPV) is one of the most relevant fields of our research. BIPV is a solution that not only generates energy but also protects facades and provides nice design [1]. Some solution adopts flexible solar cell to fill roof for temporary use or fill a surface in special shape. Architects have right to choose these solutions and materials, thus, we contacted architects who are members of our network in Denmark. They indicated their interest in environment matching, orientation of light, and energy generation by priority. They also prefered to use pictures to show their ideas, which inspired us to insert BIPV pictures in our program. See Fig. 1.

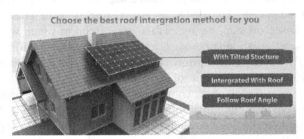

Fig. 1. BIPV example in the game-like questionnaire

We designed several posters which published on our website (http://bit.ly/U1Q2YQ) to share the aforementioned investigation to other participants, especially to the end user group, who had outdated information of solar system. To get an overview of users' feedback in Southern Denmark, we held four seminars and took turns in Odense, Sønderborg, Esbjerg, and Kolding. SydEnegi, Danfoss Solar Invertor (DSI), ProjectZero, and Mads Clausen Institute gave a presentation to household owners in their professional perspective, respectively. During these seminars, we took chance to interview participants about their perspective of solar system, invited them visit our website and try the interactive game (questionnaire), and leave emails to keep future tracking survey. We use the words "game" instead of "questionnaire" to attract people come and participate the research actively.

Many of participants considered to purchase a solar system because of the policy that equal and less than 6kW solar system for a household could get net metering. They pay close attention to the details about price and payback time. Our seminars gave the house owners a wider view for their choice. They started not only to think about total budget and payback time, but also to consider where to install the PV system and how the building looks after installation. Some of the people came and discussed their special needs with us. Some for example had to change the roof in a few years, so it could be a good idea for them to consider installing a solar system as well. It could thus reduce the overall combined cost for building material and installation labor work. A similar story can also be said about windows. Some wants to change old windows, and it might become a good idea to choose a PV window to have both functions of energy generation and shading. But feasible solutions for that are just now entering the market.

Based on the investigation in market and communication with end user group, we mapped the interest and focus of core developers, external cooperators, and end users in terms of what advantage PV can bring to our life, how to choose PV types, and how to use PV to help architectural design. The map shows the priority of the interest by the size of text as Fig 2. Consequently, these keywords showed us the most important concerns are payback time, why purchase a solar system (purpose), and appearance. We designed another section in the program that allowed participants to choose their preference in these three aspects.

Fig. 2. Keywords of participants' interest

The program combined information introduction and collection, and gave several different approaches to interact with participants. We called it as game-like, because the whole process includes a variety sections and tasks. As questionnaires give a general impression as being boring, time consuming, and long, to design the questionnaire like a game could attract participants and keep them interested in accepting and giving information. It includes choice question, sorting order question, and open discussion task. The test of the online program can be found on http://bitly.com/S38Jvq See Fig 3. The input from participants is stored in a database. So far, we collected more than 40 answers that include all different kinds of participants and show a balanced interest of design concept. The top choice of the scale of a solar system is in 40-80 square meters in size, price is between 70,000 and 120,000 DKK, and expected payback time is less than 10 years. 70% participants pay attention to a nice look from outside, and most of the people looked forward to a feature of knowing operational details of in the solar system.

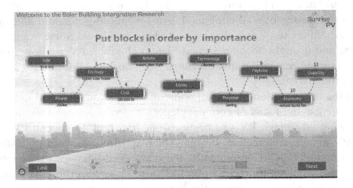

Fig. 3. A game-like questionnaire

A web based game-like questionnaire is aiming to provide an enjoyable and relaxing experience during participatory design. It clears up and re-organizes the mass of information from abundant research to help participants understand professional information easier, who are not only provide constructive suggestions, but the practical issues also rise up. This balance between negative and positive input puts the research result in a safe range and leads to later development.

4   Design and Practical Issue

Based on the overall research process, and the outcome collected from the program, we carried out several design concepts. A multifunction window that integrated PV system is one of the examples. The PV window could generate energy and provide shading at the same time. Moreover, a sun tracker system could help to adjust the angle of PV panels to improve its efficiency. A temperature sensor and a CO_2 sensor can also be used for detecting indoor air quality, which allows the window automatically to open to get fresh air in. The energy from the solar system can support the mechanical movement of the window and connect to the main power supply in house. See Fig. 4. It is an ideal concept following participants' imagination. Meanwhile it is also for developers to criticize on to get more inspirations.

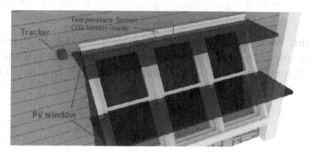

Fig. 4. Example of design concept

5   The Effect on Shading on Solar Panel

The program also gathered the concerns from professional technicians who paid attention on practical issues. One of the most-discussed issues is that shading has a more profound effect on the power generation of solar panels than one should intuitively expect. Having guided by the comments collected from the program, we did more research in this issue and found that it is due to the internal construction of solar panel with multiple individual solar cells interconnected. The participants who have technical background describe the detail to us: A single solar cell will generate a voltage of around 0.6 volt, which is too low for direct use. Solar cells are therefore in general connected in series inside a solar panel, so that a solar panel consisting of 72 solar cells will generate a voltage level of around 43 volt. If all solar cells have the same illumination, they will generate the same current, meaning that the same current will flow thru all the cells. But if some of them are shaded, they will generate less current and at the same time block for the higher current from the other cells, meaning that the resulting current from the panel is limited to the current from the cell with the lowest illumination. This effect means that even a small shadow can generate a large decline in power output, so it is important to understand that the loss in power is not proportional to the shaded area but can be much more severe. The comments from the program did not show up solution to this issue, but the expertise suggested us put the enviroment of construction in to consideration during the reasearch .

6   Conclusion

A web based game-like questionnaire can provide an enjoyable and relaxing experience during participatory design. It clears up and reorganizes the mass of information from abundant research and makes participants feel easy to understand the information, thereby bringing about more brisk ideas. The participants not only provide constructive suggestions, the practical issues also rise up. This balance between negative and positive input puts the research result in a safe range and gives us a better connection with later development. At last, at the same time, the participatory design can contribute to both of the development of this game-like program and to the research project directly.

Acknowledgement. We would like to thank our colleagues, local partners and all the participants for sharing information and conducting seminars. Also thanks to the Danish "Region Syddanmarks Vækstforum" and the European Regional Development Fund for partly funding the project.

References

1. Weller, B.: Photovoltaics: technology, architecture, installation. Birkhäuser, München (2010)
2. Solar Panels – Skive Rounds Shortly 3.000 m2, http://bit.ly/R1AHDt
3. Energi Midt Pakker og priser på solceller, http://bit.ly/R1y87v
4. Building Integrated Photovoltaics, http://bit.ly/RIwyJw
5. George, C.A.: User-Centred Library Websites: Usability evaluation methods, ch. 4 excerpt. Chandos Publishing, Oxford (2008)
6. Webb, A.: Project Management for Product Innovation. Gower Publishing, Ltd., Aldershot (2000)
7. Dix, A.: Human-Computer Interaction. Pearson Education, Harlow (2004)
8. Henry, P.: User-Centered Information Design for Improved Software Usability. Artech House Publishers, Norwood (1998)
9. Hyun-Chan, A., So-Hyun, P.: Design Tools and Three Steps in Participatory Design Processes. In: Proceedings of the 6th Conference of the Pacific Rim Community Design Network, Quanzhou, Fujian, China, June 18-21 (2007)
10. Photovoltaic panels on grid, private residence, http://bit.ly/WtVO9C

A Design Science Approach to Interactive Greenhouse Climate Control Using Lego Mindstorms for Sensor-Intensive Prototyping

Rasmus Ulslev Pedersen and Torkil Clemmensen

Dept. of IT Management, Copenhagen Business School,
Howitzvej 60, 2000 Frederiksberg, Denmark
{rup.itm,tc.itm}@cbs.dk

Abstract. In this paper, we describe a design science framework for the use of interactive, sensor-intensive prototypes to develop interactive greenhouse climate management systems. We emphasize the ways in which design science, and in particular what we call micro information systems, may enhance the human-computer interaction (HCI) aspects of emission control performance through better interactive control interfaces and the utilization of sensor network technology. By applying guidelines suggested in design science to the case studied, we identify a number of interactive prototypes that successively address core issues in this particular setting. Starting from a simple human-computer interaction with a one-sensor-one-output prototype made in Lego Mindstorms NXT, we end up with a custom made sensor that addresses interaction with our particular user profile: the gardener. Thus, we provide a reference platform for combining micro information systems and human-computer interaction in design science research into environmental sustainability research.

Keywords: Sensor prototypes, design science, HCI, embedded systems.

1 Introduction

As the importance of eco-sustainable growth becomes increasingly important, the human-computer interaction and micro information systems research communities must address environmental sustainability challenges. In this paper, we describe a design science framework for the use of interactive, sensor-intensive prototypes to develop greenhouse climate management systems. Consequently, this study emphasizes ways in which applied design science can enhance indoor greenhouse climate management performance through the utilization of sensor network technology.

We identify the need for a design science framework for sensor-intensive systems and we provide a proposed reference platform for design science research into environmental sustainability using a series of greenhouse prototyping studies.

In order to contribute to the body of knowledge on environmentally sustainable HCI [22] and environmental informatics [1], we propose to combine HCI and micro-IS. This then forms a representation of a design space for green micro-IS system.

P. Campos et al. (Eds.): HWID 2012, IFIP AICT 407, pp. 73–89, 2013.

This combination can then be used as a point of reference for further relevant work. The fundamental questions for design-science research are:

1.   What utility does the new artifact provide?
2.   What demonstrates that utility?

We use these questions for guidance in our research into interactive greenhouse climate management and control.

2   Background

This paper has been inspired by recent developments in design science research as described by Hevner, March, Park and Ram [3]. Design science research (DSR) is a model for evaluating novel artifacts. Therefore, it is different from other IS/HCI research methods that mainly direct attention toward observation. A DSR project creates – or generates – an artifact that is then assessed – or evaluated – with regard to its contribution to rigor and to relevance. In other words, the DSR artifact uses scholarly literature to form theories regarding the artifact that is created, and its ultimate test is the proposed relevance for use with practitioners.

In line with common DSR guidelines, we want to design rigorously. A part of this is to be able to reproduce prototypes and user-oriented evaluations of them. We propose to use what we call "throw-away" sensor-intensive, interactive prototypes. We suggest that reproducibility in sensor-intensive prototypes can be achieved by using re-buildable Lego NXT prototypes with instructions in terms of video clips showing how to build prototypes. In addition, we provide open source code of programs used to collect and display sensor input.

There are examples of DSR within neuroscience [2] and in sustainability research, such as Watson et al.'s environmental framework [1] using the design science guidelines provided by Hevner et al. in their seminal MIS Quarterly article, "Design Science in Information Systems Research" [3].

In HCI, DSR has been proposed to test the proposition that incorporating user modeling and usability modeling in software requirement specifications improves design [4], and more generally, HCI has been suggested as a design science discipline [5].

2.1   Micro Information Systems

The embedded and sensor context for this paper is greenhouse monitoring systems and management of same. Micro-IS research in this area also focuses on sensor-intensive systems [6]. On an even wider scale, OECD [7] presents sensor technology as a fundamental enabler for addressing global challenges with regard to global warming.

We conducted this particular evaluation using a micro information systems design science framework [8-10] that shows how it is possible to incorporate micro-IS into existing frameworks. Our focus here is on rigorous design, as listed by the 5th Design Science guideline published by Hevner et al. Our artifact-driven approach in the creation of the micro-IS design framework, the reference platform, the generate/evaluate tool, and the demo application are captured by Guideline 1: Design as an artifact. The instantiation is a demonstration of the usefulness of the generate/evaluate method.

We recognize the importance of other disciplines; two such examples are decision support systems [11] and embedded networked systems [12]. Design science, as discussed in IS [13], guides the design of the artifact and the constructs, models, methods, and instantiations that sum up this meta-artifact.

At that point, the demands and needs for our prototypes are mostly related to size, form, and function for the designed artifacts. The design theory nexus is able to cope with multiple requirements [14]. It forms a method for adapting and extending the micro-IS framework. These constraints form the search space for an acceptable solution to the part of the real world business problem that the micro-IS is intended to solve. We created several prototypes, and for each evolution, we refined the next prototype on the basis of previous knowledge.

Eventually, an acceptable solution was reached by generating/building solution candidates and evaluating/testing them in the greenhouse information systems context. This approach ensures that future micro-IS projects are understood from an HCI and IS perspective rather than from a technical one. This micro-IS meta-artifact provides some function which is to be aligned with the requirements of the IS context. This forms the combined utility of the information system.

The micro-IS context might be best addressed with a more technology-focused design framework [3], and the HCI/IS context is best addressed with an action design framework [15].

2.2   HCI in Interactive Climate Management

In relation to design science, HCI has, for long, been conceived of by some researchers as a design science [16]. The iterative cycle of generate and evaluate designs of design science is at the core of HCI's user-centered design [4, 5]. However, the importance of combining embedded sensor-intensive systems with consideration of users' interactions with such systems has appeared more recently [17]. Within the climate control community (not in the HCI community), Van Straten et al. [18] proposed that the interactive use of sensor-intensive information about crop growth would allow greenhouse control strategies to become more optimal in an economic sense. Both long-term and short-term dynamics of the crop and greenhouse and external weather conditions could be considered in such interactive control strategies. However, a major challenge in the development of interactive control strategies is the lack of reliable crop development models for the wide variety of crops encountered in real settings and the consequential need for a sensible allocation of tasks for the human grower and automatic control systems. One proposed solution is a two-systems approach, an interactive sensor-intensive control system for day-to-day climate control, and another more decision- support-like system to consider the long-term effects of climate management on crop production [18]. Within such a grower-oriented framework, the grower interacts with the system by setting constraints on temperature, humidity, and other evapo-transpiration variables over a period of interest.

The grower is supported by a model-based simulation system that predicts how these settings influence energy consumption, photosynthesis, and condensation [18].

In the HCI community, related work has been done by Pearce et al. [19, 20], who studied interactive gardening. They wanted to use what they called "everyday simulations" to allow non-specialists to experiment with and in an interactive way learn optimal strategies for watering gardens. In order to develop such a tool, they noticed "...the absence of design processes specifically tailored to this type of project..." [20], and suggested areas to consider in terms of developing a design process for such a tool. Among the identified challenges were how to allow HCI designers to develop a necessary level of understanding of the horticultural domain and in particular how to do this within a reasonable time period. The solutions included letting the domain specialists automate a large number of decisions and allowing the end-user to only gradually take part in the decision making as he or she becomes more knowledgeable. Secondly, the HCI designers tried to embody material constraints in the design, as suggested by work domain analysis [21]. In the end, they designed a software tool called SmartGardenWatering, which works as decision support for gardeners when defining watering schedules and use. In a study of 20 gardeners using the tool, the researchers identified issues of trust and confidence in the underlying horticultural models and their interactive use. They concluded that the outcome of the interaction with the software should not challenge "idiosyncrasies in existing practice" [19, p. 224] and that gardeners wanted models with higher granularity than those provided by the tested system.

More generally, the whole idea of designing interactive systems for sustainable environments and global climate management has been outlined by leading HCI researchers. Dourish [22] took the opportunity to explain how ICTs can be used to promote environmental sustainability on the part of IT users, but also warned that current HCI research is not sensitive enough in reference to the political and cultural contexts of environmental practice. The idea has also found support in the IS community, where researchers have proposed that information system design can be a catalyst for environmental sustainability as an expression of value-sensitive design [23]. Thus, the role of IS design in developing interactive systems for sustainable environment is being pressed in both IS and HCI communities. So far, most of this work has been on a grand scale of proposals, but the first steps toward meeting the new challenge in the creation of interactive systems, environmental sustainability, have been taken, e.g., [24]. However, rather than focusing on the grand global climate management challenges, in this paper, we report from the perspective of a micro-climate control (greenhouse and plants) research project [25].

METHOD

We introduced design science in the background section. From this window-accepted framework, we extracted the generate/evaluate activity [3]. The reason for doing so was the need for a clear way of combining the development of micro information systems and thus information systems with an embedded systems component, and the human computer interaction field.

The separation of generate and evaluate activities is useful because it allows us to assume clear roles in each sequential prototyping effort. Moreover, we do not necessarily assume the same roles across all sequential prototyping efforts. In the very beginning, the HCI researcher may create throw-away prototypes using paper or clay. Later in the process, it could be that the HCI researcher is now in the evaluation role, while the other researcher generates electronic prototypes using Lego Mindstorms NXT. What separates these two activities is that each prototype is evaluated and the feedback is used in subsequent prototypes. The HCI evaluation activity covers both an activity where the HCI researcher is acting as an end user and, later, the HCI researcher will act as part of the design group which is sitting in the generate/evaluate new box.

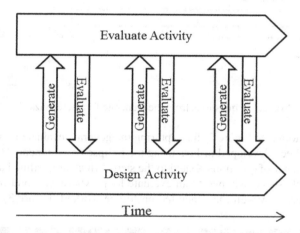

Fig. 1. Design activity and evaluate activity connected by generate and evaluate processes

In Figure 1, we describe how evaluate and generate activities are the two processes that connect the micro-IS and HCI activities. That is the subject of the following section. Each of the generate processes outputs a prototype which is then evaluated. This process is repeated, and the prototype is matured over time.

The process that we followed is this:

GENERATE approach:

1. Select a prototyping platform and design the new artifact: assemble, disassemble, construct, tear down, and work with the construction pieces while following through the steps below.
2. Refine the main IS problem and IS context and the information and control flows in the micro-IS system.
3. What are the basic phenomena to be monitored? To be controlled?
4. What set of sensors can monitor those phenomena?
5. What set of actuators is needed to regulate the physical entity?

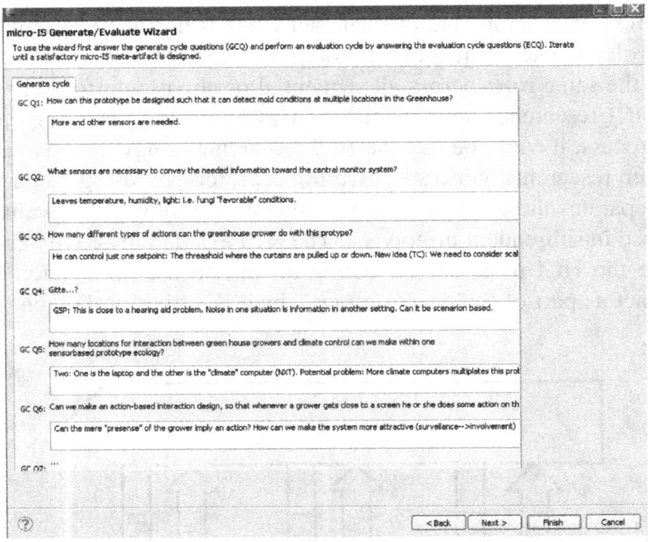

Fig. 2. Six questions from the Generate/Evaluate Wizard

We created a tool (see Figure 2) for capturing the generate/evaluate loop of our design process that had been developed in Java using the Eclipse environment. The tool asks the participants a number of questions related to the steps, which are outlined above.

Then the emphasis is switched to an evaluate loop, where a second set of questions is asked to capture how well the generated prototype worked (Figure 3). Besides these

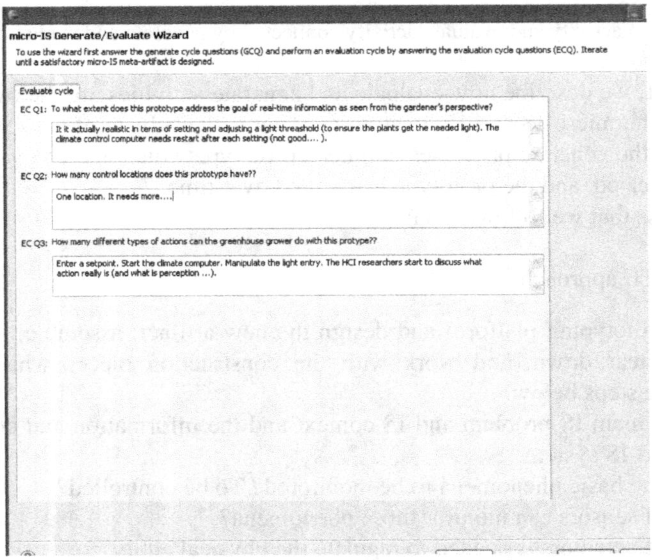

Fig. 3. Evaluate cycle from the Wizard

evaluations questions, we also used any other means of evaluation available to us. The evaluate cycle follows the generate cycle.

To use the micro-IS framework, we suggested the constructs, models, and methods to be added, removed, or adapted. We suggest the use of a minimalistic approach: new artifacts should be added to the micro-IS framework only if they are essential to solve a given problem.

3   Prototypes

3.1   Prototype 1 – Proof of Concept

The first prototype was a "proof of concept" prototype. It was a simple text-output prototype that served to show that it was meaningful and technically possible to make an interactive sensor-intensive prototype to conduct climate management (Figure 4). The prototype was evaluated by internal discussion in the research group using the generate/evaluate tool, Figure 2 and Figure 3, with the aim of conducting a rigorous evaluation. We decided to go on with the LEGO due to its ability to connect to the minds of many people with little technical knowledge and its flexibility in programming capacity, both of which had previously been demonstrated [8, 9].

Lego Mindstorms NXT is the unit that we used to model the sensors and the actuators (motors). The unit has four input sensors, which are in the standard kit: touch (shown in Figure 5), light, sound, and a distance sensor.

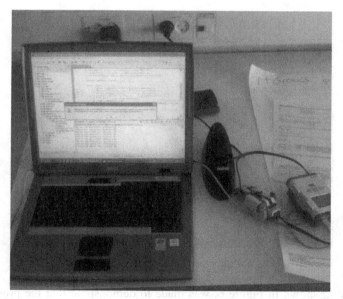

Fig. 4. IT Grows prototype 1 – demonstrating sensor-based climate management prototyping with Lego Mindstorms

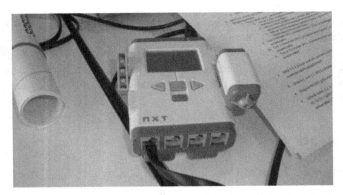

Fig. 5. LegoMindstorms NXT as the platform for prototyping

3.2   Prototype 2 – Exhibition Demo Prototype

We used the standard Lego Mindstorm educational kit to prototype an interactive climate management system in a greenhouse (Figure 6). The model greenhouse has one motor that imitates a motor controlling a roof window. When the light sensor values raise above a pre-defined trigger point, the motor opens the window. The opposite event takes place when the monitored light drops below a pre-defined set point: the window closes. A wind speed sensor is mounted on the top of the roof, but, similar to other imaginable relevant sensors, this was not connected to the climate computer (the Lego Mindstorms NXT) in this prototype version.

Fig. 6. Prototype 2 - Model of greenhouse

Prototype 2, shown in Figure 6, was made to demonstrate that the prototype was easy to disassemble and reassemble in new contexts and that it would allow different users and other stakeholder groups to interact with the prototype. Prototype 2 was exhibited at two major international exhibitions for commercial climate management systems (Figure 7). The evaluation was done by the first author via an email interview with the senior project leader in the company who had taken the prototypes to the exhibitions. Somewhat against expectations, the project leader reported that the prototype was never made to run in the sense of having the LEGO Mindstorm computer operating, but she said that it nevertheless generated plenty of interest from conference participants, who easily could imagine interacting with the demo climate management system.

Fig. 7. Lego greenhouse climate management prototype displayed at greenhouse grower exhibition.

3.3   Prototype 3 – Functionally Working Climate Control

The third prototype was aimed at generating relevant functions that would allow greenhouse growers to interact with real sensor data. A single temperature sensor was installed on top of a simulated standard greenhouse table with potted plants, Figure 8. The evaluation was done by the first author in the role of expert programmer. It revealed the need for programming specific object classes for the temperature sensor in order to calculate the level of photosynthesis and generate data that the greenhouse growers would be able to evaluate. We also found that the model table (see Figure 8) was not sufficient. It needed to be larger and to hold biological plant material.

3.4   Prototype 4 – Interacting with a Climate Consultant

The fourth prototype was made in order to interact with a greenhouse grower consultant. He examined the prototype and suggested a number of uses and improvements. He showed real engagement in terms of its use. The evaluation was done by a group discussion between the authors and the consultant. One point was that the prototype should be taken seriously as a potential way to generate innovations in reference to

Fig. 8. Prototype 3 - The simulated plant table that should hold plant material for obtaining real sensor data

climate control. For example, the prototype generated group discussions and shared sketches about how exactly to locate and use multiple sensors inside and outside real greenhouses (Figure 9). Secondly, the need for going beyond simple data logging and moving toward more advanced data visualization when supporting interactions with climate management specialists became evident.

3.5   Prototype 5 – Showing Relative Data from Many Sensors

Prototype 5 was developed with the purpose of simulating the more realistic scenario of managing several sensors from several greenhouses. Additional Lego blocks were needed. In addition, we attempted to add plastic to simulate the climate screen (This did not go so well) and we installed more sensors. A new programming environment (Lejos) replaced the LEGO Mindstorm software. The evaluation focused on the "realness" of the data; again, a greenhouse consultant interacted with the prototype.

The use of "real" electronic components at this point in the prototyping process was introduced to experiment with the sensitivity and usefulness of sensors. For each new component, it was necessary to first (1) go through the work of finding an (electronic) component and then to start the actual process measurements, confirming that they worked, and calibrating each sensor. With respect to a light sensor for an example of the process, see Figure 10, Figure 11, and Figure 12.

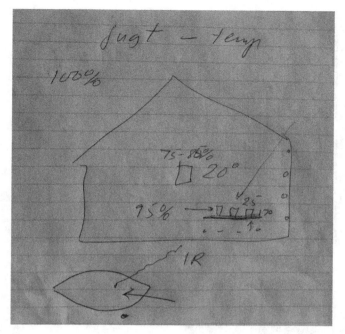

Fig. 9. Group discussion sketch of simulated greenhouse prototype 4

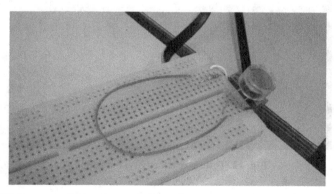

Fig. 10. Prototype 5. An electronic "breadboard" with a light-sensitive resistor

Figure 12 illustrates the Lejos development environment and how the Java code was used to read periodic readings from Lego Mindstorms NXT. For example, a temperature-dependent resistor was used to measure the temperature in the green model greenhouse. Before this was used, we experienced one minor setback with respect to this temperature sensor: it was not directly possible to find a way to interface Lejos with this sensor. A secondary potential challenge was that the original Lego temperature sensor was becoming an added expense since the micro-climate controller in further prototyping should be using several temperature measurements.

Fig. 11. Testing and calibrating the light sensor

Fig. 12. Testing connectivity to a laptop

3.6   Prototype 6 – Students' Cognitive Walkthrough of a High Fidelity Prototype

Prototype 6 was a high fidelity prototype of a part of the to-be-designed climate management system, the "side-bar" which gave decision support to the grower based on model simulations of the climate (Figure 13). Three student groups from a second year computer science and business administration study from the second author's course conducted a cognitive walkthrough [26] of the prototype in Figure 13.

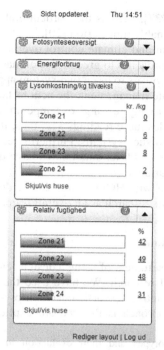

Fig. 13. The current running conceptual prototype of the decision support part of an interactive sensor-intensive climate management system (courtesy of Agrotech)

The results of the cognitive walkthrough were sent to the developers, who stated that some results – that is, some design suggestions in reference to consistency, level of detail, and scalability of graphs were particularly useful in the further development of the system.

4   Discussion

We have described the complete development flow of a sensor-intensive prototype within a DSR generate-evaluate process (Figure 2). Table 1 provides an overview. Among the possible points for discussion are:

-      The use of LEGO Mindstorm as a sensor-intensive prototyping tool is, we believe, the first attempt to make "throw-away" sensor-intensive prototypes. It is easy to assemble, disassemble, move, and re-assemble; in that way, we were able to repro-duce the different LEGO Mindstorm sensor-intensive prototypes. Hence the evalua-tion results can potentially be repeated and easily reproduced by other researchers.

-      The "throw-away" nature of the prototypes, that is, the easy reproducibility of the sensor-intensive prototypes, may, among other considerations, provide a solu-tion to the problem raised in related HCI research: How to allow HCI designers to develop a necessary level of understanding to design relatively simple user interfaces for complex work domains [27], such as the horticultural domain, and, in particular, how to do this within a reasonable time period [20].

-        Climate management and climate control overlap in our proposed combination of micro-IS and HCI approaches to greenhouse climate. Thus, we accommodated the proposals [18] to allow growers to use a two-system approach.

-        In operational climate management, the actions taken by the one(s) using the systems are dependent upon timely readings of temperature, humidity, light intensity, etc. Lego Mindstorms provides these readings and, thus, it provides the dynamic picture which is a requirement of such systems. Furthermore, Lego Mindstorms can control the greenhouse prototypes with its motors. We have used the motors to simulate the opening and closing of curtains.

-        Combining Micro-IS with HCI research can be done by using design science and the related process for this research as an overall framework.

4.1   Research Contributions

We have demonstrated the usefulness of using a design science research framework to combine Micro-IS with HCI research. We have used the Micro-IS/HCI approach in the development of six interactive sensor-intensive throw-away prototypes. A special valuable property of our approach is that we are explicit about the roles that are

Table 1. Generation of prototypes and their evaluation in growers' work domains and interaction design evaluation

	Work domain and task evaluation	Generation of prototypes	Interaction design evaluation
T **I** **M** **E**	Field test in greenhouse	**Prototype 6 -** Decision support part of system	Cognitive walk-through by students of HCI
	Review by expert in sensor information	**Prototype 5 –** Light sensitive resistor	-
	-	**Prototype 4 -**Sketches of model greenhouse simulation	Evaluation of sketches by greenhouse consultant
	Group discussion with greenhouse grower consultant	**Prototype 3 -**Simulated plant table	-
	Presentation of LEGO greenhouse climate management for industry	**Prototype 2 -** Model of greenhouse	-
	Within project team, evaluation of sensordata collection by generate/ evaluate tool	**Prototype 1 -** LEGO Mindstorm unit	Within project team, evaluation of interaction design by generate/evaluate tool

assumed by each type of generate/evaluate activity throughout the process. This allows for the creation of a lightweight log book of how a project develops over time and the possibility of going back in time to restart the design at a given point.

The design science research in IS has provided us with the established research from which we have focused on the generation of prototypes and the subsequent evaluation of same. We have noted who conducted the creation and evaluation at each point in time. Our generate/evaluate tool is an Eclipse plug-in, which can be provided upon request. This tool was easy to use and served to visualize the process of capturing the generation and evaluation, activities in addition to our videotaping of same.

Sensor-intensive prototyping involves electric engineering and computer science in addition to HCI and end user involvement. We believe that this type of development is different from traditional computer interaction, partly because of the dynamics of the sensor-intensive user interaction compared to a traditional series of screens. With the label "interactive, sensor-intensive prototypes," we want to provide a method that can be used to facilitate collaboration across multiple disciplines.

5   Conclusion

The application of a design science framework for combining micro information systems with human-computer interaction approaches adds structure to the design process. In terms of the rigor and relevance research questions that we raised in the beginning of the paper, we have achieved more than we expected.

By adhering to a lightweight process that concentrated on the generate/evaluate process, we were able to undertake a series of prototyping efforts over a period of 18 months and keep track of the progress. The relevance of the "interactive, sensor-intensive prototyping" approach has been confirmed by the exhibition of one prototype at a large agriculture exhibition. The rigor has been described in terms of design science, micro information systems, and the ability to reproduce sensor-intensive prototypes.

Acknowledgments. This research was supported by a grant from The Danish National Advanced Technology Foundation (Højteknologifonden) to the itGrows-project.

References

1. Watson, R.T., Boudreau, M.C., Chen, A.J.: Information systems and environmentally sustainable development: energy informatics and new directions for the IS community. MIS Quarterly 34(1), 23 (2010)
2. Liapis, C., Chatterjee, S.: On a NeuroIS Design Science Model. In: Jain, H., Sinha, A.P., Vitharana, P. (eds.) DESRIST 2011. LNCS, vol. 6629, pp. 440–451. Springer, Heidelberg (2011)
3. Hevner, A.R., March, S.T., Park, J., Ram, S.: Design science in information systems research. MIS Quarterly 28(1), 75–105 (2004)

4. Adikari, S., McDonald, C., Collings, P.A.: Design Science Approach to an HCI Research Project. In: Proc. OZCHI 2006, pp. 429–432. ACM Press (2006)
5. Carroll, J.M.: Creating a design science of human-computer interaction. Interacting with Computers 5(1), 3–12 (1993)
6. Guinard, D., Trifa, V., Mattern, F., Wilde, E.: From the Internet of Things to the Web of Things: Resource Oriented Architecture and Best Practices. In: Architecting the Internet of Things, ch. 5. Springer (2011)
7. OECD, Smart Sensor Networks: Technologies and Applications for Green Growth. OECD Digital Economy Papers (2009)
8. Pedersen, R.U.: Tinyos education with Lego Mindstorms NXT. In: Learning from Data Streams. Processing Techniques in Sensor Networks, pp. 231–241 (2007)
9. Pedersen, R.U., Nørbjerg, J., Scholz, M.P.: Embedded Programming Education with Lego Mindstorms NXT using Java (leJOS), Eclipse (XPairtise), and Python (PyMite). In: Proceedings of Workshop on Embedded Systems Education, WESE. ACM (2009)
10. Pedersen, R.U., Pedersen, M.K.: Micro Information Systems: New Fractals in an Evolving IS Landscape. In: Integrated Information and Computing Systems for Natural, Spatial, and Social Sciences. IDG Global (2012)
11. Sprague Jr., R.H.: A framework for the development of decision support systems. MIS Quarterly, 1–26 (1980)
12. Pottie, G., Kaiser, W.: Principles of Embedded Networked Systems Design. Cambridge University Press, New York (2005)
13. March, S.T., Storey, V.C.: Design science in the information systems discipline: An introduction to the special issue on design science research. MIS Quarterly 32(4), 725–730 (2008)
14. Pries-Heje, J., Baskerville, R.: The design theory nexus. MIS Quarterly 32(4), 731–755 (2008)
15. Sein, M.K., Henfridsson, O., Purao, S., Rossi, M., Lindgren, R.: Action design research. MIS Quarterly 35(1), 37–56 (2011)
16. Carroll, J.M.: Conceptualizing a possible discipline of human–computer interaction. Interacting with Computers 22(1), 3–12 (2010)
17. Clemmensen, T., Ulslev Pedersen, R.A.: Human Work Interaction Design (HWID) Perspective on Internet - and Sensor Based ICT Systems for Climate Management. In: Ørngreen, R., Wong, W., Rooney, C., Barnett, J., Hvannberg, E., Clemmensen, T. (eds.) Post-Workshop Proceedings for: Crisis management training, design and use of online worlds, http://pure.au.dk/portal/files/44017637/Crisis_Manageme nt_Training_Post_Workshop_Proceedings.pdf
18. Van Straten, G., Challa, H., Buwalda, F.: Towards user accepted optimal control of greenhouse climate. Computers and Electronics in Agriculture 26(3), 221–238 (2000)
19. Pearce, J., Smith, W., Nansen, B., Murphy, J.: SmartGardenWatering: Experiences of Using a Garden Watering Simulation. In: Proc. of OZCHI 2009, pp. 217–224. ACM Press (2009)
20. Pearce, J., Murphy, J., Smith, W.: Supporting Gardeners to plan Domestic Watering: A Case Study of Designing an "Everyday Simulation". In: Proc. of OZCHI 2008, pp. 227–230. ACM Press (2008)
21. Burns, C.M., Hajdukiewicz, J.R.: Ecological interface design. CRC (2004)
22. Dourish, P.: HCI environmental sustainability: the politics of design and the design of politics. In: Proc. of DIS 2010, pp. 1–10. ACM Press (2010)

23. Nathan, L., Friedman, B., Hendry, D.: SUSTAINABLY OURS: Information system design as catalyst: Human action and environmental sustainability. Interactions 16(4), 6–11 (2009)
24. Mankoff, J.C., Blevis, E., Borning, A., Friedman, B., Fussell, S.R., Hasbrouck, J., Woodruff, A., Sengers, P.: Environmental sustainability and interaction. In: Ext. Abstracts CHI 2007, pp. 2121–2124. ACM Press (2007)
25. Körner, O., Clemmensen, T., Petersen, R.U., Ottosen, C.-O.: itGrows - Module-based IT Platform for Optimizing Horticultural Production. The Danish National Advanced Technology Foundation (Højteknologifonden) (2010)
26. Mahatody, T., Sagar, M., Kolski, C.: State of the art on the cognitive walkthrough method, its variants and evolutions. Intl. Journal of Human–Computer Interaction 26(8), 741–785 (2010)
27. Clemmensen, T.: Designing a simple folder structure for a complex domain. Human Technology: An interdisciplinary Journal on Humans in ICT 7(3), 216–249 (2011)

Empirical Evaluation of Complex System Interfaces for Power Plant Control Room Using Human Work Interaction Design Framework

Anant Bhaskar Garg[1] and K.K. Govil[2]

[1] Centre for Information Technology,
College of Engineering Studies,
University of Petroleum & Energy Studies, Dehradun, India
[2] Power Plant Consultant
anantgg@yahoo.com

Abstract. This paper first discusses two cognitive science paradigms and then present third approach related to interaction with the world as known as embodied cognition. The focus is to analyze work settings with the help of cognitive work analysis and human work interaction design approaches. The case of power plant control room is discussed and analyzed in the context of human system interactions, work and task analysis. This approach helps in reducing cognitive workload on operator which can result in reduction in errors in managing the control room of the power plant.

Keywords: Cognitive Work Analysis, Embodied cognition, Human Work Interaction Design, Power Plant Control Room, Ecological Interface Design.

1 Introduction

In the year 1956, two different conferences and seminars gave birth to two new research areas known as Artificial Intelligence and Cognitive Science. They stress that brain functions like a computer that specifies symbols can be processed and manipulated and known as cognitivism. This view that thought is manipulation of abstract symbols, algorithmic computation in the same way as computer does. All meaning arose via correspondences between symbols (words, mental representations) and things in the external world. The mind was seen as a mirror of nature, and human thought as abstract and disembodied. Therefore, in principle, a computer could replace a brain, and in particular computers can do anything that brains can do. But this give rise to symbol grounding problem and unable to explain how we get meaning of objects.

The two main approaches (symbolic and connectionist) study cognition of an individual being but as we live in the world, environment and interaction with others play an important role. This thinking leads to theories of embodied and situated cognition, where cognition is seen as taking place not only in the brain, but also in interaction with the world supported by the body [1], [2]. Moreover, this may suggest that neural

P. Campos et al. (Eds.): HWID 2012, IFIP AICT 407, pp. 90–97, 2013.

processes not only generate sensory experiences, but also help in exploratory interaction with the world that guides action or behavior. This paradigm finds applications in various research projects notably robotics, autonomous agents, and interactive interfaces [3], [4]. This requires awareness of the relationship with the world especially work, physical movement, action, and other affective behavior reactions. Everyday human activities include all of above states that we can understand through work analysis, and embodied cognition – both are prominent paradigm in cognitive science. Embodied cognition, CWA, and Cognitive System Engineering (CSE) [5] provide a new framework for Human Work Interaction Design (HWID) research. A more detailed HWID framework is given by [6] (as shown in figure 1).

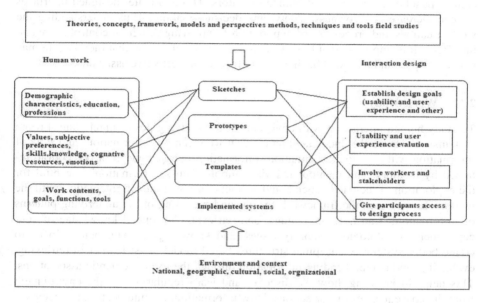

Fig. 1. A Framework of HWID [6]

To represent organizational settings that describe work processes we need to understand role of information and functional demands of the dynamic work environment. Mapping of information to features must show underline semantic structure of the work domain. This require nesting of information which implies meaning inherit in the work processes. For this, we require knowledge and understanding of objects. Objects are those with which we deal in everyday world. How we acquire the meaning and refer to the symbol or sign. Informatics and cognitive science deal with problems representation, semantics of computation and their application to create technology.

2   HWID Framework for Control Room

All this depends on perception of objects and conception of object that has been embedded in commonsense discourse. Mental phenomena, spoken & written language, and systems of signs & codes are intentional. According to Brian Smith, how we represent objects of the world and real-world situation in the computer is the vital point in understanding human functioning. So he says that experience we have with constructing computational (intentional) systems may open a window onto something to which we would not have any access [7]. Therefore, present research will suggest ways to design and develop systems, which are more suitable for varied situations and users.

Above research work is related to field of Man - Machine Interface (MMI) / Human - Computer Interaction (HCI), HWID in particular with the installation and operation of machines in the power plant. Here design of interfaces and interactions with control panel effect working of human operators. Through better-designed interfaces we can increase effectiveness, safety, and decision-making. Thus understanding the work situations and processes are important for improving design of control room and interfaces. It is important that how we could design machines so that they help human in every aspect and they will be their most efficient and effective assistants.

2.1   Work Study

To study human interaction with environment for studying power plant control room systems we require the understanding of what we mean by 'information' and flow of information within particular situation. Information is experienced in perception, retained by memory, and manipulated via symbols. Thus, 'information' is central for the exploration of technical, social, and aesthetic bases of human interaction with the world. This provides the framework for our understanding of the underlying patterns of 'information' transmission, storage, and retrieval. Conceptual knowledge of concepts such as ontologies, usability issues, and knowledge management help us to create better systems. Conceptual structures based model assist learner in retrieving, evaluating, and comprehending information through the use of semantic associations. This helps in knowing, how we discover and learn regularities in the environment from the consequences of our actions. How information, communication and technologies (ICT) can best be used for effective and efficient transmission of information to all irrespective of socio-cultural background and abilities? The above analysis is based on some goals and performance measures and their understanding. How interface design can be improved through approaches such as ecological interface design [8]? What are testing methods & situations that show the effectiveness of the interfaces?

Further, this problem is not simply programming but it involves cognition, our spatio-temporal movements, and our awareness of the environment in which we work. Therefore this problem includes representation of the world, processes involved, and comes under multi-disciplinary Cognitive Work Analysis (CWA) and Human Work Interaction Design (HWID) frameworks [6]. The problem requires understanding of the relation between human and machines that we can study in a complex socio-technical system such as control room of power, oil, and gas industries or particularly energy sector. Here our aim is to analyze the whole system not just human operators or machines in isolation but complete work settings so that individuals can act more effectively and preserve system safety and efficiency. We are analyzing work domain of the hydropower plant control room as shown in figure 2

Fig. 2. Control Room Panel of a Hydropower Plant

3   Human System Interfaces Based on Ecological Interface Design

To study work environment and particular situation we are using CWA and HWID frameworks and focusing on guidelines related to Human System Interfaces (HSI). Embodied view provides a sharp contrast from the standard information-processing viewpoint, in which cognition is seen as a problem of recovering details of the pre-given outer world [2]. In this light, the mind is no longer seen as passively reflecting the outside world, but rather as an active constructor of its own reality. The mind thereby becomes a distributed entity, an emergent characteristic of the whole sensory-central-motor neural system, existing in the elaborate network of interconnections that extend throughout the body. The philosophy of embodiment also stresses temporal, physical, and socio-cultural-technical situatedness. And, quite significantly, the embodied view in cognitive science allows for direct social and cultural interaction, which is crucial for understanding work situations.

In any power plant control room there are two objectives: first is to present to the operator components of plant and second is to minimize information or Cognitive overload on operator. To exhibit this, traditional display is shown in figure 2 and ecological display in figure 3 based on ecological interface design (EID) [9]. EID presents intangible abstract concepts visible and meaningful to operators [8]. For analyzing work situations in control room following questions are important:

- Objects representation and their meaning
- What makes us to acquire knowledge about the objects in the world, their specific relations, and properties
- How we extract information, its meaning
- Ontology of objects

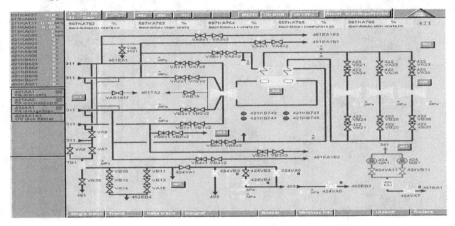

Fig. 3. A traditional display for the steam system [10]

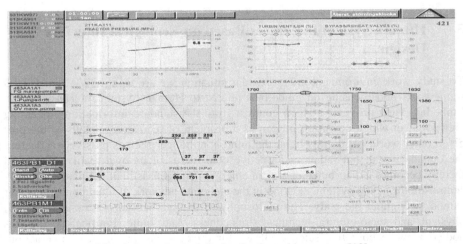

Fig. 4. An ecological display for the turbine system [10]

Ecological display clearly represents reactor pressure, enthalpy, temperature, pressure, and mass flow balance for better decision making. Through this work in progress, we would like to improve information displays, layout of system information, processes, and alarm system of a complex system such as power plant. Besides this study intend to find link between electricity distribution and control room status. These are larger unit of analysis and involve social-technical and cultural issues.

4   Research Analysis and Discussion

Hutchins tried to show that the cognitive science approach could be, with little modification, applied to a unit of analysis, which is larger than an individual. The unit of analysis here is a larger cognitive socio-technical system, such as an automated industrial setting (electricity distribution system [11], [12] power plant control room) [10], [13] and airline cockpit [14]. This approach is related to cognitive work analysis of studying processes in work environment. In both approaches, the question remains the same: what are the structures and processing of representations, which are internal to the system? To explain information-processing properties of individuals or larger systems, it is difficult to infer what is inside their mind [15] [16]. But for larger socio-technical systems, it is possible to directly observe the different representations that are inside the system, despite being outside the brain of individual. The above objectives can be attained through analyzing the various contributions of the environment in which work activities take place. Such as representational media (e.g. instruments, displays, manuals, navigation charts), the interactions of individuals with each other and their interactive use of artifacts (computer systems). Simultaneously, how information necessary to cooperate is propagated through the system by representational states and across machines is analyzed.

CWA is a work-centered conceptual framework developed by Rasmussen, Pejtersen, and Goodstein. Through CWA designing of constraints based interfaces is possible and such interfaces support operators in dealing with uncertain events and proved to be useful not just usable interfaces [17].Through CWA & HWID we analyzes the work people do, the tasks they perform, the decisions they make, their information behavior, and the context in which they perform their work [18]. CWA is a holistic approach and examines several dimensions: the environmental, organizational, social, activity, and individual. Therefore, we require a multi-disciplinary approach to apply concepts of CWA to study complex system [5].

In present research, we apply HWID framework for power plant control room panel interfaces to design the information system interaction and activities. As we live in the world, environment and interaction with others plays an important role. Thus both the paradigms find applications in various research projects and areas notably are studies of work domain analysis, robotics, autonomous agents, and interactive interfaces. These research directions will also be central for future developments of man-machine interaction, studying and enhancing the limits of information processing capacities of human and machine. These understandings result in better cooperation between human and computer that will enhance our capacities as supported by technology. Present research work explores the complex work environment to study cognition, cognitive tasks, and mental representations that will result in computational model of control room interactions and work setting for information handling based on CWA [19] & HWID (as in fig. 5). Further application is using Abstraction

Hierarchy method for the redesigning of the Control System Man-Machine Interface (MMI) of the Medium Tension Distribution Network of the Public Power Corporation of Greece [20].

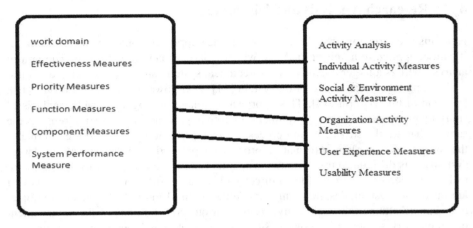

Fig. 5. Framework for Work – Activity Measure Analysis

5   Conclusion

This research provides understanding of cognition underlying human interactions with machines to improve design of both machines and work situations. We need interfaces and work situation, which reduces error and cognitive overload on human. Thus use of cognitive system engineering in the energy sector will helps us to analyze, model, design and evaluate effective human integration in complex socio-technical systems. The role of human operators in power plant control rooms is not only to control plant but also to meet market conditions and goals. With the advent of new Information Technology infrastructure we need to assess information requirements to manage control room that suits both human, machines, and economies.

Acknowledgements. First author would like to thank Prof. Torkil for helpful in writing and completing the paper. Also thankful to Dr. S. J. Chopra, Chancellor, and Dr. Parag Diwan, Vice-Chancellor, UPES for their encouragement and support.

References

1. Clark, A.: Being There: Putting Brain, Body and World Together Again. MIT Press, Cambridge (1997)
2. Varela, F.J., Thompson, E., Rosch, E.: The Embodied Mind. MIT Press, Cambridge (1992)
3. Brooks, R.A.: Intelligence Without Representation. Artificial Intelligence Journal (47), 139–159 (1991)

4. Dautenhahn, K.: Embodiment and Interaction in Socially Intelligent Life-Like Agents. In: Nehaniv, C.L. (ed.) CMAA 1998. LNCS (LNAI), vol. 1562, pp. 102–142. Springer, Heidelberg (1999)
5. Fidel, R., Pejtersen, A.M.: From information behavior research to the design of information systems: the Cognitive Work Analysis framework. Information Research 10(1) (2004)
6. Clemmensen, T.: A Human Work Interaction Design (HWID) Case Study in E-Government and Public Information Systems. International Journal of Public Information Systems (2011)
7. Smith, B.C.: On the Origin of Objects. MIT Press, Cambridge (1996)
8. Burns, C.M., Hajdukiewicz, J.R.: Ecological Interface Design. CRC Press, Florida (2004)
9. Memisevic, R., Sanderson, P.M., Choudhury, S., Wong, W.: Work domain analysis and ecological interface design for hydropower system monitoring and control. In: Jamshidi, M., Tunstel Jr., E., Anderson, G., et al. (eds.) Proceedings of the IEEE International Conference on Systems, Man and Cybernetics, October 10-12, pp. 3580–3587. IEEE, Big Island (2005)
10. Burns, C.M., Skraaning, G., Jamieson, G.A., Lau, N., Kwok, J., Welch, R., Andresen, G.: Evaluation of Ecological Interface Design for Nuclear Process Control: Situation Awareness Effects. Human Factors 50(4), 663–679 (2008)
11. Hay, S.L., Ault, G.W., Mcdonald, J.R.: Process of Simulating Novel Control Room Scenarios for Future Active Networks. In: 20th International Conference on Electricity Distribution, Prague, June 8-11 (2009)
12. Memisevic, R., Sanderson, P.M., Wong, W., Choudhury, S., Li, X.: Investigating Human-System Interaction with an Integrated Hydropower and Market System Simulator. IEEE Transaction on Power System 22(2) (May 2007)
13. Braseth, A.O., Nihlwing, C., Svengren, H., Veland, O., Hurlen, L., Kvalem, J.: Lessons Learned From Halden Project Research on Human System Interfaces. Nuclear Engineering and Technology 41(3) (April 2009)
14. Hutchins, E.: Cognition in the Wild. MIT Press, Cambridge (1995)
15. Garg, A.B.: Can Vision Provide Answers to Consciousness. In: International Conf. on Theoretical Neurobiology, NBRC, Manesar, Haryana, February 24-26 (2003)
16. Garg, A.B.: Design of Information System Interfaces: Using Human Computer Interaction and Cognitive System Engineering Paradigm. In: 2nd Uttarakhand Science Congress, Nainital, November 15-17 (2007)
17. Vicente, K.J.: Cognitive Work Analysis: Toward Safe, Productive, and Healthy Computer-Based Work. LEA, Mahwah (1999)
18. Sanderson, P.: Cognitive Work Analysis across the system life cycle: Achievement, challeneges, and prospects in aviation. In: Pfister, P., Edkins, G. (eds.) Aviation Resource Management, vol. 3. Ashgate, Aldershot (2003)
19. Jenkins, D.P., Solutions, S., Stanton, N.A., Salmon, P.M., Walker, G.H.: Cognitive Work Analysis: Coping with Complexity. Ashgate (2008)
20. Drivalou, S., Marmaras, N.: Tracing Interface Design solutions for an Electricity Distribution Network Control System Using the Abstraction Hierarchy. In: Proceedings of the XVth Triennial Congress of the IEA. The Ergonomics Society of Korea, Seoul (2003)

Natural Interactions:
An Application for Gestural Hands Recognition

Ricardo Proença and Arminda Guerra

Instituto Politécnico de Castelo Branco, Escola Superior de Tecnologia,
Av. Do Empresário, 6000 – Castelo Branco, Portugal
ricproenca@gmail.com, aglopes@ipcb.pt

Abstract. This paper presents a system for the development of new human-machine interfaces focused on static gestures recognition of human hands. The proposal is to aid access to certain objects to the occupant of an intelligent wheelchair in order to facilitate their daily life. The proposed methodology relies on the use of simple computational processes and low-cost hardware. Its development involves a comprehensive approach to the problems of computer vision, based on the steps of the video image capture, image segmentation, feature extraction, pattern recognition and classification. The importance of this work relates to the need to build new models of interaction that allow, in a natural and intuitive way, to simplify the daily life of a disable person.

Keywords: Human-Computer Interaction, gesture recognition, computer vision, disabled person, assistive technology.

1   Introduction

In face-to-face communication verbal and non-verbal modalities are used to complement each other. When we intend to transpose natural communication into communication with the machine, several difficulties occur, for example, those that concern user experience and, in particular, those that do not permit social inclusion.

We know that some people do not have the ability to handle some devices, but they possess enough ability to interact with a system of recognition of gestures [1]. It becomes evident the necessity to build models of Human–computer interaction through gestures that allow, in a natural and intuitive way, to these people, to easily interact with the machines.

The image acquisition and processing technologies evolution permit to build a system that enable computers to understand the sign language. Different types of algorithms for gesture recognition are being studied, but the challenge lies in the fact that this interaction becomes independent of devices that assist the identification of the human hand, such as gloves or sensors for motion capture.

The proposed work is the development of a system for static gesture recognition with one hand only, located in front of a webcam, in a simple and uniform background scenario, without the support of assistive materials. This interface could be

P. Campos et al. (Eds.): HWID 2012, IFIP AICT 407, pp. 98–111, 2013.

applied to an intelligent wheelchair in order to facilitate disabled peoples' quality of life.

2   Related Work

Several gestural proposals for various areas, such as entertainment, medicine, marketing, smart home control, elderly and disable care [2], [3] as well as intelligent wheelchairs [4], [5], [6], [7], [8] were found in literature review. However, the majority of studies are exclusively related to the chair's movement and we did not find the complete mobility concerns. We also noticed the existence of wheelchair-mounted robotic arm applications [9], [10], [11], [12] that uses different interaction devices (such as joystick), but none so intuitive that could be considered natural (to humans).

In fact, this relation is not fully effective to personal conflict resolution without considering mobility. Some people, for example, do not hold the necessary dexterity to handle these devices, but they have enough ability to interact with a system for gesture recognition [1] that certainly minimizes many of the difficulties and inhibitions.

3   The Context: Assistive Technology

We are daily faced with several examples of people who suffer road accidents. The consequences fully affect the mobility of the individual either physically, psychologically and socially. This situation promotes numerous side effects, some of which demand alternative means of mobility such as wheelchairs.

The increasing number of people with mobility disabilities requires assistive technologies to provide their quality of life improvement. However, there are many obstacles to use technology solutions because they require expensive resources or further studies in order to improve every citizen access.

4   Proposed Solution

We considered the case of an individual who needs to have access to an object placed on a surface with a large area, inhibitory of normal and autonomous actions.

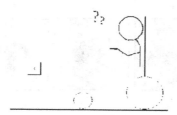

Fig. 1. Problematic situation

It is our understanding, according the research we did, that image acquisition and processing technologies' evolution, allows building a computational system that makes the machine to recognize human gestures. However, the construction of this system requires the use of various programming algorithms quite complexes. We list general procedures that entail: (1) image capture, (2) human hand segmentation, (3) feature extraction, (4) classification of gestures.

We considered the gestural algorithms development, based on low cost webcams, a great stimulus in Human-Machine Interaction.

Given the results we obtained in the course of this investigation, we propose a system to help the occupant of a wheelchair to interact with the world, especially, to have access to certain objects in order to facilitate their daily life.

In terms of hardware, the prototype consists of an intelligent wheelchair, a laptop with a built-in webcam and a robotic arm. As to software, this system consists in static gesture recognition, performed in real time, through a hand located in front of a webcam.

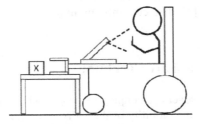

Fig. 2. Proposed system

Our concept of mobility will be based on the transposition of each executed gesture to a robotic arm action. This transposition is set from 6 gestures that we present in fig. 3, fulfilling each a specific function in the context of facilitating the mobility of the person: (a) pause; (b) stretch mechanical arm with speed 1 (c) stretch mechanical arm with speed 2 (d) open claw, (e) close claw; (f) move arm to the starting position.

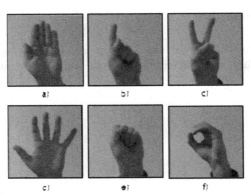

Fig. 3. Hand recognition gestures

With this method, we intend to show that it is possible to construct a human-machine interaction system, facilitating the life of the person with inhibitions, with an acceptable level of environmental restrictions.

Again, we can prove that the fact that a person has to use a glove, or any other device that aids the identification of the human hand, is inhibiting the free, systematic and autonomous individual action.

The scope of this work is limited to the recognition of gestures; we want to identify the static gesture shown by the occupant of the wheelchair, between a set of pre-defined gestures system. The prototype that we outlined has not been built so far.

Finally, we launched the challenge to awake attentions and possible interests for the implementation of this type of equipment that will allow, in our view, more disinhibiting action of the individual, because it determines the elements that are not always available to anyone of us, even in conditions of normal mobility.

5   Natural Interactions

Natural interaction is considered through the way people naturally communicate through gestures, expressions, movements, and see the world by looking around and manipulating physical artifacts; the key assumption is that people should be allowed to interact with technology as they are used to interact with the real world in everyday life.

Our focus is on gestural communication. The gestures can naturally increase the interaction between the user and the computer, replacing devices such as the mouse, keyboard, joystick or buttons in machines control. However, a great incitement for gestural interfaces development comes from the growth of applications for virtual environments [13], such as surgery simulation. In the majority of these applications, the gestures are seen as triggers to virtual objects control, simulating the 2D, 3D or abstractions of real objects, such as robotic arms.

5.1   Gestures

There are many definitions and debates about the meaning of gesture. Pavlovic [14] presents a definition of hand gesture that combines the development of posture and position in time, with the intention of communication or manipulation.

In Human–computer interaction field, gestures imply the use of the hands to instruct a machine. Its meaning depends on the system that integrates and evaluates them. Point or rotate actions are representative actions of this type of gestures.

We can differentiate the gestures in two types: dynamic and static. The dynamic gestures, necessarily, involve time evolution [15] and require movement to transmit the intended message. The gesture to say "goodbye" is an example of a dynamic gesture performed with an open hand and is only meaningful if done with movement.

Furthermore, static gestures do not include movement to transmit the message. The same static open hand, with no motion made, forward the information to "stop".

In Computer Vision, we can state that static gesture is a configuration of the hand pose represented as a single image. A dynamic gesture implies movement, represented by a sequence of images.

However, in this work, we will limit ourselves to the static symbolic gestures performed by one hand.

5.2   Static Gesture Recognition

Static gesture is represented by an image; the recognition is based on feature extraction discriminants of the image. We can, for instance, to extract features from the directions of the fingers or the contours of the hand.

The position of the palm of the hand and of the fingers has been widely used for gesture recognition [16], [17]. We can also treat other information about the hands as the angles [18], roughness [19] or sampling points on the boundary region of the hand [20], [21].

Another category of resources abundantly used implies the notion of moment. It is a weighted average of the pixels intensities of an image, usually chosen to have some interpretation. We can find statistical moments [22], Zernike moments [23] and Hu moments [24] , which are more used.

Fourier analysis can also be applied for representing the limits of the hand [25] .

The feature extraction is a complex computational problem because it requires perfect background characteristics and high computational resources. Disorganized background images with changes in lighting conditions become very difficult to handle.

Allied to this, the used algorithms require loading the whole image into memory, which complicates the computer resources management.

After extracting the features, then we can classify the gestures. The more simplistic way of static hand recognition is to count the number of fingers [17]. Nevertheless, recognition can be seen as a matching process, applying cluster algorithms [25], [26]. In this case, recognition consists of finding the best match between images that represent static gestures. We may also do the same correspondence with Chamfer distance algorithm [27]. In addition, the Neural Networks are widely used in the hand postures detection and classification [28], using two or three layers of neurons. More recently, techniques of face detection have been applied to this problem. The Viola and Jones system that leverages the features Haar [29] is a consensus for subject researchers.

6   Interface Design: Process Description

Based on [30] , the proposed method for symbolic gesture recognition follows a logical and complementary tasks' sequence in terms of digital image processing. The fundamental steps for the proposed work are presented on fig.4.

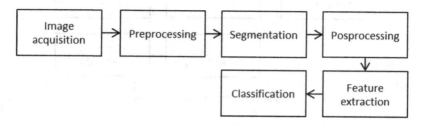

Fig. 4. Fundamental steps for the proposed work

The image acquisition is made by a low cost webcam. The preprocessing and post processing use image enhancement and noise reduction techniques by analyzing environmental lightning conditions and background colors. This happens due to difficulties in illumination. The image segmentation obtained by Computer Vision algorithms, allows the separation of full human hand in a simple and uniform background scenario, without benefit of supporting devices. The features to extract are based in the geometric shape of the hand, fast enough to be applied in real time. The classification step is based on the use of the recognition patterns classifier for training and to classify the input data.

6.1   Image Acquisition

The process starts with the gesture acquisition by the webcam and presented through video images (fig. 5).

Fig. 5. Captured frame

6.2   Segmentation

Segmentation is the main part of the entire process and it assumes a sequence of tasks (Fig. 6). This stage makes the human hand recognition by skin color detection.

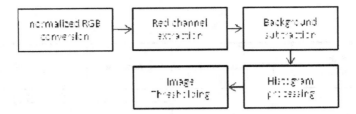

Fig. 6. Key steps of segmentation

The procedure starts with the frames conversion captured for the normalized RGB color space. Knowing that the majority of human skin color tends to cluster in the red channel, we extract this channel and then, we subtract the background of the extracted red channel image. Background subtraction allows us to obtain a greyscale image with color intensity changes between the background and the hand, as shown in (fig. 7).

Fig. 7. a) Normalized RGB image b) Red channel extracted c) Background subtracted

Then, we design the image histogram and compute the optimal thresholding value. We used the Method of the Valley that consists in checking how many regions there are (peaks and valleys) in the histogram and use the valley information to set the value of the threshold. Fig. 8 shows the histogram and optimal threshold value identified.

Fig. 8. Image Histogram with optimum threshold identified

Finally, we use the found threshold value to binarize the image (fig. 9).

Fig. 9. Binary image

6.3   Feature Finding

The previous step provides an image where we can find the edge pixels that separate the hand from the background, but without information about the edges as entities in themselves, thus, the next step is to be able to gather the whole pixels on the edge contours surrounding the stain of segmented hand.

Fig. 10 shows that trough the extracted contour we can calculate several structures such as convex hull, contour edges, fingers and surrounding rectangles.

Fig. 10. Calculated structures to feature extraction

6.4   Feature Extraction

The feature extraction lets obtaining a set of feature vectors, also called descriptors that can distinguish, accurately, each hand gesture. Our approach proposes the use of geometric features with Hu invariant moments [24]. The presented features are the most discriminatory from the six gestures chosen: contour size; contour circularity; contour eccentricity; convex hull size; bounding box proportion; bounding box area; rotated bounding box area; main inertia axe; Hu Moments.

Some problems during the gesture recognition may occur if there is a large rotational movement, because the shape and proportions of features that represent the gesture may change.

We noticed that these features are easy to extract, are independent and are sufficient to distinguish the amount of gestures chosen by us, however, these are not suitable for all types of gestures.

6.5   Classification

For pattern recognition and classification, we choose the Support Vector Machines (SVM) machine learning technique that has been recognized in recent years. This technique is used in various pattern recognition tasks, always with results superior to those achieved by similar techniques in many applications. Its use comes from some of its main characteristics [31] :

- Good generalizability;
- Robustness in larger dimensions;
- Well-defined theory in Mathematics and Statistics.

7   Tests

The system performs well as long as the skin-like colors in the background do not exist and if it is tested indoor. Results pointed for a good removal of luminosity influence during the segmentation process, so it becomes less dependent on the lighting conditions, which has always been a critical obstacle to the image recognition. The system operates in real time with around 30 frames per second, requiring an effort to minimize time processing of the tasks.

We saved 100 images representing each gesture to our database. For testing we have also saved 100 images for each gesture of 5 different people.

Table 1 summarizes the results of the hand classification tests.

Table 1. Gesture classification results

Gestures	Frames	Correct	Incorrect	% Correct	% Incorrect
A, B, C, D, E, F	3000	2974	26	99.1%	0.9%

8   Tasks and Activities to Build the Prototype

The main goal of the proposed work was the development of a system for recognizing static gestures of human hands of different people, situated in front of a webcam.

The choice of appropriate technology for this type of system could limit the development and visualization of the results.

This section presents and clarifies the work context for the development of the proposed system. Considering the literature review process carried out, we discovered interesting and innovative approaches for the application's development based on the gestural recognition. However, we found an absence of this type of systems for assistive technologies regarding wheelchair intelligent robotic arms.

Based on the lack of information, we create our design process for the proposed system. The decision about the software and hardware to be used on the development of our system was the main concern. Conversely, we needed to consider the basic principles defined previously: the system should operate in real time with minimal restrictions and the system should have a low cost demand in order to be applied in everyday life by a significant number of users who needed it.

Based on these decisions fig. 11 presents the first phase of the design process:

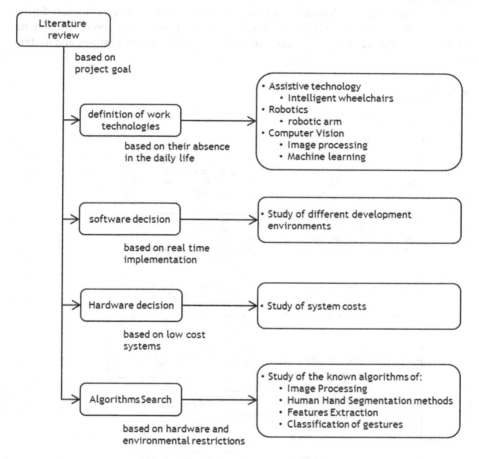

Fig. 11. The design process – first phase

After acquiring the theoretical knowledge about the subject, on literature review process, based on our project goals, the next step was the definition of the technologies that should be chosen considering the facility of their use in a daily life purpose by all kind of users. An intelligent wheelchair with a robotic arm and using image processing technology was the defined goal. Then, the main argument for the choice of the software was made after the study of different development environments based on real time implementation. The study of the system cost, the lowest one, contributed to the hardware selection to be used. Finally, we searched for the most used algorithms for each experiment steps (image processing, human hand segmentation methods, feature extraction and gestures classification) taking into consideration environment restrictions.

The relationship between quality and performance for the real-time system was taken into account.

Fig. 12 shows the implementation task process referring the decision taken during each task: image acquisition, color space conversion, histogram processing, hand segmentation, feature finding, feature extraction, classification of gestures and system tests.

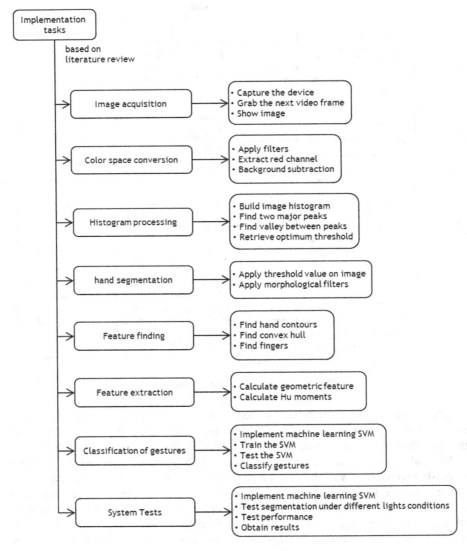

Fig. 12. Implementation task process

Some potential users of the system, around twelve, were, informally, interviewed, at the beginning of this project and later on a prototype phase. They considered that the proposed solution will be important since it preview affordance for a highest number of people who have social, financial or accessibility restrictions.

9 Conclusions

It has been shown that it is possible to interact with a machine naturally and intuitively through hand gestures without requiring support material such as gloves or markers. And that there is a possibility to develop Computer Vision interactive systems based and implemented on conventional computers using inexpensive devices, accessible to all, facilitating, especially disable mobility people with an acceptable level of environmental restrictions.

The proposed system produces satisfactory results with fixed constant lighting conditions, with a non-skin color scenario. However, the method used for skin segmentation exposes some flaws, mainly caused due to lighting variations causing glare, reflections and shadows. These shortcomings are minimized applying morphological filters and smoothing filters.

Conversely, the systems works with quite different hand gestures, but it shows some weakness when using more identical gestures such as sign language. Thus, the scope of this work is limited to the recognition of gestures; we wanted to identify the static gesture shown by the occupant of the wheelchair. The prototype that we outline has not been built so far.

In future work, the study of methods that may respond better to lighting variations, to different scenarios and how to be more effective in identifying the skin, even from other races would be helpful. The gesture recognition through dynamic movement analysis can also be a target for further investigation. However, we launched the challenge to awake attentions and possible interests for the implementation of this type of equipment that will be, in our point of view, more disinhibiting action of the individual, because it determines the element that are not always available to anyone.

References

1. Pausch, R., Williams, R.D.: Giving CANDY to Children: User-Tailored Gesture Input Driving an Articulator-Based Speech Synthesizer. Communications of the ACM 5(5), 58–66 (2012)
2. Lande, M., Samvatsar, M.: Multimodal System using Human Computer Interface. International Journal of Engineering and Innovative Technology (IJEIT) 1 (2012)
3. Chhabria, S., Dharaskar, R.: Multimodal Interface for Disabled Persons. International Journal of Computer Science and Communication V, 223–228 (2012)
4. Zhang, Y., Zhang, J., Luo, Y.: A novel intelligent wheelchair control system based on hand gesture recognition. In: IEEE/ICME International Conference on Complex Medical Engineering, CME (2011)

5. Kobayashi, Y., Kinpara, Y., Shibusawa, T., Kuno, Y.: Robotic wheelchair based on observations of people using integrated sensors. In: IROS 2009 Proceedings of the 2009 IEEE/RSJ International Conference on Intelligent Robots and Systems, pp. 2013–2018 (2009)

6. Simpson, R., LoPresti, E., Hayashi, S., Nourbakhsh, I., Miller, D.: The smart Wheelchair component system. Journal of Rehabilitation Research and Development 41, 429–442 (2004)

7. Jia, P., Hu, H., Lu, T., Yuan, K.: Head Gesture Recognition for Hands-free Control of an Intelligent Wheelchair. Industrial Robot: An International Journal 34, 60–68 (2007)

8. Kumar, K., Dinesh, M.: Hand Gesture Recognition Wheelchair Control by Digital Image Processing Technique. International Journal of Communications and Engineering 4, 67–71 (2012)

9. Hillman, M., Hagan, K., Hagan, S., Jepson, J., Orpwood, R.: The Weston Wheelchair Mounted Assistive Robot - The Design Story. Robotica 20, 125–132 (2002)

10. Tsui, K., Yanco, H., Kontak, D., Beliveau, L.: Development and Evaluation of a Flexible Interface for a Wheelchair Mounted Robotic Arm. In: Proceedings of the 3rd ACM/IEEE International Conference on Human Robot Interaction (2008)

11. Palankar, M., De Laurentis, K., Alqasemi, R., Veras, E., Dubey, R., Arbel, Y., Donchin, E.: Control of a 9-DoF Wheelchair-mounted robotic arm system using a P300 Brain Computer Interface: Initial experiments. In: Proceedings of the 2008 IEEE International Conference on Robotics and Biomimetics (2009)

12. Touati, Y., Ali-Cherif, A.: Smart Powered Wheelchair Platform Design and control for People with Severe Disabilities. Software Engineering, 49–56 (2012)

13. Krueger, W.M.: Artificial Reality II. Addison-Wesley (1991)

14. Pavlovic, V.I., Sharma, R., Huang, T.S.: Visual Interpretation of Hand Gestures for Human Computer Interaction: A Review. IEEE Transactions on Pattern Analysis and Machine Intelligence (1997)

15. Birk, H., Moeslund, T.B., Madsen, C.B.: Real-Time Recognition of Hand Alphabet Gestures Using Principal Component Analysis. In: 10th Scandinavian Conference on Image Analysis (1997)

16. MacLean, J., Pantofaru, C., Wood, L., Herpers, R., Derpanis, K., Topalovic, D., Tsotsos, J.: Fast Hand Gesture Recognition for Real-Time Teleconferencing Applications. In: IEEE ICCV Workshop on Recognition, Analysis, and Tracking of Faces and Gestures in Real-Time Systems, Vancouver (2001)

17. Kim, H., Fellner, D.W.: Interaction with Hand Gesture for a Back-Projection Wall. In: CGI 2004 Proceedings of the Computer Graphics International, Washington (2001)

18. Sato, Y., Saito, M., Koik, H.: Real-Time Input of 3D Pose and Gestures of a User's Hand and Its Applications for HCI. In: 2001 IEEE Virtual Reality Conference, Yokohama (2001)

19. Jang, H., Jun-Hyeong, D., Jin-Woo, J., Bien, Z.Z.: Two-staged hand-posture recognition method for softremocon system. In: 2005 IEEE International Conference on Systems, Man and Cybernetics, vol. 1 (2005)

20. Hamada, Y., Shimada, N., Shirai, Y.: Hand Shape Estimation Using Sequence of Multi-Ocular Images Based on Transition Network. In: International Conference on Vision Interface (2002)

21. Hamada, Y., Shimada, N., Shirai, Y.: Hand shape estimation using image transition network. In: HUMO 2000 Proceedings of the Workshop on Human Motion (2000)

22. Lee, L.K., Kim, S., Choi, Y.K., Lee, M.H.: Recognition of hand gesture to human-computer interaction. In: 26th Annual Conference of the IEEE Industrial Electronics Society, vol. 3 (2000)
23. Sribooruang, Y., Kumhom, P., Chamnongthai, K.: Hand posture classification using wavelet moment invariant. In: Virtual Environments, Human-Computer Interfaces and Measurement Systems (2004)
24. Hu, M.K.: Visual Pattern Recognition by Moment Invariants. IRE Trans. Info. Theory IT-8, 179–187 (1962)
25. Licsár, A., Szirányi, T.: Dynamic training of hand gesture recognition system. In: 17th International Conference on Pattern Recognition (ICPR 2004), vol. 4 (2004)
26. Zhou, H., Lin, D.J., Huang, T.S.: Static hand gesture recognition based on local orientation histogram feature distribution model. In: Conference on Computer Vision and Pattern Recognition Workshop (CVPRW 2004), vol. 10 (2004)
27. Athitsos, V., Sclaroff, S.: An appearance-based framework for 3d hand shape classification and camera viewpoint estimation. In: Fifth IEEE International Conference on Automatic Face and Gesture Recognition (2001)
28. Marcel, S., Bernier, O., Viallet, J.-E., Collobert, D.: Hand gesture recognition using inpu/output hidden markov models. In: Fourth IEEE International Conference on Automatic Face and Gesture Recognition (2000)
29. Jones, M.J., Viola, P.: Face recognition using boosted local features. In: International Conference on Computer Vision (2003)
30. Gonzalez, R., Woods, R.: Digital Image Processing, 2nd edn. Addison-Wesley (2002)
31. Smola, A.: Geometry and invariance in kernel based methods. In: Advances in Kernel Methods: Support Vector Learning, pp. 89–116. MIT Press (1999)

UCD Guerrilla Tactics

A Strategy for Implementation of UCD in Sweden's Military Defense Organizations

Elina Eriksson[1] and Anna Swartling[2]

[1] Media Technology and Interaction Design – MID, KTH - Royal Institute of Technology,
SE-100 44 Stockholm, Sweden
elina@kth.se
[2] Scania CV AB, SE-151 87 Södertälje, Sweden
anna.swartling@scania.com

Abstract. The problem of how to implement user-centred design (UCD) is well established as a research topic within HCI. Yet there are unresolved issues in order for UCD to actually be used in practice. This paper will present a case study within Sweden's military defense organizations, concerning the introduction of UCD. The overarching goal of the research was to bridge the gap between work practices and systems development; focusing the efforts on introducing usability work in the procurement process. We concluded early on that we needed to develop and formulate an approach that is probably common in practice but not described or used in research. We call this strategy UCD guerrilla tactics, which entails to do the unexpected, to work pragmatically with change, and to use user centred methods to introduce UCD. Our main target group was future users and procurers of UCD methods. We aimed at demonstrating and involving them in the work through user centred activities. The tactics is also a reflexive and flexible approach based on continuous evaluation of what is feasible and potentially gives the largest outcome. This paper describes the guerrilla tactics, how it was applied in a case study and factors that should be considered when using it.

Keywords: User-centred design, procurement, usability, organizational change, case study, work practice.

1 Introduction

User-centred design (UCD) is well established within the HCI research field. It can be perceived as an umbrella concept for a variety of methods, techniques, processes and approaches. Often when UCD is mentioned it is not used for a particular process, but refers to a situation in which methods with a focus on users have been used. For example in a study that surveyed people attending CHI2000 [1], several methods were included: field studies (including contextual inquiry), user requirements analysis, iterative design, usability evaluation, task analysis, focus groups, formal heuristic evaluations, user interviews, prototype without user testing, surveys, informal expert

P. Campos et al. (Eds.): HWID 2012, IFIP AICT 407, pp. 112–123, 2013.

reviews, card sorting, and participatory design. There are also influential attempts to define it more specifically e.g. [2-4]. But even though UCD is established within the HCI-field, it is still difficult to make UCD work in practice [5-7]. There are numerous studies presenting cases where UCD has been used or been introduced in organizations [8-10]. However, there exists no silver bullet, in the sense of a context free and all encompassing way to do the introduction [11]. Several attempts seem to use a subtle approach, like Kujala's Trojan Horse [12] where the field study method was simplified and the results presented in a familiar form.

UCD is by tradition often included when there is a concrete systems development project [13]. But there are many activities concerning work practices and requirement formulation taking place before the start of a project, which means that UCD activities might come into play too late. There is a need to bridge the gap in the procurement process (sometimes referred to as acquisition) between work practice, organizational development and systems development [14, 15]. Moreover there is a lack of techniques and methods supporting procurers to incorporate UCD and usability into their processes [16, 17].

Furthermore, our focus is not only to include UCD in individual projects but to establish a user-centred attitude within the organization [4] with the aim of changing the overall work processes for procurement and development of IT-systems. But how can that be achieved? If the traditional way of introducing UCD is failing, i.e. introducing it in the formal system development process, might there be another way?

User-centred guerrilla tactics is not a concept commonly used within HCI research, though similar terms are frequently used in industry to describe how to introduce usability within organizations. There is no clear common definition, more than that it comprises using a subtle approach and sneaking usability into the systems development process. Perhaps the most cited use is Jacob Nielsen's text on "Guerilla HCI" in which he advocates for gradually introducing usability by "... starting with the bare minimum and gradually progressing to a more refined lifecycle approach" [18].

Based on the second author's previous research in Sweden's military defense organizations [19] we aimed at developing the early phases of systems development: the procurement process. We developed a strategy especially focusing on what can be done when the resources are scarce. We call this strategy UCD guerrilla tactics.

The UCD guerrilla tactics is a *pragmatic* approach focusing on what is feasible and potentially gives the largest outcome with few resources. This meant for example in our case, targeting change projects, key people and being open to unconventional activities. To succeed with this, we continuously *reflected and evaluated* whether we were successful or not with our chosen activities. If not, we adapted or changed what we were doing. When choosing activities we based our actions on the context and the situations that were available.

Furthermore, the strategy initiates a change by using *user centred methods for introducing UCD*, i.e. treating the respondents as both participants and recipients. We did this by involving them in user centred activities but also through demonstrations of how usability methods could be used in the procurement process.

To conclude, the purpose of this paper is to present an approach for implementing UCD. We do this by describing our case study within Sweden's military defense organizations. The purpose of this paper is not to describe a detailed work analysis but rather to analyze prerequisites for UCD in general where work analysis is a part of the methodology. This paper does not elaborate on the result in terms of the degree of UCD actually implemented in the organizations. Rather, we reflect on the approach chosen and the consequences thereof.

2   Research Settings

Sweden's military defense setting comprises several organizations where two of the most prominent are the Swedish Armed Forces (SwAF) and the Swedish Defense Materiel Administration (FMV). SwAF is the authority that carries out international missions, protects the integrity of Swedish borders and supports the society in major crisis. FMV is Sweden's oldest civil governmental agency and its main task has remained the same over time: to strengthen the operational capability of the defense system by acquiring materiel (i.e. the equipment and supplies of a military force) in a cost-effective way. In most cases, FMV works as a middleman between the armed forces and the system developers.

SwAF procures IT systems from FMV, which in turn executes the procurements through contracts with industry. FMV does not usually do any development on its own; its responsibility is to initiate and supervise contracts with industry based on the procurements from SwAF. For this work, FMVs tradition is to employ engineers who analyze requirements and manage projects. Many formal processes have been defined and the procedures for handling procurement and systems development are extensive.

The individual units within the armed forces are the end-users of the IT systems; they inform the people in charge of procurement at SwAF headquarter (HQ) of the needs that arise during the evaluation and use of the systems. They are also in close contact with FMV as it evaluates both old and new equipment. Finally, during implementation FMV often engage them to evaluate the system. The units can also have direct contact with industry if they experience problems with an existing system and report them to the companies in charge of maintenance and support.

2.1   Research Method

The case study presented in this paper was conducted in Sweden's military defense organizations from the autumn of 2009 to the spring of 2011. The procurer of the research project was FMV. Several other research collaborations with FMV had preceded this project with the main aim of understanding usability issues in relation to the procurement process [19]. However the focus of this project was somewhat different. The project manager at FMV wished that our research should be more aimed at making a change rather than just reporting the current state. Thus the over-arching aim of the project was to introduce a higher focus on user-centeredness in the early phases of the requirement and procurement processes at SwAF.

The empirical material was collected through semi-structured interviews with the procurer, IS strategists, enterprise architects, development personnel in units and usability experts. We have also collected data through workshops with the same kind of participants. All respondents were given information about research ethics such as confidentiality and anonymity. The workshops and the interviews were in all cases except one audio recorded and transcribed. Furthermore, we have at all times been using research diaries, in which we have written down thoughts, conversations etc. as well as more structured field notes when doing participant observations. Moreover we have reviewed an extensive amount of written documents and presentations from the organizations. The overall data analysis has been iterative and we have revisited the material many times during the course of the project.

3   Result: Tactics in Practice

The core aspect of the strategy is to shift focus from the end-users of IT-systems to the users of the UCD methods or the recipients of the result such as procurers, strategists, project managers or system developers. Furthermore, it is about using classic participatory methods. The aim is to design a version of UCD that can work in a specific organization and to achieve that through collaboration with the people affected by the new work practice. Here we will describe how we tried to achieve that.

3.1   Reflexive Pragmatism

In comparison to traditional UCD introduction, which in general have a set agenda, we continuously reflected on how we could adjust our approach so that we could achieve the largest outcome. When we encountered problems we regrouped and found new activities that we thought could be more feasible.

From the outset we considered action research [20] as a suitable methodology for the project. Albeit in the initial discussions, it became clear that this was not possible due to politics within the defense organizations (the politics and the organizational structures are interesting in this case, see Debriefing and Discussion). This was one of our first situations in which we had to adjust to the situation given to us. We discussed the issue and pragmatically adapted our approach. In consequence, we decided to work as an action research project, but without actually talking about it as such. We still had a dual aim of both solving a problem in practice as well as a research problem [21], with the drawback of not being able to collaborate to the extent optimal for an action research project.

Within Sweden's military defense organizations several terms were used that relates to usability and usability work, some examples are Human Factors (HF), Human-Computer Interaction (HCI), and Human-Machine Interaction (HMI). The usage of this terminology was not clear, as in this quote from one of the respondents: *"We usually say Human Factors, and I don't know if people honestly know what it means, or if people just pretend that they do. [...] We use it and people nod and smile but perhaps they just don't understand what we do."* Furthermore, in the previous studies of Sweden's military defense organizations [19], the second author had observed that the meaning many respondents gave usability differed from the one the HCI community gives it. Therefore, in line with our pragmatic approach, we decided to start using a somewhat new terminology in this research project, primarily Human-centeredness (HC).

3.2   Pilot Project

At the start of the research project, it was not clear how we were supposed to accomplish the change in work practice that the project strived for. SwAF is a large organization and we concluded that aiming for changing it in its entirety was not an option. We decided instead, based on our pragmatic approach, to find an on-going development project where we could have an impact. We found a project with the aim to implement enterprise architecture (EA) in SwAF (here named the EA project). They were working on future rules for how SwAF should be described, a local EA framework, and a methodology for using architecture within the procurement process. We hypothesized that we could gain something from introducing UCD while the organization was changing its work practice anyway.

3.3   UCD with UCD

One major part of the tactics was to initiate change, that is, introducing UCD, through user centred methods and a user centred attitude. With this we mean treating the respondents as both participants and recipients. Or expressed differently, we considered the possible users of the usability methods and activities as exactly that: users. Hence, we involved them in user centred activities, but also in demonstrations of how usability methods could be used in the procurement process.

We wanted to introduce both classic UCD methods as well as new methods that we thought might fit this particular organization and these particular participants; we chose to explore case study [22], personas [23], scenarios [23], conceptual sketching [24], coaching [25], and Cynefin inspired methods [26]. Several other activities were also conducted. For example, we commented on and proofread several relevant documents produced by others. Furthermore, the first author interviewed usability professionals within SwAF and FMV.

The strategy resulted in us working with UCD on many different levels: 1) integration of UCD in new formal structures; 2) using user centred methods when working with the project to define and implement new formal structures (with project members and end-users of the formal structures); 3) using UCD methods with end-users of technical artifacts related to the new formal structures.

4   Debriefing and Discussion

We will here reflect on our application of the UCD guerrilla tactics in relation to the empirical data. By analyzing and describing the barriers it is possible to get a deeper understanding of the problems and the potentials of this strategy but also the introduction of UCD in general.

4.1   Usability Competence

FMV had a declining number of usability professionals in the years preceding this research project, with a maximum of ten usability professionals among its 1500 employees. There were also a non-active network of people interested in, and working with usability issues. Since the usability professionals were few they could not participate in many projects and had little time for policy creation or strategic usability work. At SwAF there was a great lack of usability professionals and usability competence. In many of our interviews, with stakeholders from both SwAF and FMV, the responsibility for including usability in procurement was put on SwAF but it was also acknowledged that there is nobody there to take on this responsibility. There were some that had training in systems theory where Human Factors had been a part, but according to our respondents they were scarce and dispersed and mainly working with other things.

We tried to engage the usability professionals and succeeded to some extent. They participated in several workshops and one of them acted as a co-facilitator in a couple of workshops with end-users. But in the end, we researchers were the main actors and the majority of activities were done by us alone. So in this respect, the UCD guerilla tactics was not enough. We needed more support and engagement from the organization than was possible.

The lack of usability professionals had serious implications for the introduction of UCD primarily as we had no one to collaborate with. Research show that usability practitioners are important [27], not only for collaboration, but also for ensuring a sustainable change in the organization. Someone have to continue to work with these issues after the research project has ended.

4.2   Organizational Structures and Politics

The division of responsibility was sharply divided between the defense organizations; regulated by formal documents from the government and by historical aspects. SwAF is the only authority in Sweden engaged in armed combat, but they were not allowed to perform any kind of development of artifacts supporting combat. The situation was similar for FMV. In general, they were not supposed to develop any artifacts for combat themselves; instead they acted as a support organization for SwAF directing procurements to industry. The interaction between the organizations were settled in collaboration contracts, but also deduced to routines and established practice. Several of our respondents expressed that working with user involvement was difficult for several reasons. One was the distance between users and the development project. When involving users, it was FMV who formally requested resources from HQ. It was not possible for the units or HQ to demand user involvement in a development project. Instead, if they wished that end-users should be involved they had to ask FMV to include it in their offer to SwAF. Sometimes FMV requested user groups and user representatives but never more elaborate and efficient ways of UCD. In some cases, different stakeholders bypassed the routines and through personal contacts made sure that end-users were included in development projects or that personnel from FMV were included in the early requirements process.

SwAF was a very hierarchical organization. For example, the EA project was explicitly told not to contact people working at HQ or in the units. Politics was always present during the research project. At one time, after most project members had been asked to leave from a meeting with the procurer of the EA project, one respondent explained: *"This is about P-O-W-E-R."*

Our research interest was to bridge the gap between work practice and systems development within Sweden's military defense organizations. Our starting point was in FMV within a research project. This made sense in some regard, since FMV did work with development and procurement of materiel and there existed at least some usability professionals. However, in order to introduce a higher focus on usability in the earliest phases of systems development much of our attention should be directed at SwAF. With all the organizational and political hindrances mentioned above, the starting point was perhaps not the best for this project. But not all research projects start off in the right situation, e.g. [27]. However, it is difficult to see what would have been better with an enterprise as big as Sweden's military defense. For us, there was no other choice at this point in time. As a result, we used the guerrilla tactics, working pragmatically with the possibilities given.

More explicit support from higher management could have been beneficial in this [4]. We tried to address this issue both before and during the project. For example, we approached and collaborated with people who either worked closely with higher management at SwAF or was part of it. We succeeded to some extent as human centeredness was included as a core premise in the project assignment for the EA project but it was far from enough.

4.3   Terminology

As described above, we explicitly decided to stop using "user centred" in favor of "human centred". We could immediately observe that this label generated more relevant discussions within the organizations. It also resulted in the integration of human centeredness in the procurer's project directive for the EA project.

4.4   Following a Project

We engaged in many different UCD related activities with the EA project. In the beginning the most central project members were interviewed and we constructed a plan for UCD activities. We also participated in project meetings and analyzed existing HCI related work to see if parts could be applied to the EA approach. Moreover, we did presentations of HCI methodology and a workshop with the aim of conceptualizing what user-centeredness could be and the expectations of the project members. The first author also performed an interview study with one of the end-user groups of the EA methodology; officers working in the early phases of procurement.

In this context, we encountered yet another taboo situation: due to politics we were not allowed to use the word "coaching". But our continuous presence in the EA project led to several informal coaching situations which we took advantage of. We were also asked to explain issues concerning usability or to come with suggestions for further work. At one point the EA project were writing a RFI (Request for Information), a pre-acquisition document and we were asked to evaluate it. This led to usability requirements (both in terms of functional requirements and requirements for a user-centred developmental process) were added in the document.

At the very end of the research initiative, the EA project was given new directions aiming primarily to formulate a change plan for SwAF as well as deliver a prototype of a technical portal, a system for accessing and working with the architecture framework. We identified this as an opportunity to exemplify a more complete UCD process and it was decided that we were to make personas, scenarios of future work and conceptual sketches of the prototype. The work with the personas are described in [28].

Our main goal with follow the EA project was to promote our ideas and change the practice. There are several advantages to working with an existing project; for example, one gets an organizational context to work in. However we also got associated with this particular project, and when it fell out of grace it was reflected on our work. Furthermore in our case we had to balance the needs from the EA project with the demands from the research project. The deliverables in the two projects did not always overlap, and financially the research project had precedence. Another problem with following a project closely is the detachment needed when doing research. Responsibility concerning for example confidentiality and anonymity did not always match the interests of the project we followed. This is a problem described by Walsham [29]: even though you withhold the names of the respondents there is always a risk that the receiver of the information makes an informed guess. This was accentuated at times when we as researchers got information that would benefit the EA project, but due to research ethics could not be shared with them. To what extent should a researcher act as a go-between in organizational politics?

Unfortunately SwAF terminated the EA project prematurely, and the potential for an introduction through that particular change project was lost. In line with the UCD guerilla tactics we would have investigated other possibilities to direct our attention to, but the research project also ended at about the same time.

4.5   Working with UCD Methods

The most successful method we used was the persona method, both in terms of engaging end-users in discussions of future work practice and technology use and as a communication tool with the strategic group planning the future work. The scenarios and conceptual sketches developed were also well received by the strategic group that was planning to develop a prototype.

In the previous studies of Sweden's military defense organizations [19], the second author had concluded that it could be a good idea to try out other methods than traditional UCD methods when working with strategic personnel. In this effort we decided to try out a framework which included a whole battery of workshop methods and was based on similar theoretic premises as we have in our research. This framework is called Cynefin [26]. One interesting event was a breakdown of a workshop held with the strategic group in the beginning of the persona activities. In the workshop we used narratives of the end-users work situation (inspired by the Cynefin framework [26]).

From these narratives, the workshop participants were asked to specify characters (someone doing something) and activities (what is getting done) on sticky notes. Then they were asked to relate these to each other, with the focus of understanding the concrete work of the officers in the procurement process. The participants in the workshop protested to the open-ended situation and the language we used in the workshop. We usability researchers used the words "concrete" and "details" in order to direct the participants towards describing the actual people doing the work, and the actual work they were doing. The participants, who were all focused on EA and strategic planning, used the same words, but with the meaning of doing more detailed flow charts and UML diagrams on roles and processes which we consider a generalized way of describing work.

We also used the Cynefin method for alternative history [26]. It was used in the beginning of the project in order to gain a better understanding of the participants' views on UCD and their expectations for the project. Several obstacles for introducing UCD were visualized and in fact, many of them turned out to be problems during the course of the research project.

The least successful method was a traditional case study with interviews followed by a written report of the findings. Even though we could later use the interview data for the work with personas and scenarios, the recipients did not see any use of the report. This might be related to the dominating way of communicating findings and ideas within SwAF and FMV being presentation slides, which is a less dense format.

It was interesting that within these organizations that emphasize rationality and facts, the report as a method, which often is perceived as "factual", was not successful while the persona method which explicitly is described as subjective was more successful.

For us, the main point in practicing these UCD methods was to demonstrate different possibilities for SwAF in general and the project members specifically. But when it came to the report as a method it was not perceived as an example. Instead the interviews showed that several people saw it as a failure for human centeredness in general and did not see the point of it at all. We often have noticed that negative results are generalized while positive results are constructed as unique successes. It was therefore important for us to continue striving for a multitude of different examples and methods so that the unique in the end would be perceived as a range of possibilities instead of unique instances.

4.6   Multitudes of Levels

During our research we have been grappling with an elusive meta-level. The supreme goal of our research was that the end-users, the soldiers, should have usable technical artifacts, but we were not working with the development of these artifacts. Our focus was rather the people developing these artifacts and our mission was to develop the work practice and the methods for them: the users of our methods. We were trying to work in a user-centred manner with these users in focus, to make them work more user-centred with their users in focus. This notion was not always easy to convey.

An example was a recurring discussion we had with representatives from FMV. They argued that our focus was wrong and wanted us to define what benefit the end-users would get from our research. We tried to explain that the end-users would get a benefit in the end, but that our research result was a step in the right direction rather than contributing to technical artifacts in that particular moment in time.

Many of the activities we did were directed towards getting research data or information for the EA project. But at the same time offering an example for how they could work in a user-centred manner. Difficulties arose when trying to report back to the EA project. What should we emphasize: the results from the UCD activities, i.e. the information the EA project were mostly interested in, or the UCD methods themselves which was something we wanted them to include in their visions for future systems development?

We do believe that UCD with UCD can be a successful way of introducing UCD but it was not clear to us how difficult it would be for both us and our collaborators to understand all the levels that this implies. In future work, we would emphasize this to a much greater extent than we did in this case study.

5   Conclusion

We have explored a pragmatic reflexive user centred approach to the introduction of UCD, which we call UCD guerrilla tactics. It was used as a way to initiate a change process within a large complex organization by the use of very small resources. More intuitive versions of this strategy are probably applied in industry on a daily basis but it is seldom used (or at least not acknowledged) in research. We wanted to explore it in a structured way in order to analyze its potentials. It is also a contribution to those who focus on HCI research closely related to practice.

A successful outcome of a change project such as this, would be to see changes on both a macro and micro level [30], that is in the organizational culture and the formal documentation and routines, as well as on a level of actual practice. Consequently, this case study was not successful since we did not see any changes on macro level during the project. This was partly due to the EA project being prematurely ended. However, we did observe changes on a micro level, within the EA project. The people involved in the project started to ask for our advice and our research data. In their sense making of such concepts as usability and human centeredness, they started to change their vocabulary, using words and descriptions that we would choose. Furthermore, we have observed how they rephrased their work in presentations, using terms such as "work practice" and "user focus".

Our research has confirmed previous research that it is not enough only with guerrilla or project activities, you need management support and an organization that is involved in the specific activities. But we have also found that the guerrilla approach has effect in the small perspective. We therefore argue that UCD guerrilla tactics is a necessary pragmatic contribution. We conclude that a successful implementation of UCD requires three things: 1) explicit widely communicated support in the organization; 2) a local infrastructure with usability competence and well defined UCD methods; 3) guerrilla activities where UCD is tried and exemplified in any opportunity given.

We argue that one important part of guerrilla tactics is adaptability. Due to the rapidly changing environment, it is important to at all times be prepared to change focus or search for new strategies for UCD work, to do the unexpected (in the sense of making pragmatic unconventional choices) in order to survive. In this, a constant reflexive process is needed: continuous evaluation of the situation in order to adapt to the changing situation. Most of all, to be able to come up with new solutions and be prepared to let go of some prestige, as we did for example when we changed our terminology.

Ultimately, when introducing UCD with UCD we have learnt that it is important to not underestimate the difficulties with multitudes of levels: working both with methods and processes on a general level and with the result from using them. We argue that one cannot be too obvious when it comes to these different levels. Would we do the project again, we would be more aware and clearer in our communication with the organization on what we mean by introducing UCD with UCD and we would try to visualize it in a better way.

Acknowledgements. We would like to thank all the respondents and collaborators within Sweden's military defense organizations. A special thanks to Jan Gulliksen and the anonymous reviewers who have given feedback on earlier versions of this paper.

References

1. Mao, J., Vredenburg, K., Smith, P., Carey, T.: User-centered design methods in practice: a survey of the state of the art. In: Proceedings of the 2001 Conference of the Centre for Advanced Studies on Collaborative research, Toronto, Canada, p. 12 (2001)
2. Gould, J., Lewis, C.: Designing for usability: key principles and what designers think. Communications of the ACM 28(3), 300–311 (1985)
3. ISO: 13407:1999 Human-centred design processes for interactive systems. International Organization for Standardization Geneva, Switzerland (1999)
4. Gulliksen, J., Göransson, B., Boivie, I., Blomkvist, S., Persson, J., Cajander, Å.: Key principles for user-centred systems design. Behaviour & Information Technology 22(6), 397–409 (2003)
5. Cajander, Å.: Usability - Who Cares?: The Introduction of User-Centred Systems Design in Organisations. Doctoral Thesis, Acta Universitatis Upsaliensis, Uppsala (2010)
6. Rajanen, M., Iivari, N., Keskitalo, E.: Introducing usability activities into open source software development projects: a participative approach. In: NordiCHI 2012, pp. 683–692. ACM (2012)
7. Mao, J.Y., Vredenburg, K., Smith, P.W., Carey, T.: The state of user-centered design practice. Communications of the ACM 48(3), 105–109 (2005)
8. Lauesen, S.: Usability engineering in industrial practice. In: INTERACT 1997 - IFIP TC13 International Conference on Human-Computer Interaction, Sydney, Australia, pp. 15–22 (1997)
9. Boivie, I.: A Fine Balance: Addressing Usability and Users' Needs in the Development of IT Systems for the Workplace. Doctoral Thesis, Uppsala Unversity, Uppsala: Acta Universitatis Upsaliensis, Sweden (2005)
10. Marti, P., Bannon, L.J.: Exploring User-Centred Design in Practice: Some Caveats. Knowledge, Technology & Policy 22(1), 7–15 (2009)

11. Iivari, N.: Representing the User'in software development—a cultural analysis of usability work in the product development context. Interacting with Computers 18(4), 635–664 (2006)

12. Kujala, S., Kauppinen, M., Nakari, P., Rekola, S.: Field Studies in Practice: Making it Happen. In: INTERACT 2003 - IFIP TC13 International Conference on Human-Computer Interaction, pp. 359–366. IOS Press, IFIP (2003)

13. Seffah, A., Gulliksen, J., Desmarais, M.C. (eds.): Human-Centered Software Engineering - Integrating Usability in the Software Development Lifecycle. Springer, Dordrecht (2005)

14. Artman, H., Zällh, S.: Finding a way to usability: procurement of a taxi dispatch system. Cognition, Technology & Work 7(3), 141–155 (2005)

15. Markensten, E., Artman, H.: Procuring a usable system using unemployed personas. In: Third Nordic Conference on Human-Computer Interaction, Tampere, Finland, pp. 13–22 (2004)

16. Markensten, E.: Procuring Usable Systems-An Analysis of a Commercial Procurement Project. In: HCI International Conference, Crete, Greece, pp. 544–548 (2003)

17. Peppard, J.: Managing IT as a Portfolio of Services. European Management Journal 21(4), 467–483 (2003)

18. Nielsen, J.: Guerrilla HCI: Using Discount Usability Engineering to Penetrate the Intimidation Barrier. In: Bias, R.G., Mayhew, D.J. (eds.) Cost-Justifying Usability (Interactive Technologies) (1994)

19. Swartling, A.: The Good Person in Information Systems Development: A Reflexive Investigation of HCI in the Acquisition Process. Doctoral thesis, KTH, Sweden (2008)

20. Rapoport, R.: Three dilemmas in action research. Human Relations 23(6), 499 (1970)

21. McKay, J., Marshall, P.: The dual imperatives of action research. Information Technology and People 14(1), 46–59 (2001)

22. Walsham, G.: Interpretive case studies in IS research: nature and method. European Journal of Information Systems 4(2), 74–81 (1995)

23. Cooper, A.: The inmates are running the asylum. SAMS Publishing, USA (2004)

24. Tohidi, M., Buxton, W., Baecker, R., Sellen, A.: User Sketches: A Quick, Inexpensive, and Effective way to Elicit More Reflective User Feedback. In: NordiCHI 2006 (2006)

25. Cajander, Å., Eriksson, E., Gulliksen, J.: Towards a Usability Coaching Method for Institutionalizing Usability in Organisations. In: Forbrig, P., Paternó, F., Mark Pejtersen, A. (eds.) HCIS 2010. IFIP AICT, vol. 332, pp. 86–97. Springer, Heidelberg (2010)

26. Kurtz, C., Snowden, D.: The new dynamics of strategy: Sense-making in a complex and complicated world. IBM Systems Journal 42(3), 462–483 (2003)

27. Gulliksen, J., Cajander, Å., Sandblad, B., Eriksson, E., Kavathatzopoulos, I.: User-Centred Systems Design as Organizational Change: A Longitudinal Action Research Project to Improve Usability and the Computerized Work Environment in a Public Authority. International Journal of Technology and Human Interaction 5(3), 13–53 (2009)

28. Eriksson, E., Artman, H., Swartling, A.: The secret life of a persona - when the personal becomes private. In: CHI 2013 (accepted, 2013)

29. Walsham, G.: Doing interpretive research. European Journal of Information Systems 15(3), 320–330 (2006)

30. Wiley, N.: The micro-macro problem in social theory. Sociological Theory 6(2), 254–261 (1988)

Feedback in a Training Simulator for Crisis Management Compared to Feedback in a Real-Life Exercise

Olga Druzhinina and Ebba Thora Hvannberg

University of Iceland
Dunhagi 5, 107 Reykjavik, Iceland
olgaromanovna86@gmail.com
ebba@hi.is

Abstract. Designing feedback to trainees in a training simulator for complex cognitive domains is demanding but has not been given adequate attention. This paper aims to understand the importance of early work analysis in a real context during the design of such a simulator. More specifically, the aim of this research was to learn whether there were differences between the types of feedback given to the learner in an already planned design and a real-life training exercise. Therefore, a comparison between feedback given to trainees in a real-life training exercise and feedback planned for a virtual environment supporting training of crisis management was made. The results showed that there were several significant differences.

Keywords: Feedback, work analysis, human computer interaction, interaction design, virtual environment, training simulator, crisis management training.

1 Introduction

While training for crisis management in the advent or after an airplane crash is vital, it is complex and resource demanding, involving many organisations such as medical, police, rescue, airlines and airport operators. The tasks of operational units involve field work, such as medical aid, transportation of casualties and triage of wounded. Coordination and decision making are also important tasks [1]. Training is carried out regularly in comprehensive real-life exercises, with tens or even several hundred participants, trainees, instructors and organizers. Trainees representing emergency personnel engage in activities where fast situation assessment and reaction are the main tasks [2]. To keep the cost down, while maintaining the level of training requirements, simulators have been developed [3, 4].

Designing such simulators is a difficult task, since crisis management requires not only knowledge domain of managing crises, but also skills that enable workers to respond to unexpected and variable events and situations which neither may have apparent causes or foreseeable consequences to reactions [1]. Another aspect of the design of such a simulator is to decide the instructional design. Instructional design is a systematic practice of analysing learning requirements and based on them, designing a set

P. Campos et al. (Eds.): HWID 2012, IFIP AICT 407, pp. 124–138, 2013.
© IFIP International Federation for Information Processing 2013

of instructional specifications [5]. Instructional design models span over the lifecycle of an educational artefact through the stages of planning, designing, developing, implementing and updating where applicable. The instructional design of a crisis management simulator needs to provide trainees with experiential learning, variable uncertainty of events and situational complexity [6].

Crisis management involves teamwork in a safety critical domain requiring actors to collaborate and communicate to manage information, make decisions, plan and delegate tasks. Teams are formed at different levels. There are organizational teams, e.g. fire fighters, medical personnel and police, and there are actors from these organizations which form teams at various posts, e.g. at command centres or at the accident site. In crisis management simulation, the activities of trainees are divided into two main categories: field and command[2][14](Hansen & Satria, 2011)(Hansen & Satria, 2011)(Hansen & Satria, 2011)(Hansen & Satria, 2011)(Hansen & Satria, 2011). Field activities are carried out by trainees representing emergency personnel, who aim to learn to assess and respond to a situation as effectively and quickly as possible. These activities mainly involve rescue, triaging casualties, providing medical aid, transporting resources and casualties. Command activities involve the command and coordination staff, who is responsible for planning, strategizing, decision making and coordinating on a larger scale. Command activities include organizing resources, e.g. people, transportation, medical aid and hospital resources, mitigating risks, assessing situations, responding to them and planning [2]. A wide range of expertise appears during training and operations of crisis management, where responders and commanders include novices to experts [7]. Furthermore, to add to the heterogeneity some are professionals but others are volunteers from search and rescue organizations, Red Cross etc.

In addition to simulating work and situations, simulators need to include a stimulating and rewarding training environment for trainees. Experience has shown that during simulator tenders technical issues are prioritised over functionalities for supporting training [8]. To encourage better practices, Naikar and Sanderson [8] have illustrated how work domain analysis [9] can be extended to define training needs. They have argued that common techniques such as Instructional System Development (ISD) [10], which has been applied extensively by the air force in military training, is inadequate since they do not support work that is characterised by cognitive work, adaptive behaviour, random events and unpredictable situations.

Besides identifying training needs, designers of simulators have to decide how to deliver training. Training needs to be planned, carried out and assessed. Much has been written on professionals' reflection in action [11] and practitioners' ability to self-assess or self-monitor [12]. Feedback is one of the most powerful techniques to help students learn. It provides learners with information on their performance when gaining or applying new knowledge and can help them finding the right answers [13, 14]. Feedback is an essential aspect for any learning environment, as it provides assessment of the learner's progress and results, motivates the learner, and enhances learning [15]. Either feedback can be intrinsic, that is available in a normal job situation, or extrinsic, which is available from an instructor either during or after a training exercise [16]. The latter one is also termed explicit feedback [17] which can come from a human tutor, a pedagogical agent, disembodied coach or other intelligent tutor

[18]. Feedback can be provided by peers and is one of the five components of team-work [19, 20]. Since teamwork is prevalent in crisis management, looking at such feedback becomes even more important than feedback provided in a single learner situation. As mentioned above, real-life training has many drawbacks, e.g. the costs of equipment and organization, and menace to environment [1]. However, it remains unclear whether the level of feedback delivery in a simulation, an essential part of training, may be the same or comparable as in a real-life exercise.

To meet this requirement of learning through feedback, most educational systems need to provide information on the assessment of learning to the trainee in some form [21], whether it is given by the system, or by a person, e.g. either a teacher/instructor or a fellow student. Although a simulator for crisis management training is not a game, we expect that knowledge from that field can be adopted. Researching designs of learning in games, Liu et al. [22] state that assessing the progress of a player´s learning activity is one of the most rewarding interactive behaviour. To assist the player in the learning experience [23], such systems should provide appropriate feed-back and they should ensure continuous flow to motivate the player to proceed [24].

Despite the substantial emphasis on including feedback in games or simulators, it seems that its design, or methods for its design, has not been given as much room as required [25]. However recently, there have been examples of methods to provide in-game assessments of objects and actions taken in real time. These assessments correspond to logged, time-stamped events that undergo statistical analyses that are displayed in real time or during a review after the game [3].

Motivated by the above need, the objective of this research is to compare, in terms of feedback, a plan for designing a training simulator to data gathered in a real-life training exercise for responding to an airplane crash. Thus, through an extensive analysis of the crisis management work domain and training exercises, we hope to learn about the kinds of feedback learners receive during training. The rest of the paper is organised as follows. After describing forms of feedback as they appear in the literature in the next section, the methodology of the research study is detailed in section 3. Section 4 describes the results of the research study which is a case study of a comparison between two different training environments. In the discussion of the results in section 5 we compare them with a feedback framework and suggest a theory of feedback. The paper concludes with section 6 presenting its contributions.

2   Forms of Feedback

Feedback in any learning environment may be categorized [15]. For example, feed-back may be qualitative or quantitative, e.g. "Good", or "65 points" [26]. It may be negative, positive or neutral [25, 27]. Also, feedback can be corrective and/or motiva-tional, where corrective feedback has the purpose to correct the learner when he/she has made a mistake, while motivational feedback motivates the learner, based on his/her individual preferences [28]. According to Pivec and Dziabenko [29], learning by mistake is a primary way for trainees to learn and motivating them to keep on trying.

Feedback may be in a form of elaboration or verification. Verification feedback refers to a notification of the result of the learner´s answer, i.e. whether it is correct or not. Elaborative feedback provides an explanation of the result of the learner´s answer and can give a hint to a solution [30, 31].

In a team, the process of providing feedback is not the same as in single person-to-person communication. According to Sonntag [32], in unidirectional teaching environment, where feedback is teacher-to-student and vice versa, feedback is a simple process, while in multidirectional environment (in a team) feedback becomes a more complex process. While Sonntag has looked at the integration of aspects within the teaching environment, the issues raised are relevant to a training simulation. To pass the right message onto students, Sonntag has emphasised a teacher's coordination of students and organization of materials and feedback in a multidirectional environment. The main concern is that students may misinterpret, underestimate or ignore bits of information [32]. In a similar manner, crisis trainees may misinterpret or not respond to information from an operational unit. Or, for example, if a trainee receives contradictory information from two other trainees, s/he may be left confused unable to proceed in such a case. Thus, unlike unidirectional feedback, multidirectional ones hold a rather arduous character due to the distributed interaction nature of the environment. Therefore, when designing scenarios, an important aspect of crisis management training is learning how to deal with wicked problems due to multi-directional feedback. Since unidirectional feedback occur in crisis handling as well, the two need to be distinguished. Another type of a teaching strategy is called peer-review, an approach when student-to-student interaction is used to provide feedback and advice [33]. Peer-review feedback exhibit similar complex behaviour of a multi-directional environment and poses a risk of credibility of information provided by the student.

Above, we have described some types of feedback in the learning context. More generally, feedback is provided in conversations, and more specifically in the context of systems, such as in the context of human computer interaction, where feedback is a report issued by the system as either a reply to the action of a user or a notification of the progress of a user's task [34]. Hence, when discussing feedback in the context of learning systems, all these aspects come into play.

Looking more closely at the system aspect, feedback in a virtual environment can be categorized according to senses, i.e. visual, haptic, or sound [22, 23, 33]. Further, there are two types of feedback in virtual environments, either immediate (real-time) feedback that can be issued to the player during the game or delayed or archival feedback that is issued as a summary upon completion of a task or a game [15, 35]. Immediate feedback which is automatically generated by an application can be of any form mentioned above, while delayed feedback is usually given in text or graphical, form [15, 22, 25]. For example, action feedback is an immediate interactive response in real-time, while text feedback can be both immediate and delayed [22]. Immediate feedback may be provided during the execution of a task, usually when the task is complex, or after task completion if the task is relatively straightforward [25]. For example, in a car simulator, the player may get immediate haptic feedback in the form of vibration during the execution of a task.

Table 1. Feedback forms as discussed in the literature

	Brief description	Learning	System / Virtual environment
Qualitative	Textual	Yes	
Quantitative	Numerical	Yes	
Positive	Positive outcome of assessment	Yes	
Negative	Negative outcome of assessment	Yes	
Corrective (explicit)	Give a correct solution	Yes	
Motivational	Encouraging to proceed	Yes	
Unidirectional	Teacher to student or vice versa	Yes	
Multidirectional	Teacher to a team	Yes	
Peer-review	Among peers	Yes	
Visual/graphical	Visual representation		Yes
Textual	Textual representation		Yes
Haptic	Touch and kinaesthetic		Yes
Immediate, automatic	Right away by the system		Yes
Delayed or archival	After the training session		Yes

Liu et al. [22] and Kiili [23] state that feedback is accepted more seriously by the player if it is provided immediately, instead of being issued after the game completion in the form of instructional text material. Also, according to Garzotto [36], when an action taken by the player is incorrect, it may be necessary and more effective to provide immediate than delayed feedback, since the player might later forget the incident, and, hence, not learn from delayed feedback. However, Renaud and Cooper [25] argue that archival feedback is also important, and may be presented in the form of text and/or graphically. Where appropriate, graphical feedback is more helpful than text, as it depicts the information as a whole [25]. Furthermore, feedback may be provided as an action replay in the form of a video [25]. Table 1 summarises the different forms of feedback described in this section divided into two categories depending on the source of introduction. By no means are the categories mutually exclusive, e.g. a qualitative feedback can be positive and delayed.

3 Research Methodology

The research method is a work analysis of trainees' performance during the real-life exercise of emergency management. The feedback in the real-life exercise is compared to a system master plan of a virtual environment of a crisis management training simulator using categories from the literature. The real-life exercise training was conducted at an international airport in Europe and included almost 250 participants, with 90 participants creating the training scenario and serving as instructors, and the rest training for crisis management. The main exercise lasted 4-5 hours and included all organizations involved in a regular response to an aircraft incident. Seven participants of the CRISIS project served as observers, taking written notes and photos. The CITE system from VSL was used to enter notes during and after the exercise. In total, 548 observations were made for four hours at five different locations of the exercise: Emergency Operations Center (EOC), Casualty Assembly Point (CAP), Rendezvous Point (RVP), On Scene Command (OSC), and Accident Site. In addition, a few observations were made by instructors of the exercise, who were using the CITE system as a pilot.

Partners of the CRISIS project have collaboratively developed a virtual environment training simulator (CRISIS VE) for responders and commanders responsible for crisis management. The target sector is transport security, such as at for airport and railway operations. CRISIS VE was designed to support the 4C/ID instructional design model, which is meant to be used for long-period training with multiple complex tasks and learning objectives [30]. The 4C/ID instructional design model focuses on complex learning tasks and comprises four components, a) learning tasks, b) supportive information, c) just-in-time information and d) part-task practice [5]. Early on in the project, a system master plan (SMP) was written of the CRISIS VE including a detailed description of the system design and architecture, description of key concepts, such as events, variable uncertainties, and the CRISIS training cycle. Furthermore, the system master plan includes reference scenarios and example scenarios. Finally, it contains a list of roles for each of the scenarios and extensive lists of functional requirements for different modules and technologies of the simulator. Comprising well over 300 pages, the system master plan, is written after a thorough requirements analysis including site visits, interviews, questionnaires and a visit to one real-life exercise.

The classification of the feedback data from the real-life exercise and its analysis was carried out independently by two researchers. Each researcher classified data according to different feedback types, which are based on an analysis of the literature presented in section 2. Afterwards, they discussed and merged their results. Out of 548 observations noted down by observers, 49 observations on feedback were made.

Table 2. Feedback forms in the SMP

Feedback form	Description or purpose
Qualitative AAR	Comments by instructor
Quantitative AAR	A summary report
Immediate Visual	Verification
Immediate Action	Preventing mistakes
Verbal feedback	Communication with fellow trainees
Unidirectional	One-way feedback comments by instructor
Multidirectional	Discussion with instructor
Peer-reviewing	Feedback by fellow trainees

4   A Case Study

4.1   An Analysis of a System Master Plan with Respect to Feedback

In this section we describe an analysis of the SMP [2] to see what requirements have been specified for the feedback available to the trainee. CRISIS VE supports functions to diagnose and to make a full After Action Review (AAR) of a trainee's action, decision and behavior based on data collected throughout the simulation game. Thus, the AAR module provides a quantitative summary report of the trainee's overall performance and details of an exercise. Based on this data, the instructor submits his/her own qualitative comments on the trainee's performance.

CRISIS VE supports **immediate visual** and **action feedbacks**. CRISIS VE supports immediate visual feedback, e.g. when a trainee places a Casualty Assembly Point (CAP) at a location, the system immediately draws a CAP object on the screen. An example of how CRISIS VE supports immediate action feedback is when the system prevents the trainee from placing the CAP in an area too close to the site of an accident, since it would endanger the casualties in case of fire spreading. Thus, the system **prevents** the trainee from making **a mistake**, but signals him or her implicitly that an incorrect action has been carried out. Furthermore, CRISIS VE facilitates, by supporting communication with fellow trainees, learning by mistake. Trainees will be able to receive real-life **verbal feedback** through communication devices implemented in the simulator, such as radio or mobile phone, from other trainees or instructors. CRISIS VE also supports both **unidirectional** and **multidirectional feedback** between the trainee and the instructor, as well as **peer-reviewing** between all trainees.

CRISIS VE does not support sound as a form of feedback. Although it includes sounds to resemble the real-life environment [37], it does not notify the trainee of the success or failure of a task completion. While some research is underway for using haptic equipment, i.e. for sensing heart beats of casualties [38], the SMP does not include such support for physical sense feedback. **Error! Reference source not found.** presents an overview of the feedback forms found in SMP.

4.2   An Analysis of a Real-Life Exercise with Respect to Feedback

Using the data from a real-life exercise, this section describes feedback a trainee gave another trainee or an instructor gave a trainee or trainees. We have put feedback types, either from the literature or the real-life exercise data, in bold. Quotes from the data are presented in quotes and italics. **Error! Reference source not found.** gives an overview of the feedback types.

All 49 instances of feedback during the real-life exercise were **verbal** and **qualitative**. An AAR was presented to trainees **verbally** at a meeting after the event, but a written report was planned as is customary in such exercises.

Trainees were **not rewarded**, i.e. they were not provided with positive feedback, upon the successful completion of a task. Although there were many examples of **verification feedback** (19), such as when one commander tells the other that they "*need better information on weapons*", most instances were of **elaborative feedback type** (29) with an explanation of the error or the problem, such as when "*airline operator discusses with Red Cross commander how to send the list*" after feedback had been provided on not receiving the list although, reportedly, it had been sent. Another example of **verification feedback** was when the commander made decisions and organized the other trainees after having concluded: "*transport capacity is not enough to transport all red casualties*". **Elaborative feedback** occurred during every status meeting.

Many of the feedback during the exercise were of a **corrective character** (20): "*Wounded still on the scene*", implying that they should not be on the scene, and only a few feedback instances were **motivational in nature** (10): "*EOC commander concludes that the transport capacity is not enough to transport all red casualties. She asks Resource manager for more resources*". Another example of **corrective feedback** was when an instructor stated that "*ambulances should already be on the scene, but they are not*".

Some of the feedback is only **unidirectional** (13), e.g. in the case of providing an assessment of the situation, at RVP: "*It took too long time for activating resources from the Rendezvous point to the accident site*", or at the OSC post: "*[We] need basic information on the status of the triage immediately in the beginning*". A further example implies **negative feedback** when commander states "*there should be better flow*". Another example of negative feedback happened when at the EOC it was observed "*NECC (National Emergency Coordination Center) has complained about not receiving a passenger list*". Feedback incidents that took place during the status meetings were **peer-reviews** with trainees explaining their current state of work and problems. Most (39) feedback instances were peer-reviews, as they involved different trainees trying to solve one task. For example: "*EOC commander concludes that the transport capacity is not enough to transport all red casualties. She asks the Resource manager for more resources. The radio operator informs that OSC has not requested* *resources, only to move existing resources closer"*. There were no multidirectional feedback instances.

In two cases we noted feedback in the form of **explicit teaching**. OSC realised that the rescue coordinator had misunderstood the role of the OSC. In response, they attempted to inform the coordinator of the correct procedures: *Commander to Planning: "How is the flow?" - Looking at an overview at the display. Planning to Resources: "Do you want to have the ambulances closer?" Commander says: "Transport coordinator should resolve this" - explains the procedure and role of transport coordinator.*

Another example of teaching trainee procedures was when a commander at OSC said: *"I want to iterate that EOC should organize transport of casualties out of the scene - this is not the responsibility of OSC but an EOC."*

Planning personnel at OSC communicated to the EOC: *"You should talk directly to the transport coordinator" - Commander looks at the hierarchy with plans and says that according to the hierarchy, the medical coordinator and the transport coordinator should organize the transport among themselves.*

Probing for information was noted as a trigger for feedback. At the OSC at a start of regular status meetings: *"We don't have confirmation that the scene has been secured. There they come (i.e. the rescue team) (Looking through the window). How much of rescue teams did he send? Do we have numbers from security coordinator?"*

During the real-life exercise, trainees were constantly burdened with various hiccups that persisted along the way, such as the equipment failure or data loss. For example, *"the police officer reports a radio problem and asks for assistance for fixing it or replacing"*. This is important to mention since it could play a big role in determining the triggers for feedback in a simulation. There were other important triggers for feedback that took place during a real-life exercise.

Many feedback instances were triggered through discussions (22 out of 49) and information sharing (42), e.g. during regular status meetings when numbers of casualties were reported. Many instances triggered reasoning (20) and organization (22) among participants of an exercise, e.g. when the commander made decisions and organized the other trainees after having concluded that transport capacity was not enough.

More examples of when feedback initiated a discussion were triggered after an issue had been raised (11). At the EOC there was an incident when *"The radio/computer operator informs that NECC has been trying to reach EOC. The EOC commander replies she is about to contact them"*. At the EOC, another example which showed feedback which raised an issue: *"We need transport capabilities from [City excluded for the sake of anonymity] - there is nothing on this in the database. This is a problem"*.

It is also important to mention that on some occasions the feedback resulted in a learning outcome. For example, in two feedback cases the trainee was learning by mistake as a result of feedback, e.g. a trainee learned not to inform patients of the death incidents as they became *"upset when hearing about dead patients over a nearby tetra unit"*.

Table 3. Feedback Forms in a Real-Life Exercise

Feedback forms	Literature / New
Verbal qualitative	L
Verification	L
Elaborative	L
Corrective	L
Motivational	L
Negative	L
Unidirectional	L
Peer-reviews	L
Explicit teaching	N

4.3   A Comparison between the Planned Design and the Real-Life Exercise

In the previous section, we presented how trainees received feedback of different types. In this section, we discuss how the design of a real-life exercise may contribute to the design of a simulation in terms of credibility of learning, by comparing it to the planned design.

Although the purpose of feedback in real-life exercise and CRISIS VE is to train participants to respond in a crisis situation, some of the feedback practices in CRISIS VE contradict with the real-life exercise. There are differences in the delayed feedback during the real-life exercise and in the training simulator. The archival feedback provided in the crisis simulator is only available in text form, and it is quantitative with the possibility that the instructor may provide qualitative comments on the performance. In the real-life exercise, the feedback which is given to the trainees as an aftermath of their performance is qualitative and is presented verbally or as text.

The immediate feedback in the real-life exercise is provided by trainees, usually in the form of elaboration, both during the task execution and/or after task completion. In the training simulator, immediate feedback is provided in the form of action by the system, and can be received through conversing with other players via communication devices. The difference here is that the trainee does not get any immediate automatic feedback in the real world, so if s/he makes a mistake, it will have consequences at a later stage of the training. The system, however, tries to prevent the trainee from making a mistake without explanations, and with no further consequences. For example in real-life, if a trainee breaks something then other trainees will have to continue without it, and will have to use another object instead as a replacement.

While CRISIS VE supports some learning by mistake function, it does not provide feedback to the trainee on the nature of a mistake. For example, in the case of placing a CAP area too close to the accident site, the simulator does not allow for the CAP to be placed. There is no explanation on why the CAP cannot be placed. Thus, the trainee may be unsure whether it is a fault in the software or if the reason is the proximity to the accident site. Although in real-life a trainee does not get any messages of the sort, in the training environment s/he may become confused if there is no message or alert generated when something is happening unexpectedly. Cyboran [15] has explained that learners do not benefit when the system does not specify its response towards learner´s action, particularly when the nature of response may not be clear or obvious. Analysing the system master plan it was unclear if incorrect actions or mistakes were logged for the AAR report.

Furthermore, the work analysis revealed that in real-life many feedback incidents are connected to unexpectedness of situations, particularly equipment failures. However, in the master plan for the CRISIS simulator, there are only some vague suggestions of triggers for unexpected incidents. While the master plan has a general design of feedback and unexpected situations, the training exercise showed that in real-life there are several typical situations that would need specifically designed feedback.

5   Discussion

In this paper we showed how feedback design may be overlooked if it is not supported by a work analysis that aids in explaining the relationship between feedback and learning during crisis management training. The current planned design reveals that the design of feedback, one of the most important learning tactics in education, contradicts with the real-life practices of crisis management training.

The work analysis has shown that during the real-life exercise feedback incidents, similar to typical of crisis management training, occurred. Such similar feedback incidents have been classified and grouped, and can be used in the design of a simulator for crisis management training. In preparation for the real-life exercise, exercise organisers said they were not expecting a lot of feedback given to trainees by instructors. The analysis reported in this paper showed that although not extensive, feedback was more apparent than expected. In future studies, it would be interesting to contrast this result to trainees' reflection on their own work [11] as professionals or in an after action review and see how trainees expertise might determine this reflection vs. feedback.

We analysed what the feedback implied in terms of learning in a real-life exercise, i.e. whether trainee would gain knowledge as a result of this feedback or get the message that training needs to be improved in the future. For example, for *assessment of a situation*, a fellow trainee pointed out to the trainee that the situation was deficient, and that in future situations this would need be avoided or improved. Or, for *raising an issue* or *probing for information*, the feedback indicated to the trainee that a problem had arisen that could be solved now but little or no instructions were provided. Or, in the case of explicit teaching, the trainee received instructions and guidance on how to accomplish a goal.

For this research, we have gathered empirical data to show how work analysis can incorporate and shape the design of the feedback incidents through comparison of the work analysis and an earlier design plan. In comparison, Narciss and Huth [30] carried out research, based on literature, to derive guidelines on how to design feedback incidents. In their research, they emphasise how the cognitive task analysis plays a crucial part in the design of feedback.

Narciss and Huth [30] proposed three facets of feedback, functions of feedback (cognitive, meta-cognitive or motivational), contents of feedback (evaluative or informative towards the knowledge of the result) and presentation of feedback contents (timing, schedule, adaptivity). Based on this framework, procedures are detailed on how to design feedback. Instruction contexts, such as objectives, tasks and errors contributed to the contents of feedback; and individual factors such as learning objectives, prior knowledge and skills and academic motivation contributed to functions of feedback. Narciss and Huth [30] viewed the contents of feedback in terms of evaluative and informative components. Comparing their classification to ours, the *assessment of a situation* and *raising an issue or probing for information* may be considered as evaluative components, while *explicit teaching* falls in the category of an informative component.

According to Gredler [39], simulations may be of two types: symbolic or experiential. Symbolic simulation presents tasks where a participant must often use or improve theoretical knowledge to solve a problem, e.g. business manager, physician, or mathematician. Experiential simulation presents tasks where a participant is trained to gain knowledge of how to operate a device or perform a set of routine tasks, which require little to no need for scientific concepts or theorems [39]. Since Narciss and Huth studied learning environments for a symbolic type of simulator where trainees solve problems by presenting knowledge of the result, such as subtraction, we do not know if their findings can be directly translated to crisis management training, which is an experiential simulator. Nonetheless, it can be valuable to compare the two types to see how well the design guidelines can be translated from one type of learning environment to another.

The research has some limitations. One limitation was that the observers may not have reported all of the incidents that occurred. Although the data set that we analysed was large, it was only from one real-life exercise. Thus, the feedback incidents retrieved are specific to that particular training scenario.

Additionally, for more detailed modelling of a learning environment in a simulation-based training, a study of gathering feedback from actual trainees, and not just observers, may need to be carried out. Castor et al. [40] performed a study for the purposes of gaining insight into the understanding of the cognitive processes of the trainees. The study was experimental in nature, and no well-defined model was derived as an outcome, although suggestions of cognitive modelling approaches were made. CRISIS VE could benefit from such an analysis in determining the functional design of artificial intelligence components within the simulator, such as for unexpected events or computer-played characters.

6   Conclusion

Previous research on feedback seems to be scattered in individual areas ranging from communication to learning sciences, onwards to system related areas such as HCI, educational technologies and learning games. And thus, the theory of feedback in the context of HCI is rather weak [27]. Furthermore, what makes it difficult is that feedback is of varying abstractions along different dimensions, ranging from low lexical level to a high semantic level, from a drill type of training to training more cognitive complex tasks in disperse application domains, ranging from Sports training [41] to Medical training [42] onwards to Pilot training [16]. This research has shown that it is possible to categorize data from a real-life exercise for use in designing a simulator. Specifically, we showed how this data may be useful in recognizing what practices in real-life are frequent and need to be incorporated, and thus should be given more attention when designing a simulation. For example, many vague suggestions of unexpected situations were provided in a system master plan, while in real-life there were several typical unexpected situations.

By comparing data from a real-life training exercise to data from a system master plan, we have shown that it is necessary to pay more attention to learning aspects of a simulator, such as feedback. In particular, since the comparison revealed significant differences between the system master plan and the real-life exercise, the research has shown that while it is vital to carry out analysis of the domain tasks, roles and scenarios, the development of a learning system needs to take into account an analysis of learning tactics provided under a real-life setting.

Acknowledgement. The research leading to these results has received funding from the European Union Seventh Framework Programme (FP7/2007-2013) under grant agreement no. [FP7-242474].

References

1. Stolk, D., Alexandrian, D., Gros, B., Paggio, R.: Gaming and multimedia applications for environmental crisis management training. Computers in Human Behavior 17, 627–642 (2001)
2. Hansen, K.B., Satria, L.R.: System Master Plan - Deliverable 3.3. of the CRISIS project (2011)
3. Raybourn, E.M.: Applying simulation experience design methods to creating serious game-based adaptive training systems. Interacting with Computers 19, 206–214 (2007)
4. Rudinsky, J., Hvannberg, E.T.: Consolidating models of requirements analysis for crisis management training simulator. In: Dugdale, J., Mendonça, D. (eds.) ISCRAM 2011. ISCRAM Lisbon, Portugal (2011)
5. van Merriënboer, J., Clark, R., de Croock, M.: Blueprints for complex learning: The 4C/ID-model. Educational Technology Research and Development 50, 39–61 (2002)
6. Wong, W., Rankin, A., Rooney, C.: The Variable Uncertainty Framework. Middlesex University (2011)
7. Dreyfus, H.L., Dreyfus, S.E.: Peripheral Vision: Expertise in Real World Contexts. Organization Studies 26, 779–792 (2005)
8. Naikar, N., Sanderson, P.M.: Work Domain Analysis for Training-System Definition and Acquisition. The International Journal of Aviation Psychology 9, 271–290 (1999)
9. Vicente, K.J.: Cognitive Work Analysis, Toward Safe, Productive, and Healthy Computer-Based Work. Lawrence Erlbaum Associates, Mahwah (1999)

10. Kirby, J., Hoadley, C., Carr-Chellman, A.: Instructional systems design and the learning sciences: A citation analysis. Educational Technology Research and Development 53, 37–47 (2005)
11. Schön, D.A.: The Reflective Practitioner: How Poressionals Think in Action. Basic Books, New York (1983)
12. Eva, K.W., Regehr, G.: "I'll never play professional football" and other fallacies of self-assessment. Journal of Continuing Education in the Health Professions 28, 14–19 (2008)
13. Alvarez, K., Salas, E., Garofano, C.M.: An Integrated Model of Training Evaluation and Effectiveness. Human Resource Development Review 3, 385–416 (2004)
14. Salas, E., Cannon-Bowers, J.A.: The Science of Training: A Decade of Progress. Annual Review of Psychology 52, 471–499 (2001)
15. Cyboran, V.: Designing feedback for computer-based training. Performance + Instruction 34, 18–23 (1995)
16. Hawkins, F.H.: Human Factors in Flight. Ashgate Burlington, VT (1987)
17. Hays, M., Lane, H.C., Auerbach, D., Core, M.G., Gomboc, D., Rosenberg, M.: Feedback Specificity and the Learning of Intercultural Communication Skills. In: Proceedings of the 2009 conference on Artificial Intelligence in Education: Building Learning Systems that Care: From Knowledge Representation to Affective Modelling. IOS Press (2009)
18. Lane, H.C.: Promoting Metacognition in Immersive Cultural Learning Environments. In: Jacko, J.A. (ed.) HCI International 2009, Part IV. LNCS, vol. 5613, pp. 129–139. Springer, Heidelberg (2009)
19. Entin, E.E., Entin, E.B.: Measures for Evaluation of Team Processes and Performance in Experiments and Exercises. In: Proceedings of the 2001 Command and Control (2001)
20. Cannon-Bowers: Team performance and training in complex environments: Recent findings from applied research. Current Directions in Psychological Science 7, 83–87 (1998)
21. Moreno-Ger, P., Burgos, D., Martínez-Ortiz, I., Sierra, J.L., Fernández-Manjón, B.: Educational game design for online education. Computers in Human Behavior 24, 2530–2540 (2008)
22. Liu, K.-Y., Yang, C.-T., Chang, K.-H.: Development of a Multiplayer Online Role-Playing Game-based Learning System for Multiple Curriculums. In: 2012 IEEE Fourth International Conference on Digital Game and Intelligent Toy Enhanced Learning (DIGITEL), pp. 62–66 (2012)
23. Kiili, K.: Digital game-based learning: Towards an experiential gaming model. The Internet and Higher Education 8, 13–24 (2005)
24. Paras, B., Bizzocchi, J.: Game, Motivation, and Effective Learning: An Integrated Model for Eucational Game Design. In: DiGRA Conference: Changing Views-Worlds in Play (2005)
25. Renaud, K., Cooper, R.: Feedback in Human Computer Interaction: Characteristics and Recommendations. In: Annual Research Conference of the South African Institue of Computer Scientists and Information Technologists, pp. 105–114 (2000)
26. Connellan, T.K., Zemke, R.: Sustaining Knock Your Socks Off Service. Amacom, New York (1993)
27. Spink, A., Saracevic, T.: Human-computer interaction in information retrieval: nature and manifestations of feedback. Interacting with Computers 10, 249–267 (1998)
28. Pyke, J.G., Sherlock, J.J.: A Closer Look at Instructor-Student Feedback Online: A Case Study Analysis of the Types and Frequency. Journal of Online Learning and Teaching 6, 110–121 (2010)

29. Pivec, M., Dziabenko, O.: Game - based learning in universities and lifelong learning: Un-iGame: Social Skills and Knowledge Training game concept. Journal of Universal Computer Science (J. Ucs) 10, 14–16 (2004)
30. Narciss, S., Huth, K.: How to Design Informative Tutoring Feedback for Multimedia Learning. In: Niegermann, H., Brunken, R., Leutner, D. (eds.) Instructional Design for Multimedia Learning, pp. 181–195. Waxmann, Munster (2004)
31. Pridemore, D., Klein, J.: Control of feedback in computer-assisted instruction. Educational Technology Research and Development 39, 27–32 (1991)
32. Sonntag, M.: Teleteaching: From Unidirectionalism to Multidirectionalism. In: Hofer, S., Beneder, M. (eds.) IDIMT 1999 7th Interdisciplinary Information Management Talks. Universitätsverlag Trauner Zadov (CZ), Linz (1999)
33. Richer, J., Drury, J.L.: A video game-based framework for analyzing human-robot interaction: characterizing interface design in real-time interactive multimedia applications. In: Proceedings of the 1st ACM SIGCHI/SIGART Conference on Human-Robot Interaction, pp. 266–273. ACM, Salt Lake City (2006)
34. Perez-Quinones, M.A., Sibert, J.L.: A collaborative model of feedback in human-computer interaction. In: Proceedings of the SIGCHI Conference on Human Factors in Computing Systems: Common Ground, pp. 316–323. ACM, Vancouver (1996)
35. von Ahn, L., Dabbish, L.: Designing games with a purpose. Commun. ACM 51, 58–67 (2008)
36. Garzotto, F.: Investigating the educational effectiveness of multiplayer online games for children. In: Proceedings of the 6th International Conference on Interaction Design and Children. ACM, Aalborg (2007)
37. Rudinsky, J., Hvannberg, E.T., Helgason, A.A., Petursson, P.B.: Designing soundscapes of virtual environments for crisis management training. In: Proceedings of the Designing Interactive Systems Conference, pp. 689–692. ACM, Newcastle Upon Tyne (2012)
38. Einarsdóttir, E.M.: Simulation of Hearbeat, Respiration and Heat using Haptic Feedback and Thermal Unit Faculty of Industrial Engineering, Mechanical Engineering and Computer Science, M.S., p. 59. University of Iceland, Reykjavik (2013)
39. Gredler: Educational Games and Simulations: A Technology in Search of a (Research) Paradigm. In: Jonassen, D.H. (ed.) Handbook of Research on Educational Communications and Technology, pp. 521–540. Macmillan, New York (1996)
40. Castor, M., Sennersten, C., Gustavsson, R., Lindley, C.: Decision processes in simulation-based training for ISAF vehicle patrols. In: NATO Research and Technology Organisation, HFM-202 Symposium on "Human Modelling for Military Application" (Year)
41. Iskandar, Y.H.P., Gilbert, L., Wills, G.B.: Pedagogy in Computer-Based Sport Training. In: 2011 11th IEEE International Conference on Advanced Learning Technologies (ICALT), pp. 403–408 (2011)
42. Cristancho, S.M., Moussa, F., Dubrowski, A.: A framework-based approach to designing simulation-augmented surgical education and training programs. The American Journal of Surgery 202, 344–351 (2011)

Library Usability in Higher Education: How User Experience Can Form Library Policy

Alison Wiles, Stephen Roberts, and José Abdelnour-Nocera

School of Computing & Technology, University of West London, St Mary's Road, Ealing,
London, W5 5RF, United Kingdom
{Alison.Wiles,Jose.Abdelnour-Nocera,Stephen.Roberts}@uwl.ac.uk

Abstract. The university library is a large socio-technical system with a vital part to play in university life. It has been described as "the social and intellectual heart of campus", with users now able to make use of both the digital and physical aspects of their library. Based on case studies in UK university libraries, this study aims to find out how and to what extent user experience forms part of university library policy, and how it can effectively be incorporated into it. Staff interviews and researcher-administered questionnaires with library users on campus will show the areas where usability issues occur and the gap between users' experiences and expectations of using libraries. These together with analysis of library policies will aim to suggest the factors that a user experience policy should cover.

Keywords: University library, usability, user experience.

1 Introduction

University libraries will vary greatly in terms of design, layout, location and atmosphere meaning that the student experience will differ greatly from institution to institution. They are the places that students will go to not only to find and borrow materials, but are also places for studying, socialising and even for sleeping [1].There are currently some 120 major universities in the UK [2], with approximately 1.8 million students enrolled as undergraduates in these institutions in 2010 [3]. There are also a further 275,000 postgraduates studying at UK universities [4], making a large and diverse user population for university libraries.

The phrase *"the heart of a university"* has been used to denote the high regard in which university libraries are held [5], and similarly they have been described as *"the social and intellectual heart of campus"* [6]. However more than 20 years ago, a study established that students had difficulties using their university library, with some experts believing they were *"virtually unusable"*[7]. Is this still the case in the early twenty-first century?

University libraries are moving rapidly towards a "self-service" culture. Whereas in the past university library staff would assist or actually carry out searches for books and literature, as well as helping with other library services, the onus is now on users to perform their own searches and find their own material using the interfaces,

P. Campos et al. (Eds.): HWID 2012, IFIP AICT 407, pp. 139–149, 2013.

databases and search engines available over the world-wide web. Similarly, they are expected to issue books using self-issue machines, and print their own articles. This has arguably simplified library use, while simultaneously bringing in a whole new set of problems.

Usability has been defined as *"the appropriateness to a purpose of any particular artefact"*[8]. It is a term widely used when referring to computer systems and their interfaces, but it can equally be applied to a non-computerised (or manual) system, or to an article such as a desk or building. Further to this, the International Standards Organization state that *"Usability refers to the extent to which a product can be used by specified users to achieve specified goals with effectiveness, efficiency and satisfaction in a specified context of use."*[9].The concept of usability can be applied to both the digital and physical spaces of a library, and it is vital that university library systems and interfaces, as well as the library buildings themselves are usable. Every university library will have the various systems and interfaces in place to support library activities with these systems potentially having thousands of users each with differing levels of computer experience, and also library experience. Similarly the physical library needs to be a usable space for both experienced and inexperienced users.

In common with other businesses and institutions, university libraries will have policies to cover areas such as circulation i.e. loan lengths and fines for exceeding these, collection development, user behaviour or conduct, and also computer use. There may also be policies which have the implicit aim of improving users' experiences. Policies have been referred to as *"...rules or guidelines that express the limits within which action should occur"*[10]. Rather than stating what should or should not be done, policies establish parameters for the decision maker [11]. By having a user experience policy, libraries can make a pledge to their users to make their systems as usable as possible and to do this on an ongoing and regularly reviewed basis, so as to create the best user experience possible.

It has been argued that there will always be a gap in understanding between technology development and its use [12]. Petre et al's [13] investigation into the total customer experience of e-commerce shoppers highlights this when it stresses the importance of thinking beyond just the web interfaces of a system to include other factors such as the delivery of the products or post-sales support. Customers have high expectations in these areas and if disappointed will not return to the website for further purchases, however usable it is. There is therefore potentially a gap between users' expectations and those of the e-commerce operator.

In a study of the usability of London transport systems, Inglesant and Sasse[14] emphasise the need for system usability to be considered and made a priority at the policy design stage. This research centred on users' lived experiences of using London transport systems such as the Oystercard and Congestion Charge scheme, with the researchers' beliefs that each system is an ecology of interfaces and media types, not just websites. In information ecologies, the spotlight is placed not only on technology, but also on the human activities that are served by technology. They are systems of people, practices, values and technologies in a particular environment [15]. An example of an information ecology is a doctor's surgery where doctors, nurses, receptionists and patients are the people involved, the practices are medical examinations and treatments, the values are to provide high-quality healthcare to improve health, and the technologies would include patients' records systems or accounting systems to track costs [12]. In the transport usability study, users of the transport systems were interviewed and asked to reflect on their experiences. Observation of users' activities was also undertaken. This once again highlighted the gap between what users and policy makers expect from a system, with the researchers concluding that usability must be considered prior to the implementation of a system [14].

The following diagram shows that there are gaps between some of the expectations of library users compared with those of the policymakers.

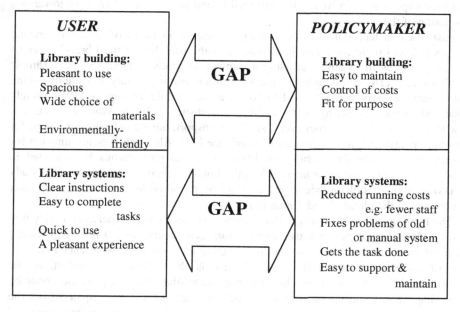

Fig. 1. The gaps between user and policymaker library expectations

This builds on the concept of technological frames which identify the goals and problems that particular groups have with technology. Members of each of these two distinct groups, users and policymakers, will have similar yet not necessarily identical degrees of inclusion in the technological frame [16]. In a library environment, users interact with both the library systems and the library building and have expectations in these areas, while similarly policymakers also have their own expectations. So for example users may expect to have a library system that is quick to use whereas policymakers hope it will fix the problems associated with the system it is replacing. Library users may want an environmentally-friendly building, but policymakers need to be aware of costs and may use cheaper materials.

2   Aim of the Study

The theme of an ecology of interfaces applied to London transport systems can equally be applied to university library systems. Library systems can be complex especially to new students or those with less library experience, with some students even feeling high levels of anxiety when using the university library. They may also experience usability issues, and problems with the library environment, but may be unaware or unsure of how to report these or who to report them to. Similarly, library staff may simply be ignorant of the usability issues that students are facing on a daily basis, and also unaware of problems that exist within the library environment. There is a potential socio-technical gap between what librarians and technologists can offer and what is socially required by users [17]. Having a stated policy regarding usability and user experience can make this gap visible and is one way of moving towards a resolution of these issues.

Past research has looked at the library experience in terms of its environmental factors [1], and there have also been studies of the usability of the library's various systems such as the website utilising a number of research methods. For example Battleson et al [18] investigated the usability of a university library website by asking participants to carry out tasks and to "think aloud", while Thompson [19] remotely observed users interacting with a library website. As previously discussed, researchers in systems in other areas, such as transport, have emphasised the need for a policy regarding usability and user experience [14]. Although it is not unusual for researchers to study the usability of library systems, past studies have tended to concentrate on one particular area such as the library website or catalogue. This study is taking a more holistic view and looking at usability in terms of overall user experience of the physical and digital libraries.

The hypothesis for this study is that a university library user experience policy will help to close the gap between user expectations and experiences. It is an exploratory multiple case study, and aims to find out whether and how user experience can form part of university library policy, and where it is absent how it can effectively be incorporated into policy. It also looks at the factors that the policy should cover by exploring the empirical foundations for such policies. This is investigated from the viewpoint of both the library users and the library stakeholders such as managers and other staff. The research questions that this study is attempting to answer are:

How can user experience best be incorporated into university library policy?

What type of user experience factors should university library policy cover?

3   Method

In order to answer these questions, this study requires data from both library stakeholders i.e. managers and staff, and also library users i.e. students, academic staff or others. Three university libraries were selected with each being treated as a case study. The cases are a range of UK university types with one being a post-1992 (or new) institution, which is a university that was formerly a college of higher education or a polytechnic, but acquired university status as the result of a 1992 act of Parliament. The second case study is a longer established university which is also a member of the 1994 group of research universities, a collection of 13 internationally renowned, research-intensive universities with the aim of promoting excellence in research and teaching [20]. The third is a specialist institution focused on postgraduate study and research. Having these three types should add more range, depth and interest than if similar types were investigated.

Library users at each of the cases were surveyed to reveal their opinions on the library's usability and their own experience of using it. This was done via a questionnaire administered personally by the researcher by stopping and asking students on campus. This is because questionnaires can have a low response rate unless carried out in this way [21], and also because university students are often asked to complete either paper-based or web-based questionnaires, and as a result some universities are actively trying to limit the number of them being carried out. Participants were selected in the library, and although this resulted in a convenience sample, it has been noted that convenience samples are very common especially in social research [22].

The questionnaire firstly asks for background information about the student, for example age, area of study and gender. There are then questions about library use in order to decide whether the participant is a regular or infrequent, experienced or inexperienced library user. The next part of the questionnaire is adapted from Koohang and Ondracek's [23] research into users' views of digital libraries. The questionnaire, designers state that, it is *"... a highly valid and reliable instrument"*. There is a series of Likert scale questions assessing the user's current views on library usability based on 12 properties, followed by more Likert scale questions evaluating the user's perceptions of the importance of each of the 12 properties. This means that it is then possible to calculate the gap between the user's experiences of the usability of the library and their expectations of its usability. The participant is asked to think about the library building and its systems as a single entity when answering the questions. The 12 usability properties include factors such simplicity – whether the library is simple and straightforward to use, user control – whether the user feels in control of his or her actions in the library and knows what to do, and navigability – whether the user can find his or her way around the library and its systems. The other nine factors are:

- Comfort – whether the user feels at ease using the library
- User-friendliness – whether the user believes the library is user-friendly
- Adequacy – does the user feel the information accessed in the library meets their needs?
- Consistency – are the words, terms and actions used in the library consistent?
- Access time – can the user find what they need in a reasonable time?
- Readability – is the information accessed readable and uncluttered?
- Recognition – whether the use recognises the features and functions of the library

- Visual presentation – is there signage and text to grab the user's attention?
- Relevancy – is the information accessed in the library relevant to the user's requirements?

Finally the participant is asked for any user experience or usability issues that they have encountered. Forty questionnaire responses have been collected at each university. Data collected was analysed statistically using the software, Statistical Package for the Social Sciences (SPSS).

Key members of staff were interviewed at each library in order to gain information about user experience policy. Usability issues are also covered in these interviews, with staff asked to discuss any known problems that occur in library and with its systems. The questions were open-ended in nature so that interviewees can be asked about facts and their opinions [24]. Three interviews are to be carried out at each library, ideally with a manager, a frontline member of staff, and an information technology or systems staff member. The interviews were recorded, transcribed and then analysed via a qualitative content analysis approach which involves searching out the underlying themes in the materials being analysed [22].

Analysis of any policy documents is also to take place at each library to ascertain what has been written regarding policy in relation to usability and user experience. Additionally a survey of all UK university libraries will be carried out to find out what policies are in place across the sector. This will be done by looking at each library's website.

As a part of each case study, empirical data is required to "set the scene" at each library. The researcher observed the day-to-day working of each library to help gather background information and to form specific interview questions for staff.

4   Findings and Anticipated Results

Currently data has been collected at the three cases. A total of 120 questionnaires have been carried out, 40 at each of the three cases. Library A is the new university, Library B is the postgraduate specialist institution, and Library C is the member of the 1994 research group of universities. Staff interviews have been carried out at Library B, and the survey of policy documents is underway.

4.1   The Libraries

Library buildings remain central to library services [5], and the allocation of space and facilities therein has impacts on how the university library is used. Students now expect different zones for individual silent study or group work. They also expect personal computers (PCs), printers and even café facilities.

Library A is housed in a building attached to other parts of the university. It has four floors, with the ground floor containing a careers advice centre for students, along with a series of library self-issue machines. The first floor is set aside for silent study and also has a number of PCs for student use as well as shelves of books. The library helpdesk is on the second floor along with the bulk of the PCs and printers available in the building. Staff offices are also based here. The rest of the space is given over to books. The third and fourth floors also contain book shelves PCs and study areas, but the fourth has provision for group work with some seminar rooms as well as large round tables with screens around to help keep noise to reasonable levels.

Library B was built in the early 1990s, is a stand-alone building on campus, and has three storeys. The ground floor has a number of seminar rooms and an area containing food and drink vending machines with a large table. The first and second floors are similar in layout, and both have individual workspaces with PCs, seminar rooms, and bookstock. Staff are based mainly on the first floor, with helpdesks and self-issue machines here too. Quiet study areas are on the second floor.

Library C is situated centrally on the university campus and has recently had a large extension added to increase the number of study spaces, PCs and group study rooms available to students. The library is now a mixture of the "old", more traditional library space, and the "new" state-of-the-art space. There are five floors in the building with silent study and group work areas. Level one is where the main entrance, self-issue machines and staff offices are located, and there is also an area containing food and drink vending machines along with seating and tables. Books and PCs are distributed across the five levels, with the third floor having a more relaxed work area containing sofas and armchairs.

4.2   The Questionnaire Participants

Questionnaire participants fall into three separate age groups with 50% aged 18 to 24 years, 37% in the 25 to 34 years age group, and 13% aged 35 years or older. Sixty per cent of participants were male and 40% were female. The vast majority of participants (84%) described themselves as frequent library building users, with only 6% saying that they hardly use the library building, while 55% were frequent users of the library website.

Fifty-nine per cent of participants were postgraduates, with 31% being undergraduates. The other 10% of the sample was made up of research students, staff and alumni. The vast majority of participants, 94%, were full-time students, and the most popular study subject areas were Engineering (24%), Business (18%), and Natural Sciences (12%).

4.3   Questionnaire Results

The three main uses of the library buildings are:

- Borrowing and returning books
- Individual study with library materials
- Accessing computers

While the three main uses of the library website are:

- Searching the catalogue for books and materials
- Searching the library databases and e-journals
- Browsing electronic books (e-books)

Looking at results in terms of user expectations of library usability, the three areas where users have the highest expectations are:

- Relevancy
- Adequacy
- Simplicity

This means that participants expect the information in their library to be relevant to their needs as well as adequate for their needs. They also expect the library and its associated systems to be simple to use.

Lesser expectations are in the following 3 areas:

- Recognition
- Consistency
- Visual presentation

Meaning that participants are less concerned that they are able to recognise the features and functions of the library, or that the words, terms and actions used in the library are consistent. They are also less concerned that there is signage and text to grab their attention.

These results show that participants are concerned about the information they access and how they access it, and less concerned about the appearance and functionality of the library and its systems. And looking at the three cases separately, the lists of user expectations are very similar suggesting that students have the same issues and concerns regardless of where or what they are studying.

The data can also be analysed by looking at the gaps between user expectations and experience of using their library. Again the results are similar for the three universities with the smallest gaps tending to be as follows:

- Comfort
- Control
- User-friendliness

So participants' expectations and experience are closely matched in terms of feeling at ease using the library, feeling in control of what they are doing, and feeling that the library is user-friendly.

The largest gaps between expectations and experience tend to occur in these three areas:

- Access time
- Adequacy
- Relevancy

It has already been established that participants have high expectations as far as adequacy of information and relevancy of information. However, these results show that their high expectations in these two areas are not being met by their actual experience thus showing where improvements are likely to be required. The largest gap concerns access time. It would seem that it takes participants much longer than they would like to find the information they need, and again this is an area where improvements are needed.

4.4   Staff Views

Interviews with staff at library B have shown that usability testing is carried out whenever possible at the library, but that this is often done in an informal way, for example by asking students to look at a new interface or system and then asking for feedback. Sometimes students volunteer information when a change is made, by telling staff their opinions, and a library Facebook page encourages feedback.

Generally staff believe that a stated policy on user experience is beneficial, and that formal usability testing via methods such as focus groups is valuable. But they also point out that while it is possible to feedback issues to a software supplier, the interface of a library software package will not usually be changed to meet the concerns of one library alone.

Library staff help and advise students with computerised systems such as the library catalogue, and also the manual systems for example the shelving classification system. They note that the library can become busy and at times there is a lack of workspace for students.

5   Discussion

Data collection in this study is still ongoing, and as yet it is not possible to fully answer the research questions or to make conclusions.

It has been seen that library users at the three cases value the adequacy and relevancy of the information available in the library, and are less concerned about the appearance and functionality of it. Further analysis of the questionnaire data by age, gender, area of study etc will add further insights, and interviews with staff will no doubt show similarities and contrasts with the students' opinions. Opinions of library usability are lived experiences in that the students or other users have used the library to try to achieve a particular goal. This goal could be as simple as finding a book on a particular topic, or as complex as writing a literature review for a Masters dissertation, but it goes beyond their experience of using a computer to include other technological and human factors along with their own experience, capabilities and values [14].

If the university library is viewed as an information ecology, it has students, academic staff, librarians and other support staff as the people involved. Its practices are the provision of information in various formats both physical and digital, while its values are to provide this information in such a way that it is easy to access, readable, relevant and adequate.

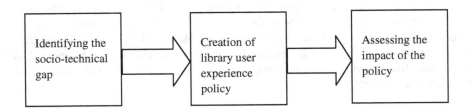

Fig. 2. Creating a library user experience policy

This study aims to shows that the creation of a library user experience policy begins with the identification of the socio-technical gap between experiences and expectations. This is when library usability opinions from staff, students and other library users are gathered, and analysed in conjunction with the existing library policies, and the existing functionality of the library building and systems. The policy needs to be a commitment to library users to continuously strive to improve the library systems and interfaces, and in order to meet users' needs its impact must be assessed on an ongoing basis.

References

1. Grimes, P., Charters, M.: Library use and the undergraduate economics student. College Student Journal 34(4) (2000)
2. UCAS. About us (2011), http://www.ucas.com/about_us/stat_services/statisticalfaqs/coverage/faq3 (accessed October 2, 2011)
3. UCAS. Students (2011), http://www.ucas.com/students/wheretostart/nonukstudents/ (accessed October 2, 2011)
4. Morgan: Fears for UK research as postgraduate rise is largely a foreign affair (2010), http://www.timeshighereducation.co.uk/story.asp?storycode=410080 (accessed October 2, 2011)
5. Brophy, P.: The academic library. Facet Publishing, London (2005)
6. Karle, E.: Invigorating the academic library experience: creative programming ideas. College & Research Libraries News 69(3) (2008)
7. Andrews, J.: An exploration of students' library use problems. Library Review 40(1) (1991)

8. Brooke, J.: SUS - a quick and dirty usability scale (1996),
   http://www.usabilitynet.org/trump/documents/Suschapt.doc
   (accessed September 29, 2011)
9. UPA. What is usability? (2012), http://www.usabilityprofessionals.org/
   usability_resources/about_usability/definitions_of_
   usability.html (accessed November 6, 2012)
10. Mintzberg, H., Quinn, J.: The strategy process: concepts, contexts, cases. Prentice-Hall,
    New Jersey (1996)
11. Robbins, S., Coulter, M.: Management, 7th edn. Prentice-Hall, New Jersey (2002)
12. Nardi, B., O'Day, V.: An ecological perspective on digital libraries. In: Bishop, A., House,
    N., Butterfield, B. (eds.) Digital Library Use: Social Practice in Evolution. MIT Press,
    Cambridge (2003)
13. Petre, M., Minocha, S., Roberts, D.: Usability beyond the website: an empirically
    grounded e-commerce evaluation instrument for the total customer experience. Behaviour
    & Information Technology 25(2) (2006)
14. Inglesant, P., Sasse, M.A.: Usability is the best policy: public policy and the lived
    experience of transport systems in London. In: Proceedings of HCI 2007 (2007)
15. Nardi, B., O'Day, V.: Information ecologies: using technology with heart. MIT Press,
    Cambridge (1999)
16. Abdelnour Nocera, J., Dunckley, L., Sharp, H.: An Approach to the Evaluation of
    Usefulness as a Social Construct Using Technological Frames. International Journal of
    Human-Computer Interaction 22(1&2) (2007)
17. Ackerman, M.S.: The intellectual challenge of CSCW: the gap between social
    requirements and technical feasability. Human-Computer Interaction 15(2) (2000)
18. Battleson, B., Booth, A., Weintrop, J.: Usability Testing of an Academic Library Web Site:
    A Case Study. The Journal of Academic Librarianship 27(3) (2001)
19. Thompson, S.: Remote Observation Strategies for Usability Testing, Information.
    Technology & Libraries (2003)
20. 1994 Group. About us (2012), http://www.1994group.ac.uk/aboutus
    (accessed November 6, 2012)
21. Pickard, A.J.: Research methods in information. Facet, London (2007)
22. Bryman, A.: Social research methods. Oxford University Press (2008)
23. Koohang, A., Ondracek, J.: Users' views about the usability of digital libraries. British
    Journal of Educational Technology 36(3) (2005)
24. Yin, R.K.: Case study research: design and methods. Sage, Thousand Oaks (2003)

Adjusting the Design Target of Life-Cycle Aware HCI in Knowledge Work: Focus on Computing Practices

Heljä Franssila and Jussi Okkonen

University of Tampere, School of Information Sciences
Kanslerinrinne 1, FIN 33014 University of Tampere, Finland
{helja.franssila,jussi.okkonen}@uta.fi

Abstract. The goal of this work-in-progress paper is to consider the utility of current theoretical and methodological HCI and work analysis approaches in understanding and supporting knowledge workers in their coping with contemporary computing ecosystems at work, and pinpoint the limitations of the design target formulation in current HCI approaches. The new approach discussed is to focus the design efforts, instead of technical artifacts, into the observation, understanding and development of *computing practices* as a resource for knowledge work. Alternative, emerging conceptualizations and methodological options to study and advice the development of everyday computing practices in knowledge work is proposed.

Keywords: knowledge work, work analysis, computing practices, design, use life-cycle, data collection methods.

1 Introduction

When considering both popular and scholarly discussion related to the most prominent determinants of work wellbeing and performance of contemporary knowledge workers, certain themes recur with accelerating frequency. Information overload, interruptions, multitasking, work fragmentation, always-on availability and the growth of the computing ecosystem versatility are characteristics of everyday work potentially challenging the knowledge worker's sense of control in their work. All of the above mentioned challenging phenomena are more or less related to interaction between the human and the computing environment. Computing environment stretch the operational limits of human attention, concentration, memory and self-control, be it subjectively experienced or objectively measured. The change rate of the environment of knowledge work is high. New ways to do and organize work combined with constant evolution of computing environment shape the means of maintaining sense of control and coherence all the time. Understanding the relations between the characteristics of computing environment and work wellbeing are not yet very clear.

The goal of this conceptual work-in-progress paper is to consider the utility of current theoretical and methodological HCI and work analysis approaches in understanding and supporting knowledge workers in their coping with contemporary computing

P. Campos et al. (Eds.): HWID 2012, IFIP AICT 407, pp. 150–160, 2013.

ecosystems at work. Special focus is to observe how the everyday *computing practices* of the knowledge workers is addressed in the HCI and work analysis literature. We examine how the target of design is conceptualized in HCI and in certain approaches of work analysis, and how the positioning of design target may limit the expected results of work practice design and development efforts. After that we propose an extension of the design target of HCI that we find relevant when analyzing and developing computing practices in knowledge work. To ground the feasibility of the proposed approach we discuss rather new data collection methods which serve the goals of the extended target of design in HCI. We also acknowledge certain concepts from contemporary HCI and work analysis as applicable in the newly framed HCI in work settings. The discussion is motivated by our research project related to the defining and developing information ergonomics in knowledge work settings.

2 Computing Work Practices in HCI and Work Analysis

The goal of HCI has been at least traditionally to understand, design, evaluate and implement interactive computing systems for human use. In work settings one of the more detailed goals has been enabling more productive work practices and processes [1]. HCI in work settings seeks to make work (and life) involving computing fit better with plethora of human characteristics. The time-scale of design and research approaches in HCI have lately been extended to cover also stages after the technical implementation and adoption of technologies. These stages are conceptualized as appropriation, configuring and design-in-use (see e.g. [2-4]).

The design goal of HCI - more successful interaction and use - however seems to be focused or framed in a certain way both in HCI research and practice. When considering design and development efforts, it seems that while the methods of practical HCI design aim to target *interaction*, most of the efforts of the design materialize as modified designs of the *technical applications and devices* - the computer side of the HCI concept dyad. Users and their activities, emotions and even biofeedback are shadowed, recorded, analyzed and modeled, but the implications and conclusions derived and the practical design recommendations and requirements given typically address only the computer or application side, not the human user side. This tendency can be observed for example in the literature reporting the application of participatory design in real world development projects. It is practically impossible to find a reported participatory design project related to the application of information technology, where the development effort would not have been motivated by an organizational, predetermined need to plan, develop, purchase or modify the information *technological* solution per se. Projects having as a core design goal to enhance and develop the utilization of *existing* technologies practically does not exist. Even the research interest to study the realization, details and lifecycle of IT use after system deployments in organizational contexts is very scarce (the rare exceptions are [5],[6],[7],[8],[9])

There's also strong tendency to try to model how the users will use the technical artifact in the future, and to equip the artifact with technical affordances that potentially could fulfill emerging user needs and preferences (e.g. infrastructuring proposed by [10]). When considering the quality of long-term HCI from the human side, this is somewhat desperate approach: majority of the development efforts stop when the application is released and not fundamentally changed any more (customization and tailoring functionalities are considered as features of mature application). The computer side of the relation is left practically untouched after the release of the application. After this, there's only the human side of the relation, which can be influenced.

One potential reason for the practical non-existence of approaches which seek to develop the user behavior in longer term and the human side of the HCI dyad is that underlying nearly all examinations of human-computer interaction pitfalls is the unexpressed assumption, that if the interaction fails, the weak or even evil party in the interaction process is the computer, not the user or his/her activities. Characteristics of the computing solution do not fit e.g. the work practices of individuals and groups. It is the technical solution, which needs to be fixed and which requires changes, not the human or the human computing practice. The evolving human computing practice is something that is often left to develop on its own. Often even unrealistic "abilities" are expected from the technical applications, like alertness to user's errors and capabilities to steer and advice user while he or she is computing whatever goals or tasks at hand.

Another characteristic of the conventional HCI is that it might be interested in studying interaction between human and computer in rich, "wild" computing ecologies, but typically design implications and recommendations derived from observations concern only a limited facet of the computing ecosystem the user operates, namely certain service, application or feature. The chains of real world computing activities, where the computing ecosystem is in versatile ways utilized by the user, are not considered as a development target per se. However, we believe that the human user can and will do a lot to influence the quality of HCI phenomenon after the deployment, during the life-cycle of interaction with the computing ecosystem, even though no iterations or considerable changes to the technical computing ecosystem (software and hardware) are deployed anymore.

3   Unknown Practice of Knowledge Work

Contemporary knowledge work and knowledge workers are very often characterized as creative, boundary less and free. Knowledge work and workers are often pictured as contrary to the factory workers whose manual work is highly structured, repetitive, without freedom to choose the best method, place and time for the work execution. Knowledge work, individual knowledge worker and especially workers' concrete macro and micro working and computing methods and practices are most often left untouched and unexplored – both in practice and in research. Working methods, habits and practices of knowledge workers seem to be a great black box in the research literature. Even the knowledge workers themselves can be reluctant to scrutinize about their working methods [11]. Thomas Davenport [12],[13] is one of the rare scholars who have questioned this immunity of the knowledge work and knowledge workers' working methods and practices for research scrutiny.

However, several aspects of ICT intensive knowledge work settings have been actively studied. The new mobile and distributed nature of the work, which reduces the constraints related to the place and timing of the work execution, has been extensively explored in the research literature [14]. Especially the factors shaping the way the distributed work is executed in a team level are scrutinized. It is proposed that at least the nature of team task, team structure, team work processes, workplace (physical, virtual, social), and organization contexts mould the practical performance of the work [15].

If there is a goal to develop any practical activity, there needs to be some visions what the desired qualities of the more developed activity are, and how the development can be observed and confirmed. When considering development of knowledge work, there have been several attempts to collect and define key success factors of knowledge work in general. One way to classify the factors is to divide them into input, process and output factors. Among the success factors related to the knowledge work process are management of individual work, organization of work, setting of goals, timeliness, quality of work related interaction, knowledge acquisition and sharing, team structure and continuous learning. New technologies are seen as input level factors of knowledge work process [16]. Studies exploring the impact of new technologies to the knowledge work often identify the change enabled in the organization of work, but do not elaborate the actual nature or principles of that organizing – organization of work is often undifferentiated dependent variable, e.g. [17]. Concrete practices of organizing individual knowledge work stay obscure.

The current popular and also academic concerns of the knowledge worker wellbeing and effectiveness relate to still controversial effects of work fragmentation, high amount of interruptions and multitasking [18],[19],[20]. Research conducted in real world work settings has so far been able to give evidence mainly about variable, subjective wellbeing and effectiveness responses to these new features of knowledge work. However, these new features relate to a central dimension of work practice, namely to the organization and management of individual workers' tasks. The information and communication intensive work environment where the knowledge workers are exposed to rich and frequent stimulus clearly has an impact on minute-to-minute organization of the tasks. Again, research exploring the actual organization and coordination of individual knowledge workers' task load both in macro and micro level is surprisingly scarce. Issues of organizing and coordinating tasks are detailed extensively when collaborative group work processes are studied in CSCW literature, e.g. [21], but the studies often concentrate to follow accomplishment of a certain task flow executed by a distributed group e.g. [22]. Less is known about the task organization, self-coordination and task management principles and conventions of an individual knowledge worker [23], where the individual worker organizes several personal subtasks, delegated and derived from group task flows.

It seems that continued, post-deployment *IT use* as one facet of knowledge work and its development per se in work contexts is not a prime interest of any HCI approach. The studies of appropriation, configuring and design-in-use address the rather long post-deployment period of use life-cycle, but the main interest is to understand and advice the design of deployed *technologies* or technical means to enable their technical adaptation. The detailed paths of computing activities of a user across different applications and the development potential during the life-cycle of everyday computing practices are considered rarely. We propose, that understanding computing micro-practices in detail is central when considering the work efficiency and control experiences of end-users, and when trying uncover the phenomena like the experience of information overload and interruption. HCI and work analysis seems to resist or at least hesitate to formulate human *computing practices* as a goal of design per se.

4   Promising Conceptual and Methodological Approaches for More Life-Cycle Aware HCI in Knowledge Work

In order to narrow the gap between the goal of enhancing knowledge work and the quality of HCI in real life computing environments there is a need for conceptual tools to effectively approach and characterize both knowledge work and computing. The nature of knowledge work and factors shaping its' execution can be conceptualized in several ways.   When characterizing knowledge work practices, more empirical research concerning *"how"* the everyday work of *individual* knowledge workers is executed in needed.

Certainly, classical work analysis concepts from the fields of human factors and HCI are useful when characterizing knowledge work. The concepts of goal and task are needed when observing what is done in knowledge work. In knowledge work most often the task is to produce something intangible out of intangible, namely information and knowledge. That is why it is sometimes even for knowledge workers themselves a bit hard to describe, of what kind of tasks and subtasks their work contains [24]. They might take care e.g. about maintaining productive client accounts, make different kinds of designs, plans and decision, and create various kinds of information artifacts.

Basic, rather descriptive concepts of job design could be considered, when trying to detect the patterns of individual knowledge work organization, be they planned or unplanned. Observing the everyday conventions of task load planning and scheduling, sub-tasking of one's responsibilities, task ordering, task prioritizing and management of coworker interdependencies could reveal lots about the practical realities of work organization in knowledge work. These observations could be contrasted with the expressed principles and targets knowledge workers have considering the control of their everyday work organizing and further with the potential effects the nature of the information environment have on the actual conventions.

In several HCI design approaches targeted towards developing artifacts to support work and work processes, the key analytical concepts involved are the user, role, goals, tasks and some kind of flow of events. For example the five work models of contextual design – flow, sequence, artifact, cultural and physical – detect several distinctive characteristics shaping the execution of work [25]. However, these models are targeted for understanding only certain tasks processes, with the aim of aiding the design of an artifact supporting those particular task processes. Work modeling in contextual design does not try to detect the point of view of a particular worker executing the task, but rather the processes that can be executed by any worker in a domain under the study. It is typical for task analysis applied in HCI design methodologies that the focus of analysis is either a particular task, artifact use or task/work flow, but not the individual user or worker as the more or less goal oriented integrator of all the resources and constraints provided by the computing environment, e.g. [26]. When the target is to enhance the HCI and the computing practices applied across many, even concurrent tasks, new ways to conceptualize the work execution and its determinants is needed. What matters, is what happens to an individual in a given, complex environment. Thus there is need for concepts to characterize the information environment and events in there.

When considering the understanding and the systematic development of computing practices at work, the turn to the practice and the turn to the wild [27] in HCI provide promising conceptual tools. Detailed ethnographic descriptions of work practices may serve appropriate grounding for unfolding of actual computing conventions and methods knowledge workers apply. In the studies conducted in the tradition of workplace studies [28] and distributed cognition [29] have provided vivid accounts how users and communities in workplace enact to total work environment and its computational and representational resources. In the practice tradition there is emerging quest for not only analysis but also for systematic development and reforming of social practices when applying technology into work [30]. The cognitive work analysis is explicitly concerned about how HCI can enable designing for worker adaptation [31].

A sample of analytical concepts from the IS can also prove powerful when descriptions of work to enable systematic development of computing practices in work are pursued. The application of the concept of *computing habit* in IS research has devoted more attention to the human side of HCI dyad, even though so far the approaches have mainly been explorative and descriptive, not design or development oriented [32]. Computing habits are controversial when considering efficiency of human-computer interaction. Habits make any activity effortless and fluent, but at the same time they are very sticky and conservative, hindering possibilities to learn new, enhanced methods and practices [33].

Profiling basic, industry-independent knowledge work processes and knowledge work types has been provided scantily, but the account of Davenport makes an exception [11]. Davenport tries to formulate a set of basic working modes of knowledge workers, and presents a typology of knowledge workers. In addition, when trying to find a unit of work to serve as analytical basic element for characterizing knowledge work practice in meaningful granular level, the concept of *ensemble* is proposed. Ensembles are units of work which are concrete enough to be distinguished from thick account of work, and conceptually they lay between the unit of action and the unit of activity [34].

Promising conceptual tools for development oriented analysis of knowledge work, knowledge work practices and computing practices in work can be found from rather unexpected direction. In the context of lean management philosophy and development practice, treatment of information as a resource of work process and practices has emerged. Powerful categorization of different kinds of wastes in lean management approach is applied to the analysis of work practices which involve manipulation of information. In lean information management four categories of dysfunctional information waste events are conceptualized: information excess, lack of necessary information, laborious accessibility of information and errors in information [35]. Identification of information wastes is successfully applied when analyzing information processing in order-to-cash processes of manufacturing company [36] and engineering change management in product design [37]. Even the long abandoned tradition of taylorism and especially its most well-known development method, time-and-motion studies, could be successfully adapted to the study of work processes and practices which comprise of information flow manipulation. The profound developmental goal of time-motion studies was and is even nowadays to equip workers with better and more convenient working methods. While time-motion studies traditionally concentrated into physical ergonomics of the work task execution, the similar approach could be applied for studying information and communication intensive work tasks. Especially the basic concepts related to the detection of time spending in non-value generating activities like waiting, fixing errors and moving and collecting resources to be processed are equally applicable into knowledge work as for manual work.

Common to all above discussed concepts is their potential power to detect actual working patterns, conventions and habits of knowledge work. Diverse information technological resources are involved and applied in practically every step of executing knowledge work. The critical question is, how the computing practices and habits involved in the everyday task management and execution have been developed and evolved, how they serve the expressed goals of the knowledge workers and what is their fit with the human capabilities.

5   Development of Empirical Data Collection for Studying Computing Practices

Observing and analyzing the connections between computing practices and the success of knowledge work is not straightforward. Collecting reliable empirical data in real work settings for long periods without a presence of an observing, interviewing and intervening researcher has been so far difficult in practice. On the other hand, the mere presence and activities of the researcher may alter the situation and the behavior of the person observed. Detecting and scrutinizing the detailed patterns of task organization, computing activities and event flows in the work in nearly real time disturbs the activities of the person observed considerably.

The application of earlier mentioned analysis frameworks of work and computing practice are becoming feasible because of the emergence of new commercial tools of tracking the details of everyday computing practices in work. Portable lifelogging devices (e.g. Vicon Revue) and associated analysis software, screen navigation video recording, tracking software for capturing, logging and analyzing moment-to-moment screen activities related to different software use, and portable, mini-sized video cameras leaving both hands of the user free provide powerful but unobtrusive means to study naturally occurring micro-practices of computing in work. Tracking the computing activity with these tools does not disturb normal working of the person observed.

By integrating data collected by tracking and recording tools it is possible to observe computing micro-practices in a great detail. The data from different tracking sources (e.g. screen navigation video and screen activity tracking data detecting flow of user activity across different software tools, documents and files) can be merged into a single time-stamp based database. Even the filtering confidential content, which the person observed does not want to show for analysts, is possible programmatically without extensive manual browsing of many hours of recorded data. The activities on and by the screen can be detected as a continuous process, and viewed from different viewpoints. They provide rich and objective measure about what happens in the concrete level of computing operations, enabling both qualitative and quantitative analysis. Because the data can browsed in visually natural way (e.g. watching interesting events from screen navigation video), collaborative interpretation of the data with the persons observed is possible outside the tracking and recording moment. When this data capturing "computing behavior" in naturally occurring work situations and ecologically valid environment is applied as the source material for the analysis of actual computing methods, totally unrecognized possibilities can open up to recognize the details of computing habits and micro-practices, and to understand the determinants of efficacy of human-computer interaction in the service of knowledge work.

Researching computing practices in detail requires dedicated analytical units to be observed from the collected computing event and process data. Shifts between tools and documents, sequencing and patterning of the shifts, duration of events, recurring of events, and chains of operations to reach a certain goal are just examples of potential "raw" conceptually low observations, which need to be further correlated with conceptually more abstract observations detecting phenomena under interest. When considering particularly the impact of the quality of HCI on knowledge work, these more abstract dependent variables can be the success factors of knowledge work or the work wellbeing variables.

6   Conclusions

In this conceptual work-in-progress paper we have discussed kind of blind spot of HCI and work analysis, namely the inability to systematically address the development on everyday computing practices of knowledge workers. In addition, we have discussed the state of the research evidence considering the nature of individual knowledge workers' working practices and principles of organizing their tasks in their information technologically intensive work environments. Much is still unknown about the character of knowledge work task management and practical computing methods. We still do not know how the computing practices and knowledge work success factors are related especially in the individual worker level.

When considering the life-cycle of use of any technology, the post-deployment period is the longest phase of the life-cycle of use. During the long post-deployment period, the everyday computing habits and practices evolve, and often very rapidly freeze – regardless of the affordances designed into the technical artifact potentially enabling a more sophisticated and efficient use. We have observed that development of computing practices and habits of individual users and user communities in work organizations are not central design targets of current HCI or work analysis efforts. This is an unfortunate limitation, considering the critical role the actual nature of use plays in the shaping of the overall impacts of computing for the qualities of work processes and experiences of the knowledge workers [38]. Therefore, we proposed that a central new design effort focus of HCI and work analysis should be the understanding and development of everyday computing practices of knowledge workers in their "as-is" computing environments. In addition, we proposed emerging and promising conceptual and methodological approaches to address the shortage.

Acknowledgements. This article is based on a research project "Construction of evaluation and development approach for information ergonomics in knowledge work", which is funded by Finnish Work Environment Fund, grant number 112135.

References

1. Preece, J., Rogers, Y., Sharp, H., Benyon, D., Holland, S., Carey, T.: Human-Computer Interaction. Addison-Wesley, Harlow (1994)
2. Karapanos, E., Zimmerman, J., Forlizzi, J., Martens, J.-B.: User Experience Over Time: An Initial Framework. In: Proceedings of the CHI 2009, Boston, Massachusetts, USA, April 4-9, pp. 729–738 (2009)
3. Stevens, G., Pipek, V., Wulf, V.: Appropriation Infrastructure: Supporting the Design of Usages. In: Pipek, V., Rosson, M.B., de Ruyter, B., Wulf, V. (eds.) IS-EUD 2009. LNCS, vol. 5435, pp. 50–69. Springer, Heidelberg (2009)
4. Balka, E., Wagner, I.: Making Things Work: Dimensions of Configurability as Appropriation Work. In: Proceedings of the CSCW 2006, Banff, Alberta, Canada, November 4-8, pp. 229–238 (2006)
5. Jasperson, J., Carter, P.E., Zmud, R.W.: A Comprehensive Conceptualization of Post-Adoptive Behaviors Associated with Information Technology Enabled Work Systems. MIS Quarterly 29(3), 525–557 (2005)
6. Devaraj, S., Kohli, R.: Performance Impacts of Information Technology: Is Actual Usage the Missing Link? Management Science 49(3), 273–289 (2003)
7. Carter, M., Clements, J., Thatcher, J.B., George, J.: Unraveling the "paradox of the active user": Determinants of individuals' innovation with IT-based work routines. In: Proceedings of the Seventeenth Americas Conference on Information Systems (AMCIS 2011) Proceedings - All Submissions Paper 41 (2011), http://aisel.aisnet.org/amcis2011_submissions/41
8. Saeed, K.A., Abdinnour, S.: Understanding post-adoption IS usage stages: An empirical assessment of self-service information systems. Information Systems Journal (2011), doi:10.1111/j.1365-2575.2011.00389.x
9. Burton-Jones, A., Gallivan, M.J.: Toward a Deeper Understanding of Systems Usage in Organizations: A Multilevel Perspective. MIS Quarterly 31(4), 657–679 (2007)
10. Pipek, V., Wulf, V.: Infrastructuring: Toward an Integrated Perspective on the Design and Use of Information Technology. Journal of the Association for Information Systems 10(5), 447–473 (2009)

11. Davenport, T.H., Thomas, R.J., Cantrell, S.: The Mysterious Art and Science of Know-ledge-Worker Performance. MIT Sloan Management Review, 23–30 (Fall 2002)
12. Davenport, T.H.: Thinking for a Living. How to Get Better Performance and Results from Knowledge Workers. Harvard Business School Press, Boston (2005)
13. Davenport, T.H.: Rethinking Knowledge Work: A Strategic Approach. McKinsey Quarter-ly (February 2011)
14. Vartiainen, M., Hakonen, M., Koivisto, S., Mannonen, P., Manninen, M.P., Ruohomäki, V., Vartola, A.: Distributed Mobile Work. Places, People, and Technology. Otatieto, Es-poo (2007)
15. Bosch-Sijtsema, P.M., Fruchter, R., Vartiainen, M., Ruohomäki, V.: A Framework to Ana-lyze Knowledge Work in Distributed Teams. Group & Organization Management 36(3), 275–307 (2011)
16. Laihonen, H., Jääskeläinen, A., Lönnqvist, A., Ruostela, J.: Measuring the productivity impacts of new ways of working. Journal of Facilities Management 10(2), 102–113 (2012)
17. Beurer-Zuellig, B., Meckel, M.: Smartphones Enabling Mobile Collaboration. In: Proceed-ings of the 41st Hawaii International Conference on Systems Sciences. IEEE (2008)
18. Paridon, H.M., Kaufman, M.: Multitasking in work-related situations and its relevance for occupational health and safety: Effects on performance, subjective strain and physiological parameters. Europe's Journal of Psychology 6(4), 110–124 (2010)
19. Mark, G., Gonzales, V., Harris, J.: No Task Left Behing? Examining the Nature of Frag-mented Work. In: Proceedings oth the CHI 2005, Portland, Oregon, USA, April 2-7, pp. 321–330. ACM, New York (2005)
20. Wajcman, J., Rose, E.: Constant Connectivity: Rethinking Interruptions at Work. Organi-zation Studies 32(7), 941–961 (2011)
21. Schmidt, K.: Cooperative Work and Coordinative Practices. Contributions to the Concep-tual Foundations of Computer-Supported Cooperative Work (CSCW). Springer, London (2011)
22. Franssila, H., Okkonen, J., Savolainen, R., Talja, S.: The formation of coordinative know-ledge practices in distributed work: towards an explanatory model. Journal of Knowledge Management 16(4), 650–665 (2012)
23. Bellotti, V., Dalal, B., Good, N., Flynn, P., Bobrow, D.G.: What a To-Do: Studies of Task Management Towards the Design of a Personal Task List Manager. In: Proceedings of the CHI 2004, Vienna, Austria, April 24-29, pp. 735–742. ACM, New York (2004)
24. Drucker, P.F.: Knowledge-Worker Productivity: The Biggest Challenge. California Man-agement Review 41(2), 78–94 (1999)
25. Beyer, H., Holtzblatt, K.: Contextual Design. Defining Customer-Centered Systems. Morgan Kaufmann, San Francisco (1998)
26. Courage, C., Jain, J., Redish, J., Wixon, D.: Task Analysis. In: Jacko, J.A. (ed.) The Hu-man-Computer Interaction Handbook. Fundamentals, Evolving Technologies and Emerg-ing Applications, CRC Press, Boca Raton (2012)
27. Rogers, Y.: HCI Theory: Classical, Modern, and Contemporary. Synthesis Lectures on Human-Centered Informatics. Morgan & Claypool Publishers (2012)
28. Luff, P., Hindmarsh, J., Heath, C.: Workplace Studies. Recovering Work Practice and In-forming System Design. Cambridge University Press, Cambridge (2000)
29. Hutchins, E.: Cognition in the Wild. MIT Press, Cambridge (1995)
30. Jacucci, G.: Social Practice Design (SPD), Pathos, Improvisation, Mood, and Bricolage: The Mediterranean Way to Make Place for IT? MCIS, Proceedings, Paper 19 (2007)

31. Vicente, K.J.: HCI in the Global Knowledge-Based Economy: Designing to Support Worker Adaptation. ACM Transactions on Computer-Human Interaction 7(2), 263–280 (2000)
32. Guinea, A.O., Markus, M.L.: Why Break the Habit of a Lifetime? Rethinking the Roles of Intention, Habit, and Emotion in Continuing Information Technology Use. MIS Quarterly 33(3), 433–444 (2009)
33. Carroll, J.M., Rosson, M.B.: Paradox of the Active User. In: Carroll, J.M. (ed.) Interfacing Thought. Cognitive Aspects of Human-Computer Interaction, pp. 80–111. MIT Press, Cambridge (1987)
34. Gonzales, V.M., Nardi, B., Mark, G.: Ensembles: understanding the instantiation of activities. Information Technology & People 22(2), 109–131 (2009)
35. Hicks, B.J.: Lean information management: understanding and eliminating waste. International Journal of Information Management 27, 233–249 (2007)
36. Franssila, H.: Information waste: Qualitative study in manufacturing enterprises. In: Møller, C., Chaundry, S. (eds.) Advances inn Enterprise Information Systems II, pp. 105–110. CRC Press, London (2012)
37. Hölttä, V., Mahlamäki, K., Eisto, T., Ström, M.: Lean Information Management Model for Engineering Changes. In: Proceedings of International Conference on Business, Economics and Management (ICBEM 2010), Paris, France, June 28-30 (2010)
38. Jain, V., Kanungo, S.: Beyond Perceptions and Usage: Impact of Nature of Information Systems Use on Information System-Enabled Productivity. International Journal of Human-Computer Interaction 19(1), 113–136 (2005)

Mobile Probing and Probes

Uffe Duvaa[1], Rikke Ørngreen[2], Anne-Gitte Weinkouff Mathiasen, and Ulla Blomhøj

[1] Learning Specialist, Oticon A/S, Denmark
[2] IT and Designs for Learning, Dep. of Learning & Philosophy, Aalborg University, Denmark

Abstract. Mobile probing is a method, developed for learning about digital work situations, as an approach to discover new grounds. The method can be used when there is a need to know more about users and their work with certain tasks, but where users at the same time are distributed (in time and space). Mobile probing was inspired by the cultural probe method, and was influenced by qualitative interview and inquiry approaches. The method has been used in two subsequent projects, involving school children (young adults at 15-17 years old) and employees (adults) in a consultancy company. Findings point to mobile probing being a flexible method for uncovering the unknowns, as a way of getting rich data to the analysis and design phases. On the other hand it is difficult to engage users to give in depth explanations, which seem easier in synchronous dialogs (whether online or face2face). The development of the method, its application to the two projects, and the challenges and potentials which were found are discussed in this paper.

Keywords: Human Work Interaction Design, Cultural & mobile probes, online empirical data gathering methods, multimodal methods, IT and designs for learning.

1 Introduction - Research Area and Focus

When investigating, it can be difficult for a designer or researcher to ask questions pertaining to a user's work process, task or similar, if the existence of this process or task is not known to the designer/researcher. Also, it is difficult for a user to recall and verbalize all aspects of a process or task, no matter how relevant they may be to convey to the designer/researcher, if the user's attention to issues related to these aspects are not touched upon in the dialog.

One of the authors of this paper had through previous experience from practice (research-based design and research-based consultancy) found herself in this paradox of trying to get to the "heart of things". It seems that applying traditional qualitative methodologies to a digital and online setting does often not bring about much information besides what is being asked about. Moving to more ethnographic approaches as observations and task analysis can be difficult to do online, and requires a lot of hours for both collecting and analyzing data. With methods as online interviews and focus groups, it has been difficult to bring forward the so called non-knowledge. This does not mean that the knowledge is tacit to the users; but simply that when the

P. Campos et al. (Eds.): HWID 2012, IFIP AICT 407, pp. 161–174, 2013.

questions are not asked; the issues are just not touched upon. This happened using various digital methods, as online interviews, focus groups and textual "describe your workflow" situation.

The cultural probes method is a more explorative approach, which on previous occasions has provided valuable information, in particular when combined with other inquiry- and interview-based methods in traditional face2face situations [12]. Consequently, it became relevant to look for a way to transfer these experiences to digital and mobile methods.

Based on the before mentioned difficulties with getting to non-knowledge, the first research question was to see if mobile probes can provide an adequate way forward. A second research question was to investigate, which adaptations of the method were useful when gathering qualitative empirical data from end-users, to be applied to the design process.

Two projects have been involved in this research so far. In 2010 the method was used in a project on mobile learning, where school children from the same school in 8.grade participated (young adults at 15-17 years old). Here, the objective was to gain knowledge from users, in order to inform the design process of a mobile application to be used in the educational system. The other and most recent use of the method was in 2011, where the participants were employees from a major Danish consultancy company. This project had a dual objective: One perspective was to learn about the employees' standpoint (feelings about) and use of the existing knowledge sharing platform, in relation to how they perceived the concept of knowledge sharing, and their knowledge sharing strategies in practice. The project also wanted to discover and map possibilities for mobile support of knowledge sharing in the company.

A common focus area, on the practical level of these two involved projects, has been the need to acquire knowledge directly from the end-users; on their work tasks and processes related to knowledge sharing in general and on their use of digital media, more specifically mobile phones / smart phones.

The tasks under investigation were also carried out in a very mobile or flexible environment. For example the employees in the consultancy case, worked from different locations, and only sometimes at the office. Similarly, the young adults were in and out of school, at home, with friends and so forth. Both projects wanted information about a specific group of people (contextual information) and their current use of their smart phones in general and in relation to how future use-situations could be. In the situation of the consultancy the employees were even situated in different countries, making the need for a digital empirical gathering tool, even more eminent.

Research findings from these two projects points to: applying mobile probes in an almost qualitative interview fashion, utilising the users own mobile equipment can be rewarding for the project in term of uncovering non-knowledge; and that making use of multimodal approaches in the data creation, gathering and analysis phase assist sense-making processes. However, in some situations the mobile probes are seen as too intrusive to daily practice (understood as too time consuming for users to deal with).

In the following, a brief presentation of the concept of non-knowledge and a discussion of its implications for this paper is given. Afterwards, a presentation and discussion is given of the literature and history on cultural probes as it relates to the development of this mobile probing method. Then the first research design considerations are outlined in the first use of the method.[1] Afterwards the second project and its methodological use is presented, followed by a general discussion on findings related to the mobile probing method.

2   Non-knowledge

Non-knowledge is the knowledge that depends on context, social relations and artifacts in order to become understood or recognized as significant and to be codified.

An integral aspect of the mobile probe method is its ability to help gather otherwise hard to handle knowledge. This paper does however not offer space nor is it the place for a long discussion on the differences between tacit and explicit knowledge, on codified and uncodified knowledge and on focal and subsidiarily knowing, to put it in Michael Polanyis terms, and the often used quote that "There are things that we know but cannot tell. " [16] We would however, like to establish this frame: the knowledge form, which is addressed here, is often both contextually, socially and technologically tied, which means it can be very hard, even impossible, for a participant to describe; as work processes and tasks of everyday life is tied to complex network of actions and interactions, thus it can be difficult to realize the causalities; which relations makes which difference. Non-knowledge however, can be, but is not necessarily tacit knowledge.

If space permitted, it would make sense to also discuss and refer to Ed Hutchins distributed cognition [17], as well as the larger body of knowledge sharing literature, for example Nonaka and Hirotake [18], as the concept of non-knowledge used in this paper, is closely related to the codifiability of interpersonal knowledge.

For the work presented in this paper, the postulate is that a part of the code is kept outside the person "holding" the studied knowledge. This means that this "outside", whether artifact or human, needs to be documented or brought into play, if a larger piece of the sum-knowledge (which is not an a priori definite sum) is to be shared or understood in design and design-research. This makes it necessary to identify relational ties between the studied knowledge and the context and artifact that it is interwoven with. Without gathering this data, the state of the knowledge is in danger of getting perceived as everything is tacit knowledge, which cannot be made explicit, while in fact some is pre-codified and can be "talked about", when connected to the "outside" documented nodes.

With a somewhat different objective, though not far from, Lotte Darsø in one of her earlier papers with the title: Is there a formula for innovation? Defines and describes non-knowledge as part of her model for innovation. "*Non-knowledge deals with that which we know, we do not know; that which we do not know, we do not know; and finally that which we did not have a clue about, that one could know. The problem with non-knowledge is, that is it an uncertain and fear-provoking area to be*

---

[1] Research on the first project, with a focus on the domain findings: designing for mobile learning, is published in [11].

in, and this leads to, that most people prefer to withdraw to safer grounds.. [and she continues, when referring to how we can work with non-knowledge] .... *This is primarily done by asking questions – and keep asking questions.*" (translation from [19] p.6. The term non-knowledge as used by Darsø has been developed in collaboration with her then ph.d. advisor Henrik Herlau).

An integral aspect of this view is that the design-researcher, who is in both an analytical and design activity of getting to know the users, context and technologies, and who is mindful to documentation in-situ; also need to ask question to oneself and the process: what has not yet been written, talked about, taken pictures off; which relations did I not see; what can surprise me; and what can I learn now, that I could not predict before?

3   Methodological Considerations

The Cultural Probes method was originally introduced to HCI by Gaver, Dunne and Pacenti. The method was developed using probes such as maps, postcards and other materials that were designed to provoke inspirational responses from elderly people in diverse communities [4]. The method provided empirical user generated data, whose content could not be predicted and which held valuable information about emotions, reasons as well as visual representations. This data collecting process preceded the design phase and contributed to the qualitative knowledge-base about users. [4,5].

The typical cultural probing process has used a large degree of openness and anonymity. For example the postcard could contain a statement or question, as open as "what is a living room to you", and some would return with a description of their own living room, others with a dream scenario, some focus on the layout, others on activities etc. As the post card would be pre-stamped or handed in to a box, the anonymity would be well preserved.

In the presented projects in this paper, there was a need to know something about the tasks and processes from a known and pre-defined user group, within a relatively well defined area. Anthropology, where the researcher/designer is present over longer periods of time is suitable, when investigating tasks and processes, also in our situation, where digital and mobile supported tasks and processes needed be investigated (see for example [20]). Full scale methods of "going native", being with the users (traditionally and digitally) at any time over longer periods, are often too resource consuming for many smaller research and development projects. This primarily concerns two aspects: time used to plan, conduct and analyze the data gathered, and time required from the participants. The latter was especially of concern in the consultancy case and would be in many similar situations. The anthropologist way, also lack the voices of the users'. Interviews and focus groups would be feasible, but could not stand alone, as the openness to the direction and type of data received from users as in the cultural probes was also desired.

A hybrid probing method was thus selected based on both appropriateness and scale of method according to the project size. Others have used hybrid probing methods, as using them in a game-environment, which in the cases listed significantly increased the number of responses [13], and the cultural probes have also moved to digital probing materials and in recent years in particular to focus on mobile probes using mobile phones [1]. Iversen & Nielsen applied mobile phones, as they needed to utilise a media which was suitable for children [7]. In a Finnish study by Hulkko et al, the aim was to make the probe more accessible in all contexts. Their research was rooted in a customer survey perspective, investigating the buying habits and decisions people make when buying clothes (thoughts and visual impressions). Consequently, they too digitized the cultural probes concept, handing out mobiles with attached cameras, with the intention of getting empirical data gathered in-situ [6]. The review of mobile probes studies also indicates that the method is predominantly used in the consultancy domain as opposed to the research domain where it focused more on input to practice. For example, one company developed a mobile based 'probe pack'. A tool for collecting data, with the purpose of reducing development and execution time associated with the use of probes [10].

Two arguments are used when applying the digital probe formats: it provides means for getting access to situated information, and users today recognize and are motivated by mobile phones in the same way as disposable cameras and post cards was [7].

The digital based probes are sometimes linked to Experience Sampling, used in a form of non-present observation of the everyday life of respondents. Experience sampling was originally described as: "to identify and analyze how patterns in people's subjective experience relate to the wider conditions of their lives. According to the authors, the purpose of using this method is to be as "objective" about subjective phenomena as possible without compromising the essential personal meaning of experience" [14]. However, in our context we argue, that technology focused data gathering, using handed-out technology will not provide a valid technology usage picture. Instead it will most likely give insight into the adaptation and acquisition of new technology. While the Experience sampling method seeks to minimize this by prompting for in-situ, descriptive data; But if mobile phones are handed out as part of the empirical data gathering process and the data gathering process is about mobile phones: how natural would their use be to their everyday?

That is, in the above studies the participants were given new tools (hard-/software), which they had to learn to use, before being able to respond on the probe tasks. If such a strategy is applied, it may seem extensive and intrusive to the participants, because learning a new media and being able to use it actively, is a process that takes time and energy. Even if the learning curve over time becomes shorter for some user groups (that is the time needed for acquiring the ability to use a new smartphone, may be relatively small for some user groups), it is not part of a natural work situation to carry several phones; to work on one phone while carrying out the usual digital tasks and then shift to a new phone to send data to the research project.

Furthermore, in the projects, the mobile phone was not only acting as an agent for acquiring empirical data (as the situation in hitherto mobile probe settings as seen above), the mobile was also the technological medium for which data should say something about (mobile learning and knowledge sharing / management). Accordingly, not only the content of the data but also the ways in which data was delivered and handled, provided a valuable dimension for investigating mobile use. It would not make sense to give the participants a new phone, with different operating systems and apps than they usually use, as it would say less about their everyday informal strategies.

Probes have often been applied in a manner, where participating people was probed randomly, with pre-designed probes and answer-channel (i.e. a question-probe + take picture that answers question, or a theme-probe + write a text about the theme, etc.) or by allowing participants to choose time and answer-channel [4,5,6]. There are no immediate follow up on the returning data from the participants' [1]. Boehner et al. argue for probes that work as an open conversation with the participants. A conversation, where the researchers' contribution is a response to what was expressed in the answers coming in from the participants', instead of making representations that delimit the design space [1]. As a result, a more dialog oriented approach, seem appropriate [2].

In a semi-structured interview, the interview guide is pre-formulated [8]. The guide sets the scene, but enables the interviewer to come with follow-up questions, to guide the participants in new directions or to even omit subjects from the pre-formulated guide if this is relevant in the context as the interview takes place.

An important aspect of the cultural probes method is that it does not aim at generating data, which should go through a traditional qualitative analysis; rather the objective is to make the researcher sensitive towards the emotions, experiences and causalities of the participating group [4]. The initial focus of the probes has thus newer been on the development of products, but on new understandings of users and their use of technology [5]. However, in the research and development projects outlined in this paper, the objective has been to understand users' application and utilization of existing technology in order to make future design decisions or strategies of design. This may influence the original method in terms of how the received data becomes sorted and analyzed. In "Moving from cultural probes to agent-oriented requirements engineering "Anne Boettcher discuss data collection in social environments via cultural probes and uses socially oriented requirements analysis for informed technology production [15]. However, mobile proping in these settings does not take place in a vacuum, but in projects were a number of other design activities take place. The intention would not be to let the responses to the probes be subjected to a direct translation into a design, or to see them as "correct answers to a problem". The idea is rather to support the codification and understanding of all data from all methods; to rest on a better foundation of users, their opinions and emotions, and their everyday practice.

In summary and for the outlined contexts, the combination of methods could make it possible to expand on the dialogical aspect, as the mobile phone enables a more flexible probing process than pre-printed post cards and similar material, using generic programs familiar to the participants (as sms, mms, mail etc.). Also, where interviews and surveys have a more retrospective character and ethnographic or anthropological research often requires a "researcher to go native"; in this kind of mobile probing the researcher could ask to the "here and now" of a situation and alongside the actual answers, receive valuable multimodal metadata pertaining to contextual technology usage. The probes are part of a larger set of methods applied in pre-phases and data from the probes are analyzed and joined with data from the other methods.

Consequently, for these studies the Mobile Probes uses a semi structured interview approach, combined with non-intrusive technology, namely their everyday tool, their own mobiles.

4   First Use – Mobile Learning in Schools

Through ministerial funds a project partnership was formed between a broadcasting corporation and two private companies with the objective to develop a learning application for smartphones. The vision was to combine digital information from archives with current information, and thereby support learning in multiple disciplines (as relating historical and current news shown on the phone as the user moves in the city spaces). One of the authors of this paper was invited as a research-based consultant within IT didactical design and two other authors participated as research assistants, where they applied the data in their master studies. IT didactical design refers to the theories, models and practices of teaching and learning supported by IT, focusing on the process perspectives in educational design, as activities relating to both (re-)designing, planning, running, adapting and evaluating learning processes and spaces for learning.

The pre-phase began in the spring of 2010. However, though the researchers finalised the pre-phase, the partnership between the companies dissolved and the project itself was newer finalised. Nevertheless, the process and findings were from a research perspective methodological relevant.

The project's primary audience was students at 15-17y. According to the project description: in 2009 more than 98% of these Danish students were using mobile phones, one third send photos, videos or similar and roughly one in five surf the web using their mobile phones. However, in 2010 very little was known about the informal strategies, the cognitive and subjective processes, as well as the reasons and motivations for mobile applications use. A small investigation based on the Cultural and Mobile Probe method was seen as an adequate way forward at the same time as workshops and low-fi prototypes were designed and evaluated. The research design was build on the assumption that the probe data would spread light on what are the positive and negative user experience elements, and how these components influence the students' choice and learning strategies.

Access to the potential participants, was gained through the headmaster in order to get permission to contact them during school hours. All students in the age group were presented to the project and encouraged to contact the researcher if they wished to participate. The final participants were chosen from those who replied, based on criteria's related to their access to the technology, and their experience with smartphones. Subsequently, four students from the same high school were chosen, adopting a homogenous and typical sampling based strategy [2].

The probing took place over a period of seven days in which the participants received text messages with various questions about their use of smartphones, and received tasks they should address utilising various media and generic smartphone functions. The participants received three text messages each day. The first question was typically sent in the morning, the second at noon, and the third around 6 o'clock in the evening. The first two questions were almost always the same for all participants, whereas the third was often used as a follow-up question to their previous responses, making it individual. Three questions per day enabled some of the positive aspects of semi-structured interviews, where you can make inquiries in to the essence of opinions [8].

During the seven days, 81 tasks were sent and 74 answers were received. The answers were primarily text messages, but also many pictures / screen shots. (table 1 and figure 1).

Table 1. Number and type of responses

Number of tasks send:		81
Number of responses recieved:		74
Media used in responses*;		
SMS:	57	
Audio:	4	*Some answers had both
Pictures:	19	text and pictures

Fig. 1. Example of probe response picture

From an analytical perspective, the Mobile probe method objective was not to reach a single unambiguous answer or solution, but rather the responses should let the researcher become inspired by the participants [1]. With the aim to support the project's rigidity in the analysis phase, while keeping a user-centric focus, user experience goals and cognitive process variables were applied to the analysis. The cognitive processes were identified as: attention, perception & recognition, memory, learning and problem-solving, planning etc. The user experience goals were identified, as: satisfying, enjoyable, provocative, boring, etc. (All derived from [9]).

The multimodal nature of the responses presented a number of challenges during both the collection and analysis process. The primary challenge was to organize the data in a way that would give it a uniform structure and expression, in order to compare answers and reveal trends and relations, to identify and codify the non-knowledge. Data also had to be recorded and stored during the collection process, in a way that supported the interview-based probes approach. Consequently, the project identified "probe managers", sending tasks to the participants and communicating with them when necessary. To facilitate this, an online data collection site was used, where answers and thoughts on the ongoing process was shared. This site allowed simultaneous work on the data and a kind of reflection-log.

For example a simple text-based table was used to store and organize both the pre-defined guide and questions, as well as the participants' answers; Day 1, Question A, participant 1, 2, 3, 4 - Question B, participant 1, 2, 3, 4, etc. Organizing data this way enabled an ongoing preliminary exploratory analysis during the collection phase [2]. This overview helped qualify the follow-up questions, and showed if it was necessary to deviate from the original questions. After the probing process had ended, a themat-ic analysis based on predetermined themes began [2]. The theme-set used was based on the reflective Cognitive Processes (CP) found in the participants smartphone use and the Subjective User Experiences (SUE) associated with the actual use [9]. Through physical and visual (not online) ordering of the relations in the data, it was possible to study and discuss which cognitive categories and subjective user expe-riences were dominant in the data, and gain insight into the correlations between these and different forms of smartphone interaction (figure 3).

3A3	
Answer category:	explain favorit app
Summary:	Facebook is favorit app
most used, good design and user-friendly	
SUE:	enhancing sociability
emotionally fulfilling, enjoyable	
CP:	Attention
perception and reconition	

Fig. 2. Each piece of user material was first analyzed

Fig. 3. Then all pieces were analyzed as a collective

Example: Dohn and Johnson describe m-learning strategies and the use of the stu-dents' own smartphones as an advantage. When the students already know the media, they are already competent and can rapidly decode relevant strategies and instead focus on the learning content. They found students use small one-player games, and they suggest including these in formal learning applications [3]. But what happens when one adopts the cultures and behaviors' of the informal strategies into a formal learning setting? This may be valuable, but can also be disadvantageous in some situ-ations. As such, we found in this project's mobile probe data also showed use of small one-player games. The probe process, however, disclosed that they were played as a fast game "to kill time", or while waiting for something else to happen (during trans-port etc). If designed into learning software, the culture of "beating the game" fast, rather than learning about the domain knowledge, may be inherited.

5   Second Use – Knowledge Sharing in Consultancy

This project was conducted in 2011 and it is noteworthy that the consultancy company had not asked in advance for the research to take place, but decided to use a great deal of effort and man-hours, once they were introduced to the ideas (of the whole pre-phase). The company was in the midst of reorganizing their knowledge sharing platform and had discussed the possibility for mobile support, but had not yet investigated this nor made any decisions regarding this. The total pre-phase was part of the master students' thesis, and the primary research focus was the mobile probing method and how it worked in a pre-phase.

Prior to the mobile probing process, the potential participants received an introduction to the method and to the investigation at hand. It was the employees nearest manager who decided, who participated. It was decided to keep the qualitative approach, and only 6 people participated. There were 9000 employed in the company globaly, making it a truly small, but still interesting insight in to the everyday practices and feelings towards knowledge management in the specific work-domain. For the mobile probing process a mobile probe guideline was developed, similar to the idea of an interview guide. The objective was to understand more about these employees everyday knowledge sharing practice and to learn about the terms and phrases they themselves used for processes related to knowledge sharing. The two tables below illustrate this point and summarize the number of mobile probes and responses sent. Responses were very different in nature, sometimes very concrete ways of working (as in table 3), other times with suggestions to design or just thoughts.

Table 2. Summary

Number of tasks send	90	
Number of responses recieved	86	
Media used in responses*:		
SMS	78	*Some answers used
Mail text	14	more than one mediatype
Picture	6	
Audio	2	
Video	1	

Table 3. Example of question and answer

4E3
Hi XXX. Time for thursdays last task and the last message you will get from me. Please tell me about a situation in which, input from a colleague changed your working practice. I look forward to getting your responses to thursdays tasks. /XXX
It was highlighted to me by a colleague that getting caught up in the old emailknowledge share medium was not only clogging up my mailbox but wasn't efficient. By using SharePoint to upload items, using announcements and then simply sending a link in an email should become the norm for everyone. This is now the way I communicate on the UK.

Sent	Recieved
Media:SMS	Media:SMS

Tech options - social practice - know how - internal knowledgesharing - tech effiency

In retrospect, when analyzing the time of probe distribution, it becomes obvious that the probes consistently was distributed at 9:00, 12:00 and 16:00. Though not an explicit decision, clearly the research team shared a notion on when a probe may be more or less intrusive. Already at day 1, one of the respondent expressed that the probing was a stress factor, responding with a "*I am busy these days, so please make it brief*". This adds a layer to the mobile probing process as it took place in this context, where the respondent was more or less chosen by the nearest managers and thus not volunteered. (Which also became part of the discussion in the analysis and interpretation phases.)

To use this insight in the pre-phase project results, the analysis took point of departure in a set of pre-defined themes, derived from the existing data (meeting, materials and observations from the consultancy company). A possible drawback here was an increased risk for contamination of the data analysis, by inducing ones preconceptions as they are or have been "build" in the analysis of the other data. The incremental, iterative analysis process, where the raw data is revisited and where the themes are discussed after each cycle (leading to reformulation or even to a theme being discarded), aims at minimize this risk.

Mobile probing is a method that by explicit choice is digital. Nevertheless the analysis process makes use of a physical representation and handling / re-coding process; a process that takes place after all mobile probes are collected. Good network views are available in digital analysis tools as Atlas.ti, but the bodily engagement and collaborative dialog while doing so was prioritized here. Soon, technologies may support the analyst in an acquiring equally sense of the data, but for now this was a very adequate process.

Fig. 4. Bodily engagement into the collaborative analysis

6   Discussion of Experiences and Conclusions

As every respondent participate in parallel at a given time period, the method provides a setting for getting access to people independent of space and time. The probing aspect gives knowledge about what the person is doing, but at the same time makes it possible for the researchers or practitioners to make follow-ups based on previous responses. Questions that arose were: What does this mean? Which led to an individual follow-up question; Are other people in similar situations? This led to a follow-up question to all participants. This mean the Mobile Probing method provide the possibility to work with gaining some continuity by asking every participant the same question in new ways, or new questions all together. This is different from traditional interviews, where the basis of the guide may change over time (as interviews are carried out), though follow-up questions of course can and do take place, it means starting up the relation again. Here, the continuity and changes can happen to every participant during the mobile probe period.

However, it was often difficult to receive in-depth answers. This is likely to be linked to two reasons: primarily willingness to invest time to answer the researcher/designer as seen in relation to this time could be used on tasks related to ongoing work requirements. Secondly, based on choice of medium (though not directly investigated in these two projects), in particular SMS, but also when answering mails on a phone, makes answers somewhat short. There is the same tendency in chat-interviews.

The mobile probing process as used here, made use of a large analytical phase in order to use the incoming data in the design phase, whether for design of products or design of processes. The physical sorting of data, provides the team with a very dynamic and visual representation, but at the same time this process needs logging with pictures or similar, to be preserved. And similar a cloud-based storage solution for the mobile probe materials is essential in making it possible to gain access to all the material regardless of time and location. This allowed for everyone in the project team to get an overview of all the responses, as they are received, and thereby ensured the qualification of the open and ongoing dialog.

In conclusion, the mobile probing method and the mobile probes used, differ from the existing and original cultural probes in that: During the information gathering process the mobile probes takes use of a qualitative interview-based method, with focus on an authentic dialog. This gives the researchers the possibility to get to know the researchers and the participants the researchers. Through this, the probing method can allow for facilitating the participants, pursue interesting points etc.

Secondly, the mobile probing process used a combined analysis strategy, with pre-defined themes, allowing the on-going analysis of probes as they were received and then later in a physical coding process as well. Also, making use of multimodal approaches in the data creation, gathering and analysis phase assisted the sense-making processes.

Using mobile probes can be a very rewarding for the projects in term of uncovering non-knowledge, but in some situations the mobile probes are seen as intrusive (understood as too time consuming for user to deal with).

References

1. Boehner, K., Vertesi, J., Sengers, P., Dourish, P.: How HCI Interprets the Probes. In: Proc. of CHI 2007, San Jose, CA, USA (2007)
2. Cresswell, J.W.: Educational Research - Planning, conducting, and evaluating quantitative and qualitative research, 3rd edn. Pearson, USA (2008)
3. Dohn, N.B., Johnsen, L.: E-læring på web 2.0. Samfundslitteratur, Frederiksberg (2009)
4. Gaver, D., Pacenti, E.: Design: Cultural probes. Interactions 6(1), 21–29 (1999)
5. Gaver, B., Penningtong, W.: Cultural probes and the value of uncertainty. Interactions 11(5), 53–56 (2004)
6. Hulkko, S., Mattelmäki, T., Virtanen, K., Keionen, T.: Mobile probes. In: Proc. of the 3rd NordiChi, vol. 82, pp. 43–51. ACM (2004)
7. Iversen, O.S., Nielsen, C.: Using Digital Cultural Probes in Design with Children. In: Proc. of IDC 2003, p. 1 (2003)
8. Kvale, S.: InterView – En introduktion til det kvalitative forskningsinterview. Hans Reitzels, Copenhagen (1997)
9. Preece, J., Rogers, Y., Sharp, H.: Interaction design, Beyond human-computer interaction, 2nd edn. John wiley & sons, Ltd. (2007)
10. Mobile Probes: Frontpage and product descriptions on (2010), http://www.Mobileprobes.dk (visited June 25, 2010)
11. Blomhøj, U., Duvaa, U., Ørngreen, R.: Mobile Probes in Mobile Learning, pp. 1–4. Institut for Uddannelse og Pædagogik, Aarhus Universitet, København (2012)
12. Ørngreen, R., Andreasen, L.B., Levinsen, K.: Digital storytelling: the methodology applied and example stories from Denmark, København (2010)
13. Bernhaupt, R., Weiss, A., Obrist, M., Tscheligi, M.: Playful Probing: Making Probing more Fun. In: Baranauskas, C., Abascal, J., Barbosa, S.D.J. (eds.) INTERACT 2007. LNCS, vol. 4662, pp. 606–619. Springer, Heidelberg (2007)
14. Csikszentmihalyi, M., Larson, R.: The Experience Sampling Method. New Directions for Methodology of Social & Behavioral Science 15, 41–56 (1983)
15. Boettcher, A.: Moving from cultural probes to agent-oriented requirements engineering. In: OZCHI 2006 Proceedings of the 18th Australia Conference on Computer-Human Interaction: Design: Activities, Artefacts and Environments, pp. 253–260 (2006)

16. Polanyi, M.: Tacit Knowing: Its Bearing on Some Problems of Philosophy. Reviews of Modern Physics 34(4), 601–616 (1962, 1996)
17. Hutchins, E.: Cognition in the Wild. MIT Press (1995)
18. Nonaka, I., Hirotake, T.: The knowledge creating company (1995)
19. Darsø, L.: Findes der en formel for innovation? Børsens Ledelseshåndbøger, 12 sider (2003)
20. `http://digitalanthropologist.blogspot.com/2009/11/digital-anthropology-vs-digital.html` ((re)accessed February 18, 2012)

A Framework in Support of Multimodal User Interface

Luis Velhinho and Arminda Lopes

Instituto Politécnico de Castelo Branco, Escola Superior de Tecnologia,
Av. Do Empresário, 6000 – Castelo Branco, Portugal
luis.velhinho@gmail.com, aglopes@ipcb.pt

Abstract. Technologies (IT) Companies' Frameworks have been one of the solutions for the increasing demand for new products and services that are more and more complex and need to be delivered in the least amount of time possible. This paper presents work in progress. The goal was to evaluate Frameworks used by business enterprises and to state the advantages and disadvantages in their use. The chosen methodology for data collection and analysis was the Grounded Theory Method from which it was possible to obtain some conclusions based on given answers. With this research, the intention was is to present some recommendations for companies that work with this type of products to improve their productivity and profit.

Keywords: Company Frameworks, Content Management, Graphical User Interface, Information Technologies, Work Analysis.

1 Introduction

The business market has sought, in last years, to take out advantage of new technologies as a differentiation factor for better productivity and to reach new customers. This increased demand has brought pressure to the suppliers of IT to provide products and services of greater complexity on a reduced time.

The IT companies meet their expectations supported on their customers' claims, and they found solutions thinking in profit incomes. For many companies one of the ways to be different and to respond to this challenge has been the Frameworks development which allows accumulating knowledge and experience that exist within the company and to improve their products' quality.

According IBM [5] "A Framework is a set of blocks of pre-fabricated software that programmers can use to apply, or change specific computing solutions. (…) With the Frameworks the software developers do not need to start from beginning each time they start building an application. Frameworks are built from a collection of objects, so far as the design codes to be reused."

In this research we try to analyze the impact of these types of tools inside companies, and we will try to understand the following concerns:

- To understand the segment markets where the Companies Frameworks are used furthermost;
- To identify the advantages of using Frameworks for enterprise businesses as well as for the development teams;

P. Campos et al. (Eds.): HWID 2012, IFIP AICT 407, pp. 175–182, 2013.
© IFIP International Federation for Information Processing 2013

- To understand the decision factors considered for the choice of a framework and the customers' satisfaction;
- To detect key requirements in the creation of Frameworks;
- To identify areas of improvement on the Frameworks.

2   Frameworks

Frameworks can be classified according two dimensions [7]: where the framework is used and how it is used. And they can be regarded in three distinct ways:
- White-Box - where the developer modifies or extends existing functionality by defining or overlapping methods.
- Black-Box – where the developer uses functions already presented in the Framework (the internal modules of the Framework cannot be viewed or altered and interfaces already defined must be used).
- Hybrids – has the same behavior as the White-Box and Black-Box

Frameworks are used by companies with different goals. It depends on the type of use that the company intends to do. In some cases, they only intend to have a tool that helps in a simple project's development, but in other cases, they intend to develop a tool that has a huge amount of data and logic definitions.

2.1   Framework Wizy

Wizy is an agile development Framework that we use within the enterprise. It enables rapid creation of web applications based on web front ends (Fig. 1.). It was created as a platform to allow fast development of multiple application projects. Conversely, it offers an entire multi-runtime application with embedded functionality for content

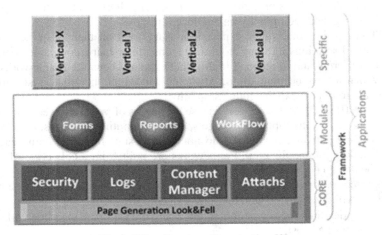

Fig. 1. Wizy Structure Organization [9]

management and workflow. The dispersed data is aggregated in a standard manner allowing content management in a flexible way, providing libraries and components that let prompt development for custom applications.

Typically, a framework is composed for several organizational layers that allow a higher abstraction view for anyone working with the Framework [6].

Fig. 2. presents an example of the Framework Wizy structured on 4 layers. The first layer, External Systems, is the whole systems that interact with Framework. The second layer, Content Provider, provides interfaces to interact with internal and external systems. The third layer, the Content Aggregation, is where all contents are aggregated into one default or custom ASPX page. The fourth layer Content Presentation is shared between Server and Client: the server sends the page on XML and applies XSLTs and CSS styles. The client browser interprets the whole data and shows the page to the user.

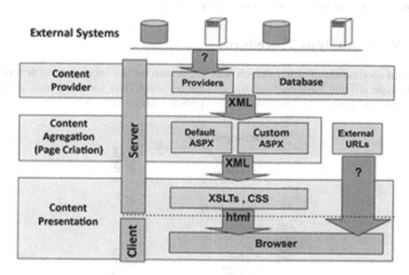

Fig. 2. Framework Wizy Layers [9]

3   Research Methodology and Methods

Grounded Theory Methodology was developed by Glaser & Strauss [3]. It is a general methodology for developing theory that is based on data systematically collected and analyzed [8]. Grounded Theory (GT) is a general method to use on any kind or combination of data, and it is particularly useful with qualitative data.

The main goal of this approach consists of a set of steps which will "guarantee" a good theory as the outcome. It involves two phases in the analysis of qualitative data. Data fragments are compared in order to derive concepts and categories which catch their analytically relevant properties. The second phase is used to elaborate, refine and reduce results of the first phase.

3.1   Research Methods

This research was prepared for business companies which mission is to invest in software development for clients who wants customized applications to manage and improve their business.

This study was conducted through the use of different research methods. Data was collected from staff interviews, observations, and surveys. Interviews were conducted with staff from 11 Portuguese companies whose core business was IT consultancy operating in several target markets with over 5 million euros.

Interviews were face to face, on a private room, and with the interviewees' authorization. They were audio recorded. Later, a transcript of the interview was made. Based on a script several questions were asked and the researcher took also some notes.

Finally, an anonymous online survey for IT developers was made through programming forums, social networks, e.g. LinkedIn. The forum's participants were software developers who worked with multiple Frameworks.

4   Work Analysis Procedures

The main motivation of this research was the researcher's concern about several rejected projects from customers at the end of an order. The intention was to try to understand and find out the reasons that led projects to this end.

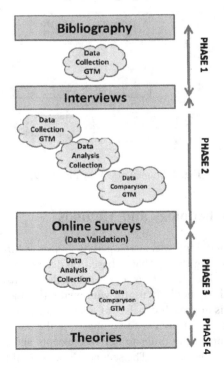

Fig. 3. Research Methodology Phases

This research was carried out through several phases. Initially, we started reading literature, namely, Fayad [2] and technical documentation about object-oriented application frameworks. When applying GTM preconceived conceptions it should not be feared but instead serve as a starting-point for looking at data. After this initial data collection and analysis phases, we decided to make interviews. Interviews permitted to have rich data through a constant comparative method which constitutes the core of grounded theory, ideas started to be organized but needed to be validated. To validate the analyzed data and to keep the GTM process of constant comparison analysis, we decided to do an anonymous online survey. Several IT companies were invited to collaborate in completing the survey. Fig. 3. presents the several phases for data collection, analysis and comparison.

On Phase 1 we start by searching and reading bibliography to begin the data collection GTM process. On Phase 2 the interviews were conducted and respective data analysis and collection was made. Interviews demanded a preparation process before: background information about Companies' Frameworks were collected through books and internet articles which permitted to understand, as well as, to describe Frameworks' components and the way they work. The researchers only considered to interview people with around six years of experience in the companies. After this data collection phase the data was compared with the previous dataset.

Online surveys for data validation, on phase 3, were designed. Phase 3 also included the data gathered analysis and respective comparison with other phases. On Phase 4 we start defining the final theories of the process.

The work analysis process, following GTM, was, initially, based on the literature, different set of profiles were identified to establish a set of questions according to interviewees' experience (see table 1.).

Table 1. Profiles Description

Profile	Description
Developer	Basic element of the hierarchy that develops projects over the Framework.
Team Leader	Coordinator element of the team development that manages the resources in accordance with the project plan.
Project Manager	Project manager who controls and analyzes the various stages of the project, is the bridge between the development team and the client.
Support	Element responsible for providing application support to the Framework or to the products built upon the Framework.
Tester	Element that performs the tests of the project according to the requirements.
Architect	Element responsible for defining the architecture of the solution. He is the person who defines the structure of the Framework and defines the features to be implemented.
Soft Director	Responsible for I&D is who controls the investment and define the product roadmap.

After face-to-face interviews, we did memo-writing which has high priority in the process of constructing a grounded theory. Memo-writing is the pivotal step between data collection and the draft. When an idea was got, "It prompts you to analyze your data and codes early in the research process" [1].

The reading and note taking processes about frameworks led to a spreadsheet elaboration with some questions that should be asked to interviewees. It was realized that their different profiles required different kinds of questions. A developer, for example, sees the Framework on a different way that a supporter or an architect do.

Defined the profiles and questions, meetings were scheduling with all the persons. It was decided to start with some of researcher's colleagues to get more experience and to help in the questions' redefinition.

When the interviews were concluded a new phase arose, the data transcription and analysis. From that moment, different codes were defined to give rise to several categories. This analysis process was made with other spreadsheet and from there charts and diagrams were constructed. An example of data analysis for one of the answered questions by interviewees is presented on fig. 4.

Question: What are the advantages of using Frameworks by business enterprises?

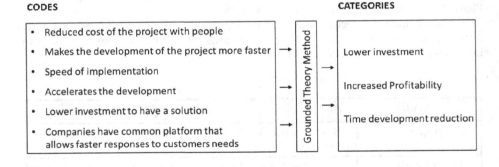

Fig. 4. Grounded Theory Method

5   Results and Discussion

After data analysis it was found that business sectors that most use Companies Frameworks are those of Telecommunications and Media, High Tech, Financial Services and Public Administration as shown in Fig. 5.

About 89% of respondents have worked with a Framework and from these 43% have between 6 and 10 years of experience.

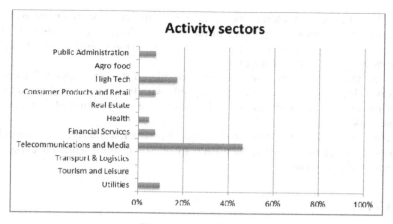

Fig. 5. Activity Sectors

Considering the main categories found within the GTM analysis we could understand that the benefits for developers who have worked with the frameworks were among others the speed of implementation, structuring, reuse and efficiency. The major identified drawbacks were the lack of documentation and the costs of introducing new features as well as versatility of the Framework in accordance with certain customer requirements.

For companies, the most obvious advantages for the use of frameworks are the increase on productivity associated with a shorter development time, the profitability improvement and the creation of standards inside the company (Fig.6.).

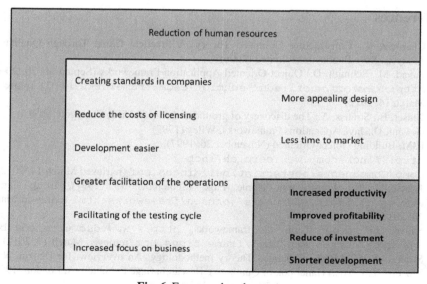

Fig. 6. Frameworks advantages

Some keys factors considered good practices to the creation of Frameworks were also identified: formation, implementation speed, performance and security. It was interesting to see that the average investment by companies on these products is between 10% and 15% of their budget.

From the interviewees' responses it was considered that the support for multiples systems is a challenge for the future, side by side with the frameworks' versatility and adaptability, and also the continuous evolution and the introduction of new features in the framework.

The companies that are betting on this type of product, a framework, although they are achieving great profitability, they need to do some more work concerning new solutions to their customers.

6   Conclusions

This research was important and it permitted to have some answers to the initial questions from the interviewees and from the online survey.

The data analysis showed that there are some activity sectors that invest more in this type of products than others, for example, the Telecommunications' sector.

Many users highlighted some key attributes on the advantages of using Frameworks like: time development reduction and the increase of profitability.

Two of the major evident concerns are the lack of documentation and learning courses about the frameworks' use. On these referred areas, companies need to do some effort to improve the quality of utilization of the Framework.

In resume the Frameworks are useful for companies, they allow to reduce costs and increase productivity, besides allowing offering new and innovative products to its customers.

References

1. Charmaz, K.: Constructing Grounded Theory. A Practical Guide Through Qualitative Analysis. Sage Publications limited (2006)
2. Fayad, M., Schmidt, D.: Object-Oriented Application Frameworks (September 28, 2006), http://www.cs.wustl.edu/~schmidt/CACM-frameworks.html (retrieved March 14, 2012)
3. Glaser, B., Strauss, A.: The discovery of grounded theory. Aldine, Chicago (1967)
4. Govoni, D.: Java Aplications Frameworks. Wiley (1999)
5. IBM. Building Object-Oriented (November 26, 1997), http://lhcb-comp.web.cern.ch/lhcb-comp/Components/postscript/buildingoo.pdf (retrieved March 14, 2012)
6. Johnson's, R.: Frameworks Home Page (September 15, 1997), http://st-www.cs.illinois.edu/users/johnson/frameworks.html (retrieved March 14, 2012)
7. Sauvé, J.P. (n.d.): Tipos de frameworks, http://www.dsc.ufcg.edu.br/~jacques/cursos/map/html/frame/tipos.htm (retrieved March 17, 2012)
8. Strauss, A., Corbin, J.: Grounded Theory methodology: An overview. In: Denzin, N.K., Lincoln, Y.S. (eds.) Handbook of Qualitative Research. Sage Publications, London (1994)
9. Wedotechnologies, Framework Wizi Portugal (2006), http://www.wedotechnologies.com/pt (retrieved January 2, 2012)

An Organizational Study into the Concept of Automation in a Safety Critical Socio-technical System

Paola Amaldi[1] and Anthony Smoker[2]

[1] School of Life and Medical Sciences, Department of Psychology,
University of Hertfordshire Hatfield AL10 9AB England
[2] NATS; Mailbox 50, Swanwick Centre, Southampton, SO31 7AY
p.amaldi@herts.ac.uk, anthony.smoker@nats.co.uk

Abstract. Although automation has been introduced in all areas of public life, what seems to be missing is a reflection at the organizational or societal level about a *policy of automation*. By this we intend appropriate declarations made at the level of rationale, future plans and strategies to achieve intended goals and most importantly how those achievements will impact on various aspects of societal life, from legal responsibilities to moral and socio economic issues. In some public spheres these issues are becoming quite controversial because automation opens up possibilities of profound structural re-organization; however, we lack a discussion across and within different work domains to help us review methods or even methodological principles needed to gather and organize knowledge towards the construction of automation policies. This paper uses the UK service organization for Air Traffic Management Domain called NATS – National Air traffic Service, as a case study to illustrate an example of an organization currently undertaking critical self-reflection about automation policy or lack of such, along with the illustration of some unresolved deep concerns raised by the development, introduction, and continued use of automation.

Keywords: Policy of automation, organizational culture.

1 Introduction

Although automation has been introduced in all areas of public life, from production to tertiary sectors, what seems to be missing is a reflection at the organizational or societal level about a *policy of automation*. By this we intend a declaration of rationale, future plans and strategies to achieve intended goals expressed not longer at a single mission level such as gate-to-gate trajectory management, but how those achievements will impact on various aspects of societal life, from legal responsibilities to moral and socio economic issues. While in some public spheres these issues are becoming quite controversial because automation opens up possibilities of profound structural re-organization, we lack a discussion across and within different work domains that help us to review methods or even methodological principles needed to gather and organize knowledge to the construction of such policy. For example, current concerns about the deep changes to be introduced in the British Public Health sector would likely benefit

P. Campos et al. (Eds.): HWID 2012, IFIP AICT 407, pp. 183–197, 2013.

from a more open discussion about the relationship between automation and higher level societal goals (see [1] Rozzi, Amaldi and Kirwan, 2010).

This paper uses NATS—National Air Traffic Service, the UK Agency for air traffic management as a case study to illustrate an example of an organization currently undertaking critical self-reflection about automation policy along with the illustration of some unresolved deep concerns raised by the development, introduction, and continued use of automation. Before discussing NATS-specific concerns we shall briefly review major issues within the cognitive ergonomic literature about the relationship between automated processes and human control.

1.1   Major Pitfalls of the Automation Process

Information and computer technologies provide an increasing number of opportunities to develop new solutions to assist operators/professionals across many domains of practice in managing complex socio-technical systems. There are, however, a number of concerns highlighting complexities and paradoxes embedded in the automation process. Bainbridge [2] discussed the unexpected consequences of technology-driven automation, which often relies on human reliability to be safely operated. One of the "ironies" is that automated systems are often introduced on the ground that humans are less reliable than automation because of "intrinsic" limitations in their ability to monitor for unexpected, unsafe events in a stream of a routine flow of events.

Paradoxes linked to the introduction of expert systems have been extensively emphasized ([3, 4, 5, 6]). Inappropriate design choices might result in an increase of operators' workload, in an excessive demand on working memory, in a difficulty to co-operate with team members, and finally it might slow down the development of expertise [7]. Automation is expected to assist operators in achieving the overall system goals in a more cost-effective way. These expectations have, at times, relied on a number of misbeliefs [8]. In fact, although it might lead to "de-skilling", automation does not decrease the requirements for expertise. Some have nevertheless been led to believe that expert systems can replace the need for or even decrease the standard of expert operators.

This claim does not consider that automation has to be constantly adapted to its operational context to be effective [9]. This is because expert systems have a limited scope with respect to the variety of objectives characterizing activities in complex socio-technical systems. This variety reflects the ability of expert operators to identify ways to improve the system performance in routine situations. The role of operators when interacting with complex technical system has often been emphasized in relation to their ability to manage exceptions. While this is true, it should not be neglected the finding that operators systematically go beyond the prescribed practices to enhance system's efficiency [10]. An old study involving observations of maintenance operators, reported that almost one third of the times operators have been observed making an informal use of available tools [11]. By informal it is meant that the tool is not used for the purposes it was designed but rather with the intent of making the corrective action more effective.

This phenomenon has already been well documented and studied within the francophone ergonomic tradition quite long ago [11, 12, 13]. The informal use of tools and procedures reflect often a search for an improved efficiency, not just a solution to unexpected problems. Similarly, the spontaneous generation of linguistic code has been observed in different operational settings [12]. Notice that deviations from standard communication patterns have generated fatal misunderstandings such as in the case of air traffic controller / aircraft pilot radio communications [14]. In spite of these fatal accidents, deviations from standard use are often generated with the aim of achieving task goals. In this respect, automation should support operators in finding the best way to achieve the goals while limiting the negative consequences of possible misfits between tools adaptations and task constraints and goals [9]. As part of the integration process operators will engage in «finishing the design» of the tool with respect to its original intended use [15], i.e., improving the fitness between the tool and the complexities of the operational environment.

1.2 Automation and Information Processing Stages

In an attempt to characterize automation with respect to models of information processing, Parasuraman, Sheridan & Wickens, [16], have used a simplified model of human decision making and problem solving. The model allows the classifying of technological innovations according to four stages:
- (i) information acquisition ;
- (ii) information analyses ;
- (iii) decision selection;
- (iv) action implementation.

The introduction of new technology might interact with cognitive processing in each of these stages with differing degrees of automation. The allocation of tasks to humans and machines depends then on the level of automation chosen. While the classification schema does offer a means to group technological innovations across different domains, guidelines for function allocation do not seem straightforward. Criteria for deciding how to do task sharing have to be based on an understanding of the impact of automation on the targeted communities of practitioners. Neglecting, for example, the crucial role of cooperation or adaptation processes like "finishing the design" does not seem a very promising start for deciding on task allocation. Further, such a simplified model of human cognition and of human-computer interaction might mislead designers and engineers to believe that a fairly simple algorithm can generate the desired answer to a very complex and still unsettled issue (see also [17]). Some examples discussed below will illustrate the pitfalls of such naïve assumption.

For example, automation concerning the (i) acquisition and (ii) information analysis stages involves the organization of incoming sensory data. A stated purpose is to decrease attentional demands of operators by highlighting or cueing relevant information while leaving the rest un-cued but still accessible. Yet, this apparently simple solution neglects considering a number of issues. The assumption here is that human information processing capacity is limited and thus the number of items that can be processes at anytime cannot exceed that capacity. While this is not wrong, this statement neglects considering that there is no an obvious way of "measuring" that capacity as it is subject to people's expertise, organization of labor and the development of new working practices. In addition filtering "relevant" information raises the issue of "context sensitivity" [18]. What needs to be noticeable depends on the situation, which includes other related data, the "history" of the process, the intentions and expectations of the observers, [19].

A higher level of automation within the information analysis stage implies the temporarily or permanently hiding of certain information. For example in Air Traffic Control (ATC), certain electronic displays of future traffic problems "hide" or "reveal" information according to the role of operator within the team. Or, the available data might be automatically organized in terms of problems to be dealt with in a given priority order. Notice that information filtering, problem formulation and priority assignment, all involve anticipating how the system under control is going to evolve. Automation of some anticipatory functions is then involved in the design of predictor displays introduced in both the flight deck and ATC to assist operators to project future courses of flight.

Automation interacting with the third stage of decision making leads to the selection of a course or several courses of actions. Automation here might assist operators in calculating the best option(s) given the constraints of the current situation. For example the Flight Management System (FMS) in the cockpit can, more effectively than pilots, calculate the most cost-effective trajectory in terms of gas consumption and timing.

In ATC, decision aids assist controllers by offering solutions to traffic problems and in this respect several systems have been proposed and evaluated (e.g., ERATO, HIPS, URET, IFACTS) [20]. At this level of automation a range of alternatives are proposed, leaving operators responsible for making the final choice. A more advanced automation would give very little or no choice to operators as to what solution to implement. This implies automating the process of evaluating costs and benefits associated with each alternative. The problem is that the criteria used in the automated evaluation process are not likely to include all of the factors included by human decision-makers. In fact there will always be a number of conditions where the automated solution would need to be adjusted to reflect local contingencies. Therefore it seems crucial that a high degree of automation at this stage of decision-making leaves open the possibility of deciding whether or not to implement the course of actions. For example a number of studies on the onboard warning called Traffic Collision and Avoidance System (TCAS) have shown that pilots do not always comply with the advice provided by the automation ([21] Amaldi, under review; [22]) unless they can verify its compatibility with other conditions. Notice that improving an understanding of the criteria underlying the solution proposed facilitates a complying behavior ([23, 24]).

Automation intervenes in the last stage of decision making through the implementation of the course of actions. For example digital data link will allow air traffic controllers to uplink a pre-edited clearance into the plane's FMS. Notice that the clearance could be a computer-selected option to an automatically identified traffic problems. Current proposals to uplink ACAS advisories to FMS are another example automaton taking over the decision making and implementing.

1.3   What Is Automation for?

What is then automation? It is a transformation of a world state accomplished by an electro mechanical device with or without human intervention. Our previous discussion aims at classifying the levels of the involvement and mode of human-automation interaction with respect to controlling and decision-making.

What is automation for then? It is the means by which we (i) extend our cognitive skills; (ii) aim at increasing the resilience of the operational system (by introducing for example, back up sub-components); (iii) aim at increasing productivity by enabling the system with new tools that increase the throughput.

What can be automated? There have been cases, in the history of R&D in Air Traffic Management when (over) ambitious automation projects have been withdrawn. Lack of mature technology or too many contingencies that made it impossible to proceduralise operational practices. One apparent rational was that whatever could be made faster and more reliable through the use of automated device, it should.

For a few decades now, ATM operations have been the object of R&D efforts to make them faster and more reliable through the introduction of automation. There was a lack of consideration of the wider impact of those innovations. For example, increasing traffic throughput en route was not connected with the need to increase airport capacity. Increasing airport capacity, however, has been the target of serious environmental concerns.

Starting on the assumption that the complexities of current system require automated aids, the coupling of computers to air traffic management has surely resulted in an increase of safety and productivity. Nowadays targeting individual human limitations with respect to system control is not longer a viable strategy for expanding current business. The main challenge seems to have shifted from designing interfaces usable or trustable (although these are still serious concerns) to mapping out the added complexities and the profound consequences of the technological innovation process. For example, recent debates by environmentalists have challenged that Civilian Air Traffic is an important contributor to CO_2 emission. To what extent, then the design of new technology should be planned to address issues of atmospheric pollution? The main point to be raised is that the human-computer interaction unit of analysis has to be embedded in a larger context to target limitations and contradictions of the entire system, rather than marginalizing the human as the 'limiting factors' to system development.

2   Organizational Culture in NATS

This is a study about NATS organizational culture. In particular what are the existing views and expectations held by the middle layer management, toward the increasing dependency on digitized information processing systems? By doing this investigation we wish to articulate the model of cultural analysis suggested by [25] and a number of researchers working in the area of organizational cultural analyses (e.g., [26]).

Culture, safety and safety-culture, have been treated as 'components' of systems and as such discussed as either the source or the cause of behavior. Further isolating components prompts researchers to treat them as measurable and manipulable to control on their 'effects' on system behavior. We are basically seeking to advance our understanding of the main claims of what a cultural analysis is NOT: (a) culture as causal attitude as the engine that pushes processes; (b) culture as engineered organization, proposing a set of indicators that verify the cultural recommendations have worked. Rather, we support the view that culture is to be understood as in a dialectic relation with practice, one cannot be constituted as an object of study without the other. Their relationship is not one of cause-effect but rather one of mutual dependency. In other words, we can't study safety culture without inquiring into those regular patterns that characterize organizational behavior. The safety culture literature, on the other hand, hardly makes reference to the following features of organizations: (i) power, (ii) group interest, (iii) conflict or (iv) inequality.

These features (organisational) are feeding the following cultural schema and interpretative mechanisms:

- Normative heterogeneity
- Competitive and conflicting interests
- Inequalities in power and authority

What is missing from a number of account on safety culture is a focus on process that produce systemic meanings where isolated factors like understaffing, excessive workload, lack of effective communication are seen as a constituent part of a general pattern ... Within the interpretative schema of a cultural analysis, these factors are not caused by a 'wrong culture' but they are a constitutive part of it, give and take meaning from it. They become 'dysfunctional' only when clashing with public images or other competing interests. Manipulating these factors as though they are independent from the historical-cultural context that did not simply *produce* them, but from which they derive their intelligibility and at the same time 'feed in' a more general patterns, is not very promising. Normalizing deviance, informational secrecy, credibility gap, are examples of mechanisms that constitute cultural schema.

Is NATS enacting a moment of critical self-reflection to unsettle what is taken for granted and make space for innovative practice?

2.1   NATS Main Concerns with Automation

NATS is currently reviewing their position and their implicit assumptions with respect to automation. At this stage NATS is seeking views in the face of unexpected side effects linked to increasing complexities from all parties involved in the design, implementation and use of the existing or planned automated systems. Such process of critical self-reflection aims at enhancing its resilience in the face of increasing complexities linked to ongoing technological innovation. The notion of organizational resilience has become popular in the area of organizational risk management [27].

The more an organization builds its own resilience, the more is capable of adaptively responding to hazardous events. We extend the notion to situations where the planning of far reaching changes cannot indeed account for in advance for all of its major contingencies. Given the increased complexity introduced by more and more powerful technology, NATS attempts to move from a rather patchwork to a more holistic approach seems worth reporting. In the following we report a two-stage data collection aiming to document NATS main concerns, suggestions, recommendations to the problem of lack of automation policy.

3   Method

The main objective of the data collection was to elicit subject matter experts a wide as possible range of issues deemed to be associated with past practices of automation development and introduction into air traffic control management. Data collection occurred in three stages.

First in December 2011 we devised a survey and distributed it mainly to NATS officials. Three main themes were suggested as guidelines but then participants were encouraged to raise any other issue and think about in terms of

a)   What the problem was—the problem statement

b)   Why was it a problem

c)   What needs to be done about it

The guidelines for reflection were centered around three main themes:

i)   What is NATS scope and vision for automation;

ii)   What is the role and responsibility of the human;

iii)   What are the skills that need to be developed and maintained.

Second, we organized a Workshop in April 2012 attended by approximately 70 people partly from NATS and partly from a number of disparate industries. Participants were asked to participate in 4 activities designed to encourage constructive and creative thinking about automation and how it should be developed, deployed and utilised. For each of these activities the following provides a brief definition of their aim and the opening question used to initiate the discussion

Activity 1: *Reversal*. Aim: elicit recommendations for improvements through identifying weaknesses. This is done by asking the opposite of the question you want to be answered, and then by reversing the results as appropriate.

Opening question: *What things can we do to make the introduction of Automation less likely to succeed and less likely to be safe? How could we make it worse?*

Activity 2: *Reframing Matrix*[1] *Aim:* Looking at problems from different perspectives. The proposed perspectives were Pilot; ATCO; SRG and NATS although groups were free to select their own perspectives.

Opening question: How should we prepare for the introduction of Automation in NATS?

Activity 3:*Brainstorming*:   Aim: Participants were asked to elicit solution to the following :

Opening question: What actions should we take to ensure Automation is introduced safely and avoid the problems we have discussed?

Activity 4: *Force Field Analysis*[2]: Aim: Understanding the pressures for and against change. Participants were asked to select ideas from their brainstorms for force-field analysis.

The stated objectives of the 4 activities were:

- To validate the draft 'Use of automation in NATS operations' position paper by exposing it to expert scrutiny
- To identify enablers and blockers to the delivery of an effective policy on automation within NATS
- To identify problems with introducing automation within NATS and create potential solutions to these problems
- To engage experts (from around NATS, the UK and the world from Aviation, Regulation, Medicine, MOD, Academia etc.) to form a community of expert resource
- To identify the risk landscape regarding automation and thus provide a metric against which safe introduction of automation can be assessed

Finally a third workshop was organized in July 2012 and attended by 25 participants, approximately. A well-known domain expert was invited as well to review and comment on main challenges/issues of automation. Participants had to rank the priority of the fourteen problem statements that were reviewed in Workshop 1. Further they were asked to write statements about potential negative outcomes of automation, along with their mitigation. Last they were presented with two definitions about automation and asked to comment on them. All comments have been transcribed.

---

[1] Adapted from
http://www.odi.org.uk/resources/details.asp?id=5221&title=reframing-matrix
[2] Adapted from http://www.mindtools.com/pages/article/newTED_06.htm

4   Findings

Stage One: Generating problem statements

In reply to the survey, NATS has compiled 14 statements that we grouped into 6 groups.

Group Statement 1. Lack of definition/vision: There is not an agreed set of definitions about the scope of automation, i.e., to what extent is mostly technology- or problem-driven. This results in confusion and lack of clarity in planning and communication. Different people have different expectations and different requirements regarding what automation will deliver. Similarly there is not a single agreed vision for automation. The scope of automation needs to be defined and agreed. Automation affects every aspect of the business – it determines how people are selected and trained; how many people remain in the system and NATS' capacity to generate income. There is no clear definition of the future levels of automation that NATS should be planning for.

Group Statement 2. Responsibility and role allocation. No single clear picture of how automation will affect MOPS[3] – in particular the responsibility of the operational staff for the decision making process. The literature previously reviewed suggests how automation can interact with the problem solving and decision making process. The introduction of new automated technology will affect the role of the human. It is vital that human strengths and vulnerabilities are accounted for in the design and attribution of roles. Also, it is vital that the resulting role is one that can be trained for.

Assumptions about role allocation are being made at the moment and are affecting how NATS plans and implements projects but these assumptions are not being made explicit.

The allocation of responsibility between the machine and the human needs to be defined clearly and explicitly over time and at each key milestone of system operation.

Group Statement 3. The introduction of automation will be neither as safe nor as effective as it could be. Automation could be used to remove risks from the current operation – unless this is done in a focused way (aimed at specific known risks) the full benefit will not be realized and, in fact, automation may add risks. Automation needs to be focused upon removing key risks from the operation and exploiting the different strengths of the human and the machine.

The operational effectiveness of our systems relies heavily upon the close relationship between the human and the machine – if this is not optimized then maximum effectiveness will not be realized. Automation needs to be focused upon achieving the most effective balance between human & machine. The cost/benefit balance of automation needs to be managed.

Group Statement 4. There is no clarity on how the relationship between the human and machine will change due to technical failure (or cyber-attack). Current

---

[3] Minimum Operational Performance Standard.

assumptions regarding the capacity of the human to revert to manual operations are likely to prove incorrect after a short while of automated operations. If this is the case, we might not have a mode to revert to.

It is difficult to place limits on the extent to which automated systems should be implemented in order to ensure that they ultimately remain under human control. In general, the greater the level of automation the further the human is removed from the control loop and therefore the harder it is for them to recover control. The skills that the human will need to exercise in order to effectively participate in Human-Automation interaction need to be identified and the impacts of automation anticipated.

Group Statement 5. Aspects of human behavior indicative of their ability to effectively use future automated systems are not receiving the emphasis required. We do not yet know the number of people and the types of skills/capabilities we will need to provide for the future ATM changes. These have been planned over the next few years and will require current controllers to significantly adapt their ways of working. The extent to which they will need to be helped to do this will depend on NATS ability to effectively assess their automation "competence".

Group Statement 6. There isn't yet an agreed and validated methodology for assuring the performance of the automated system (cooperative performance of human and automated technical system). Co-ordinative/co-operative requirements are neglected. As automation levels increase, the complexity of the emergent system interactions will also increase. Traditional methods of analysis and validation are unlikely to provide sufficient assurance that the system will be stable. It will be necessary to set and measure demanding performance standards for the total system.

NATS is planning for levels of automation that have not yet matured into operational systems. They might not mature. Automation of human-centered sociotechnical systems has far reaching consequences that can be framed only at an organizational/societal level (see [28]).

Stage Two: Automation Workshop.
There was considerable overlap between the statements generated in the two stages, so analysis of respective contents and overlap is ongoing. At the moment we have compiled a table including the frequency at which a number of activities have been suggested in order to cope with present and future challenges of automation.

Table 1. Most commonly elicited activities to cope with automation challenges

Proposed Activity	Votes
Define the future role of the controller	15
New aviation system model	13
Improve training strategy and delivery and design for automation	12

Table 1. (*continued*)

Proper R&D Phase	11
Produce NATS led industry strategy	10
Training adequate and appropriate	9
Understand system needs, requirements and levels of automation	9
Recruit and employ people with the right skills for the new operation	8

Stage Three

About 25 participants were asked to rate the importance and priority for solving 14 claims used in Stage 1. Those have been grouped into 4 main themes: (i) agreed upon vision of automation; (ii) role played by human over time; (iii) allocation of responsibility between human and artificial agents over time; (iv) supervision and leadership in team working. While they were all considered 'priority', only the lack of an agreed vision was judged an issue to be addressed immediately. Next, participants were asked to make suggestions as to how to mitigate on the consequences of some of the points raised in Stage II concerning potential negative outcomes. Ten major themes were summarized along with the most commonly cited mitigation strategies.

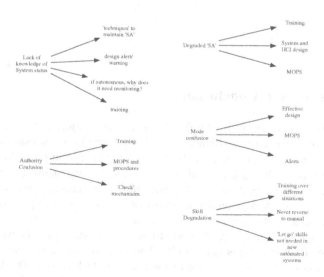

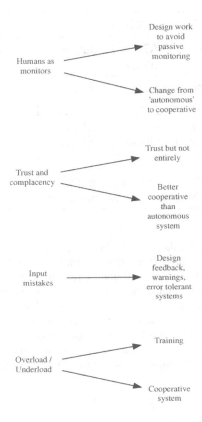

5   Discussion and Conclusion

We looked at NATS current critical reflection upon automation and its consequences as a case study of engineering resilience against unexpected and undesirable effects of automation. Given the initial stage of the work, our conclusion takes the form of a working hypothesis to be further confirmed. Given the increasing complexities of socio technical systems, traditional HCI and human-automation interaction issues cannot be handled outside a general framework of automation policy. This includes a set of goals, values, costs and strategies to cope with uncertainties and unintended effects of automation. First, NATS needs to address more explicitly what the long term and scope of automation is going to be. This goes beyond a piecemeal approach where automation innovation would be technology and task driven. The latter means that two main rationales for introducing automation i.e., availability of the technology and a focus on a specific (set of) task are inadequate. In fact the assumption that interventions on subcomponents of the system do not need to consider the long-term effects on the operations in their ensemble, seems under scrutiny. However as we stated, as automation level increases, the complexity of the emergent system interactions will also increase and traditional methods of analysis and validation are unlikely to provide an overall assurance of system stability.

Second given a better specification of NATS requirements and expectations about automation, what will be the range of roles that humans are expected to engage with? The history of automation both in the cockpit and on the ground has shown that humans act as 'mediators' [29] between the automation and the environmental contingencies and operational complexities. Typically operators have to monitor for unexpected interactions among apparently unconnected subcomponents. Further they need to reconcile the need for standardization (like the European Sky) with the need to locally tailor tools and procedures.

Third, what sort of competencies will be required; how they will affect the selection process; the training and the maintenance of them has to be informed and guided by a policy of automation. This goes beyond the specific characteristics of the system in use. For example, a recent study by [30] has documented that in the case of a National Service Provider, a vision of automation has affected decisions about changes on a specific interface and thus about competencies required in an interim phase.

Fourth, safety has reached level that can be hardly improved through the development of further safety nets alone. Rather the roles played by the various agents across the organizational levels of control have to be openly discussed, identified and defined.

Designing for human capabilities as modeled by certain computational/cognitive theories of mind, might be misleading because these theories are not sufficiently concerned with how the meaning of symbols and symbol manipulations is grounded in the goals, constraints and possibilities of the task domain ([31], Dowell and Long, 1998, p. 132). Rather the aim should be designing for automation that is fit for purpose, where 'purpose' is defined by the joint human- technical system. Focusing on requirements of either one misses the fundamentally interactive nature of human work design.

References

1. Rozzi, S., Amaldi, P., Kirwan, B.: IT Innovation and its organizational condition in safety critical domains. In: 5th IET International Conference on System Safety, Manchester (2010)
2. Bainbridge, L.: Ironies of automation. In: Goodstein, L.P., Andersen, H.B., Olsen, S.E. (eds.) Tasks, Errors and Mental Models. Taylor & Francis, London (1986)
3. Billings, C.E.: Human-centered aicraft automation: A concept and guidelines (NASA Tech. Memorandum 103885). National Technical Information Service, Springfield (1991)
4. Norman, D.A.: The psychology of everyday things. Basic Books, New York (1988)
5. Woods, D.D., Cooks, R.I., Billings, C.: The impact of technology on physician cognition and performance. Journal of Clinical Monitoring 11, 5–8 (1995)

6. Sarter, N.D., Woods, D.D.: Teamplay with a powerful and independent agent. Human Factors 39(4), 553–569 (1997)
7. Woods, D.D., Sarter, N., Billings, C.: Automation surprises. In: Salvendy, G. (ed.) Handbook of Human Factors and Ergonomics. Wiley Interscience Publication, N.Y (1997)
8. Mosier, K.L., Skitka, L.J.: Human decision makers and automated decision aids: Made for each other? In R. Parasuraman & M. Mouloua (eds.). In: Parasuraman, R., Mouloua, M. (eds.) Automation and Human Performance. Theory and Applications. LEA, Mahwah (1996)
9. Vicente, K.: Cognitive work analysis. Lawrence Erlbaum Associates, Mahwah (1999)
10. Wright, P., McCarthy, J.: Analysis of procedure following as concerned work. In: Hollnagel, E. (ed.) Handbook of Cognitive Task Design. LEA, Mahwah (2003)
11. Leport, B.: Les utilisations des outils et la fiabilité de l'organisation. Rapport interne á la CCE Roneó, Paris (1970)
12. Cuny, X.: Different levels of analyzing process control tasks. Ergonomics 22, 425–526 (1979)
13. De Keyser, V.: Works analysis in French language ergonomics: origins and current research trends. Ergonomics 34(6), 653–669 (1991)
14. Mell, J.: Emergency calls: messages out of the «blue». In Le Traspondeur. 11, INGENAC Toulouse, France (1993)
15. Rasmussen, J.: Information processing and human-machine interaction. An approach to cognitive engineering. Elsevier Science (1986)
16. Parasuraman, R., Sheridan, T.B., Wickens, C.D.: A Model for Types and Levels of Human Interaction with Automation. IEEE Transactions on Systems, Man, and Cybernetics – Part A: Systems and Humans 30(3), 286–297 (2000)
17. Dekker, S.W.A., Woods, D.D.: MABA-MABA or Abracadabra? Progress on human-automation co-ordination. Cognition Technology & Work 4, 240–244 (2002)
18. Woods, D.D., Patterson, E.S., Roth, E.M.: Can we ever escape from data overload? A cognitive systems diagnosis. Cognition, Technology, and Work 4(1), 22–36 (2002)
19. Burns, C.M., Mumaw, R.J., Roth, E.M., Vicente, K.J.: There Is More to Monitoring a Nuclear Power Plant Than Meets the Eye. Journal of Human Factors and Ergonomics 42 (2000)
20. Mendoza, M.: Current state of ATC Conflict Resolution. Eurocontrol: EEC Note 12/99 (1999), http://www.eurocontrol.fr/public/reports/eecnotes/1999/12.pdf
21. Amaldi, P. (under review): The integration of alert devices into socio-technical systems. The case of an airborne alert device (ACAS)
22. Garfield, D., Baldwin, T.: European ACAS Operational Monitoring 2002 Report. Eurocontrol EEC Report No. 393 (2004), http://www.eurocontrol.int/eec/publications/eecreports/2004/393.pdf
23. Lees, M.N., Lee, J.D.: The influence of distraction and driving context on driver response to imperfect collision warning systems. Ergonomics 50(8), 1264–1286 (2007)
24. Pritchett, A.R., Hansman, R.J.: Pilot non-conformance to alerting system commands during closely spaced parallel approaches. In: 16th DASC Digital Avionics System Conference. AIAA/IEE (1997)
25. Silbey, S.: Taming Prometheus: Talk about safety culture. Annual Review of Sociology 35, 341–369 (2009)
26. Bergström, J., Dekker, S., Nyce, J.M., Amer-Wåhlin, I.: The social process of escalation: a promising focus for crisis management research. BMC Health Services Research 12(161) (2012), http://www.biomedcentral.com/1472-6963/12/161 (last accessed October 2012)

27. Hollnagel, E., Paries, J., Woods, D.D., Wreathal, J.: Resilience Engineering in practice: A guidebook. Ashgate, Farnham (2011)
28. Rasmussen, J., Svendung, I.: Proactive risk management in a dynamic society. Raddningsverket. Swedish Rescue Services Agency, Sweden (2000)
29. Downer, J.: When failure is an option: Redundancy, reliability and regulation in complex technical systems. LSE, Discussion paper 53 (2009)
30. Amaldi, P., Rozzi, S.: Inter-organizational safety debate. International Journal of Socio-Technology and Knowledge Development 4(1), 30–47 (2012)
31. Dowell, J., Long, J.: Conception of the cognitive engineering design problem. Ergonomics 41(2), 126–139 (1998)

Author Index

Printed in the United States
By Bookmasters